ENESCO
HIS LIFE and TIMES

Б. КОТЛЯРОВ

ДЖОРДЖЕ ЭНЕСКУ

Издание второе, дополненное

ВСЕСОЮЗНОЕ ИЗДАТЕЛЬСТВО
СОВЕТСКИЙ КОМПОЗИТОР
МОСКВА 1970

Enesco

by B. Kotlyarov

Translated by B. Kotlyarov and E. D. Pedchenko

© 1984 by Paganiniana Publications, Inc.

© 1984 by VAAP, Copyright Agency of the Soviet Union, for the original Russian language manuscript.

PAGANINIANA PUBLICATIONS, INC.
211 West Sylvania Avenue, Neptune City, New Jersey 07753

Contents

Introduction 7
Chapter 1 15
Chapter 2 23
Chapter 3 33
Chapter 4 49
Chapter 5 73
Chapter 6 105
Chapter 7 151
Chapter 8 191
Notes 230
Index of Persons 238

Georges Enesco. Engraving by Cornelius Baba (1955).

Introduction

The aim of art is to lead people forward on the way to the better.
Georges Enesco

Musical art requires that he who practices it, sacrifices for its sake all his thoughts, all feelings, all his time, his very being.
Anton Rubinstein

There are in musical history quite a number of examples which show how wide in scope and range the creative activity of an artist can be, but few can rival the outstanding Rumanian musician, Georges Enesco in combining a universal gift with unfailing integrity of purpose to such a high degree. Whether in the field of composition or of concert playing, his activity was prompted by a single determination to promote beauty—determination brought about by an overwhelming inner quest for self-expression in art. Irrespective of the forms in which this quest manifested itself, it was always subordinated to a noble cause inspired by great humanistic ideals.

Enesco was a devoted servant of these ideals for more than half a century; he served them by playing his violin in small, poor provincial towns and in the world's greatest concert-halls, on the rostrum as an orchestra conductor, and at his desk, composing music. But no matter in what capacity he appeared in public, as composer or violinist, conductor or pianist, pedagogue or organizer of musical life, he was first and foremost an artist with a capital "A" and yet merely a fellow human, who saw in himself, as he used to say, "a brother of men whose mission it was to reveal to them a secret which nature had entrusted to him."[1] These words show that Enesco appreciated the cultural and educational role of art in the highest possible sense; they also help us to understand the very essence of his artistic credo in which all kinds of musical activity merged into an organic whole.

An especially important part in this complex formation was the interdependence of composition and performance which were so closely linked that it is difficult to separate them without damaging their internal entity.

It is true that Enesco, particularly in his "Souvenirs"[2] often speaks of composition as his main vocation. But would it be correct to underestimate the part played by the performing art in the process of the formation of his artistic personality?

The French writer, Alexandre Dumas Sr., once bitterly remarked that the fame of an actor was short-lived, for the memory of his art did not survive his generation. However, it is unlikely that Enesco's attitude to concert playing was influenced by such a consideration. No doubt his concerts did deprive composition of much valuable time. More than once he complained about it, expressing his misgivings in a somewhat lighthearted witty manner typical of "causerie mondaine". But Enesco passionately wanted to see his art recognized equally in all its manifestations. Shortly before his death, when assessing his life's achievement, he nevertheless found some kind words to rehabilitate the violin by saying that performing art had not, after all, stood in the way of composition.

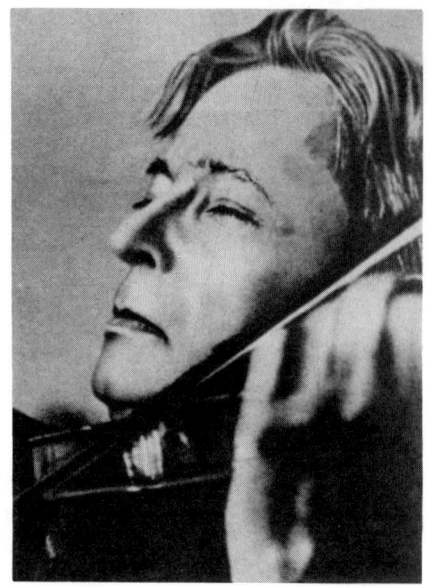

Enesco performing Chausson's *Poème*.

True enough, Enesco, with regard to his violin, would not repeat what F. Liszt had said about his piano, namely, that he was attached to his instrument as much as a sailor to his ship. Even at the start of his career in composition Enesco was attracted not by a solo violin virtuoso piece, but by large-scale symphonic and chamber music works. It is significant that among several orchestral overtures, cantatas and symphonies he wrote as a teen-ager, only one manuscript containing two movements of a violin concerto (1895) was found.[3] In this respect, he represents a very rare exception among other well-known virtuosi composers who write primarily for their own instruments.

Speaking of Enesco, it should be borne in mind that the integration of concert playing with composition had a very positive effect on the development of his talent. It was especially due to the fact that interpretation for him did not amount to a mechanical reproduction of a given musical text, but required a truly artistic rendering of its contents, and this could be achieved only when both the author's and the performer's personalities were welded together into a single concept. He felt that only then could performance become a creative process deserving to be called the art of interpretation. It is this highest synthesis of imaginative power, both in the act of creation and interpretation, that Enesco had in mind when he said: "There is no sacrilege whatsoever in merging oneself with the author of a masterpiece. On the contrary, this is a stimulating illusion thanks to which a performer can most effectively identify himself with that magician whose humble interpreter he is called upon to be. If I do not transplant myself into the eighteenth century when I play a sonata by Bach, if I do not imagine myself to be

Beethoven when I tackle the *Kreutzer Sonata,* it seems to me that I am unable to perform them well."[4]

Enesco's striking gift for transfiguration will be dealt with later on, but now it should be said that the integration of personalities, so common to his way of playing, had its bearing on his music. It was not a simple coincidence that his artistic Olympus, so far as composition and interpretation were concerned, was inhabited by the same gods. It was under their auspices that he found a breeding ground for his way of thinking in composition as well as in his manner of playing; this common source made them mutually increase their fertility. One gave his art magnitude and depth of thought, the other, a strong touch of reality.

Is it possible in Enesco's music to separate the gigantic large-scale conception and monumental proportions as in his opera *Oedipe,* or his wide-ranging symphonic thinking in orchestral and chamber music works from his style as a conductor? Were they not shaped by the same creative willpower through which he was able to chisel out his majestic tone-sculptures on a concert stage? If we examine his subtle orchestration, his manner of writing, the fine character of his instrumental texture, in short, his general way of treating musical instruments, we recognize at once the hand of an accomplished conductor, soloist, accompanist, quartet and orchestra player for whom a score is not an abstract graphic outline of voices, but an aggregate of the sounds they actually produce. Moreover, in the nature of his orchestral writing, one can detect the supreme craftsmanship of a musician who, like a medieval jeweler, takes great pride and pleasure in working out every single detail of his design. The way Enesco employed his technical skill had much in common with the folkloric background of his art, of which many features had their counterparts in the popular interpretative style. For instance, let us look at the endings in a number of melodic phrases from Enesco's A-major *Rumanian Rhapsody* (ex. n 1). Here the composer imitates

Ex. 1

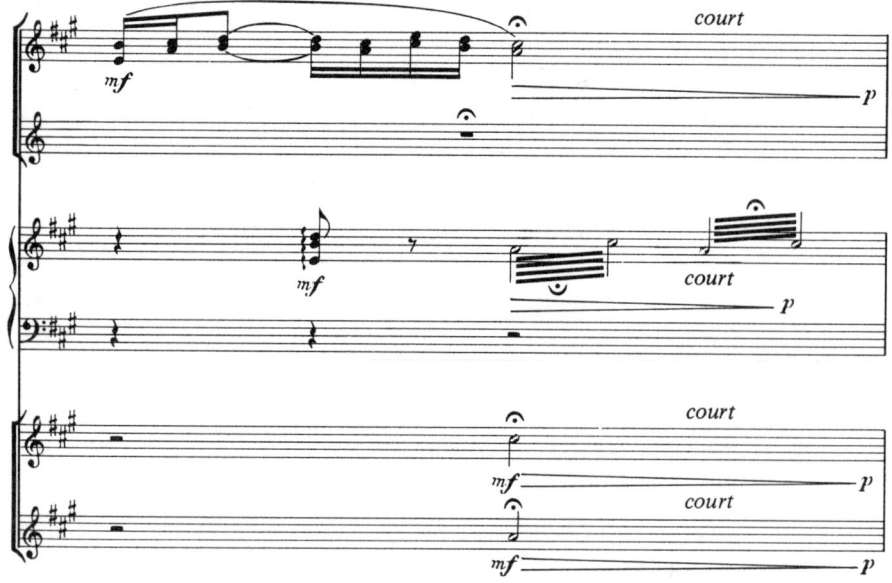

the peculiar sound of the cobza.[5] Its specific flavor is reproduced here so neatly and precisely that one has an impression of actually hearing folk-players engaged in their usual music-making.

But the influence of popular art is to be felt not only in Enesco's approach to tone-coloring; it played a substantial part in shaping his melodic style as well. In this respect the role of the violin, which for centuries had been a popular instrument in both Rumania and Moldavia, could hardly be overestimated.[6] The tuneful sound of the violin, its large-breath melodic respiration, for which Enesco as a violinist was so much admired, had a direct bearing on him as a composer. As a matter of fact these qualities contributed to the crystallization of his entire melodic style characterized by dynamism, flexibility and amplitude, neatness of melodic pattern and variety of expression. Enesco considered melody to be the basic means of expression; such an approach to it had, no doubt, much to do with his masterly way of handling the violin which is a melodic instrument.

The fact that Enesco as a youngster was attracted by the best examples of classic music—especially in his detailed study of Johann Sebastian Bach's immortal masterpieces—helped him to develop that rare quality that N. Rimsky-Korsakov had termed "the ability to hear a voice progression." The Rumanian musician possessed this quality in an equal degree as a performer and as a composer. This fully revealed itself, for example, in his interpretation of Bach's *Chaconne* as well as in the character of his polyphony which he considered to be not an artificial display of ingenious contrapuntal technique, but a living tissue made up of several melodic lines, each of which preserved its expressive quality. He had the advantage of combining a composer's know-how of viewing a musical

Georges Enesco at age 6.

César Franck, one of the few great representatives of the French Romantic school, and one whose music had a lasting impact on the artistic development of Georges Enesco.

text as a whole with the complete command of all the resources of a bowed instrument. This enabled him to achieve amazing results in cases which at first glance might seem quite unrelated to one another. The same applies to the unison prelude from his first orchestral suite, whose melodic texture seems to unfold itself as if from within, and to his truly score-like conception of the *Chaconne* written by Bach for solo violin.

To grasp Enesco's individuality, it is necessary to understand how such a synthesis of double art was brought about. As a composer he was deeply influenced by C. Franck whose music made a strong impact on his way of thinking. This is particularly noticeable so far as the character of his monothematic writing is concerned which, despite the difference in personalities of the two musicians, bears a clear resemblance to the monothematic technique of Franck. Another common feature with Franck is the fact that neither of them depended on a literary text or on a scenario to put across the programmatic contents of their works.

The integrity of purpose, so typical of Enesco in general, determined the character of his symphonic writing. Symphonism, as the highest type of musical thinking, manifested itself in his works of various kinds, provided there was an artistic need for it. It had at its root a distinct dialectical principle which implied a frequent transformation of an artistic image taking place during a process of intense development of internal contradictions potentially embodied inside a thematic nucleus. Enesco's symphonic conception, closely linked with his monothematic inclination, grew in contact with the classical symphonism of Beethoven and Brahms, having assimilated the aforementioned features of Franck's art.

As we already know, music for Enesco represented something much greater than a purely artistic occupation. In fact, he was an artist who felt himself to be at the same time a missionary. For him to have a belief meant to profess it. "Music for me is not a state of mind, but action," said Enesco, stressing the dynamic character of his artistic vision.[7] Enesco was aware of the tremendous emotional impact music could have, of its power to provoke an echo in people's souls. "To be vibrating myself in order to make others vibrate"—this was the main thing for him.[8] Thus it becomes clear what great moral satisfaction he derived from his interpretative art which gave him an almost unlimited opportunity to achieve his aspiration. For him, direct contact with the audience was an effective means of communication with people. Thus as an interpreter, he could transform himself into a relentless messenger and an inspired herald of his lifelong dream "to lead people forward on the way to the better." This was the aim he cherished most as an artist.

Guided by that lofty goal, he found in his violin not only a means to achieve it but also a source of a handsome income without which an artist cannot feel himself independent. This enabled him to concentrate on creative activity, spared him the gloomy necessity to sharply budget his time in order to earn his living. He was more fortunate than many others who, despite their determination, had to compromise by engaging in tedious private lessons, copying music, arranging someone's works or composing commonplace pieces. He was privileged to live as he liked, that is to say, serving his art and through it, serving people. He would consider himself a happy man if, thanks to his concerts in provincial towns, there appeared one more music-lover.

Enesco's way of playing, and his music, produced a strong impression on laymen and professional musicians alike. One of them, the well-known French composer Arthur Honegger wrote to Enesco on September 30, 1954: "The sound you extract from your violin, the impression produced upon me by your sonatas, symphonies, Octet and particularly by the so strikingly moving *Oedipe* have served me as guide-lights throughout my musical career."[9] This letter tells us that the call, sent from Enesco's heart, was reaching its destination, and there was no higher reward for a man who could, in the twilight

Georges Enesco in 1896, at the time of his studies in Paris

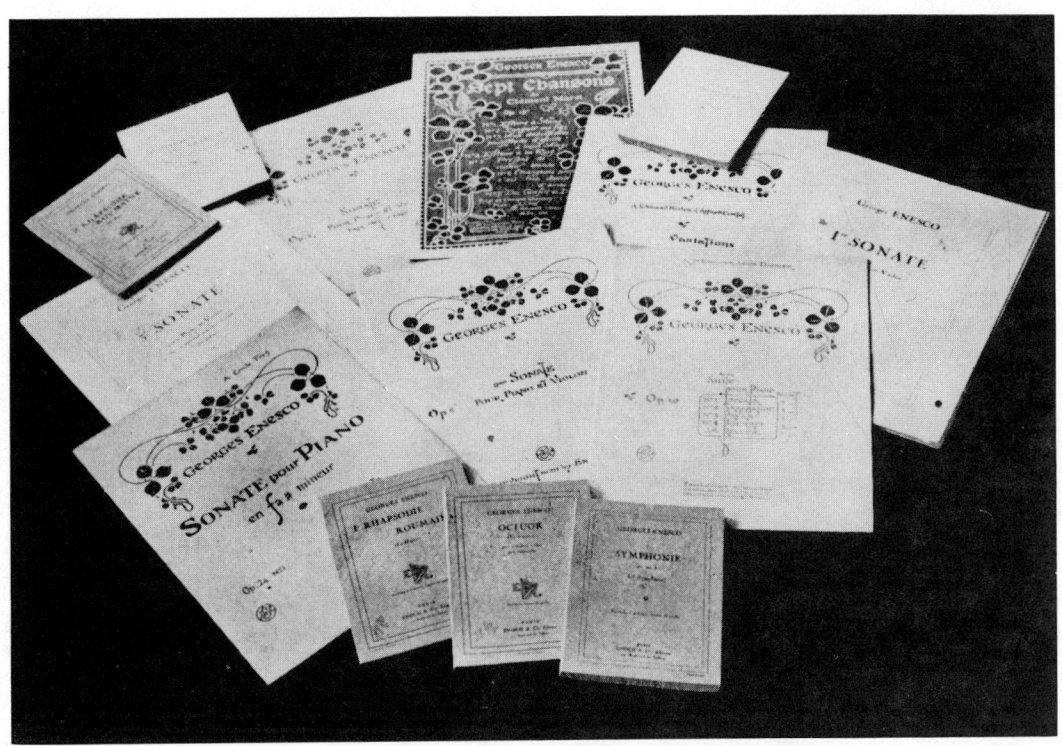

A display of the scores of some of Enesco's most significant works.

of his life exclaim: "so long as I live I shall sing".[10]

Such an expression could have been uttered only by an artist who had been nourished by a mighty vital force. How it affected the formation of his personality could be gathered from Enesco's "Souvenirs" in which he singled out with great affection the three following stages: the village Liveni, (situated in the heart of Moldova, where on the 19th of August 1881 he had been born), the charming Vienna and the dazzling Paris.

The five-year-old Enesco with his parents, Costache and Maria Enescu.

Chapter 1

Wherever Enesco was, he always kept alive in his memory the unforgettable fragrance of his native land, that pungent scent of the countryside, whose nostalgic sweetness evoked in his imagination vivid pictures from his early childhood. Steep slopes of the Carpathian mountains, as if disfigured by deep abysses, an endless steppe, crisscrossed by ravines, dark green patches of woods against the background of barley and corn fields, the dim fringe of the horizon, and, as far as the eye could see, deserted, dusty tracks, stretching out in the distance, along which in the heat of summer days karutsas,[11] drawn by sleepy oxen, were slowly dragging on—such was the landscape that remained engraved in the child's mind.

As the youngest son, and the only one to survive in a family of eight children, he grew up in seclusion without companions of his own age, without noisy games or any other children's entertainments, surrounded by the untiring care of his loving parents. Deprived of an outlet, his energy took an inward course. This made him concentrate upon himself and become thoughtful from his early days. The habit of taking everything in earnest stimulated the sensitive and vivid imagination he had inherited from his mother. All this affected favorably the development of the creative impulse in his character. It clamored to come into the open, and music, with its inherent emotional appeal, provided the much needed outlet. Thus, music served him as an "exhaust-pipe" to discharge his oversaturated sensitivity just as a safety-valve allows extra steam to escape from an overheated boiler.

To this must be added that the child's love for music had a family background. His grandfather was well-known in the neighborhood as a good singer, and his parents used to indulge in music-making in their spare time. Strolling fiddlers were welcome guests at Enesco's house, and the boy was deeply impressed by their exotic appearance and the way they played. Looking back later at those early days, Enesco would say that even then there was no line of demarcation between his life and music. From then on, the desire to compose became his sole dream.

At the age of seven, leaving for Vienna, he carried with him sweet recollections of his childhood in which the house where he had been

e house where Enesco was born
Liveni (now George Enescu).

The landscape of Enesco's birthplace, which forever remained dear to his heart.

The five-year-old Georges with a violin, his lifelong passion.

Top, facing page:
The Enescu family.
Bottom, facing page:
Georges' parents, Costache and Maria.

17

born, and the surrounding landscape, peasants singing in the evenings and the sound of the shepherd's flute merged into a single image—that of his native land.

Vienna with its picturesque environment captured the boy's imagination. Everything seemed strange to him in this huge town on the Danube, flanked on all sides by vineyards and projecting itself majestically against Bohemia, Tirol and the boundless Hungarian steppes on which, as he fancied, he could see the shadow of the galloping Mazepa. Vienna's attractive spell was also due to its colorful atmosphere. In this modern Babylon, situated at the crossroads of the Adriatic and the Baltic seas to the Danube, were strangely mingled together oriental and western influences, the remnants of the old, patriarchal way of life and the brilliance of a great European capital. Enesco grew fond of this radiant city which looked to him a little bit sad and yet frivolous, most kind and very slightly sentimental. To him, Vienna seemed a sanctuary whose atmosphere still preserved that air of intimate privacy which could be described only by the German word Gemütlichkeit (coziness, tranquility, goodheartedness).[12] But through its apparent carelessness he could see Heiligenstadt, which had become the scene of one of the greatest human misfortunes experienced by Beethoven, and the cozy bar where Schubert, already fatally ill, had played at a friendly party his *Die Winterreise* only a year before his death.

Joseph Hellmesberger, Jr., Enesco's violin teacher and mentor.

Places made famous by so many geniuses were sacred to Enesco. It seemed to him that he could see their shadows still floating over them. They became real in his imagination and made up a part of his own life. He eagerly absorbed the new impressions invoked by architecture, paintings, literature and music. Beethoven, whose austere, majestic and tragic image struck him as vividly as if he had seen the composer alive, became his idol. Already at the age of fourteen he came to regard Beethoven's art as an embodiment of the supernatural and the human, free of sentimentality, like a statue by Michelangelo.[13] Beethoven's music satisfied his longing for harmonic tension which revealed itself in the first piano pieces he tried to compose in Liveni. The impact of Beethoven on him was so strong that Enesco had the impression of knowing him very well personally. It seemed to him that Beethoven was still living, if not actually in the flesh, at least in the memory of those who had had contact with him. There still were such men at the Vienna Musical Academy where Enesco studied. Its director, Joseph Hellmesberger, Senior, was one of them. He would often tell his pupils how his father, who had been a friend of Beethoven, played in the presence of the master. The time-gap between Enesco and the giant of Bonn lessened also because the student orchestra used to play many of Beethoven's works from old hand-written copies.

Even more familiar did Brahms seem to Enesco. He saw him very often between 1888 and 1892 when Brahms used to come to the Musical Academy to supervise the student orchestra. Sitting next to

Hellmesberger's wife Wilhelmina.

Johannes Brahms, one of the idols of Enesco's youth.

the leader of the orchestra, the youngster had the honor to accompany him in his *First Piano Concerto* and to perform under the composer's direction his *C-minor symphony*. Brahms's manners, his music and piano playing fascinated him. It was not brilliancy, but profundity that he admired in Brahms. Penetrating the dense texture of his music, he felt as if in a thick forest full of wonderful perfumes. This music appealed to him by its romantic impulse and logic of expression, by its warm lyricism and emotional control. There was yet something else that made Brahms' music particularly dear to him: it was the Hungarian flavor present in a number of his works. The Andante from his *Clarinet Quintet* in B minor carried his imagination away to some distant Hungarian lands which lay beyond his native country.

It was in Vienna that Enesco first became acquainted with Wagner's music. This happened thanks to Joseph Hellmesberger Junior who was not only his violin teacher, but also the third conductor at the opera theatre. He was an excellent musician, brought up in the best Viennese traditions, and wanted to see his gifted pupil develop in the same way. He took complete care of the boy who, according to the established custom, was staying in his house which had been one of Vienna's centers of musical life. Besides giving him violin lessons, he took him regularly to his quartet and orchestral rehearsals. These gave the boy an excellent opportunity to enlarge his musical interest. Under his teacher's paternal guidance, he grew very fond of symphonic music, and the orchestra surprised him by its diversity and magnitude of sound.

A conductor having at his command this vast world of sounds seemed to him like a sorcerer with a magic power. This wonderful force captured his daring imagination, and from then on the desire to be a conductor became his most cherished dream.

In reminiscing about his early Viennese impressions, Enesco later would single out the concerts given by Hans Richter, who was a well-known conductor of Wagner's operas. He heard him direct *Der Fliegende Hollander, Tannhauser, Lohengrin* and the tetralogy, *Der Ring des Nibelungen.*

Wagner aroused in Enesco an irresistible love that persisted throughout his entire life. Wagner was for him "... an artist who, speaking about God, was addressing himself to people and appealing to what was most intimate in them."[14] Wagner's music evoked in Enesco concrete sensations. Thus, some of "Wagner's chromaticisms became"—as he put it—"a part of his vascular system."[15]

These words have a special meaning from a double point of view. They help us to understand Enesco's approach to Wagner, who, together with other great composers, played a very important role in his development. At the same time, they throw a light on the specific nature of his artistic perceptions. Wagner's influence can be seen in the early works by Enesco. These show a tendency towards elaborate forms, large proportions and intense sonority. This is obvious in a number of his symphonic overtures reminiscent of Wagner's models.

These words of Enesco also suggest that even at this early age, he had a pronounced inclination for concrete sensual forms of perception from which any art phenomenon provoked a reaction that assumed an almost bodily shape. It was prominent in perceptions of different kinds, both auditory and visual. "Already in Vienna"—he says—"certain combinations of color in painting provoked in me a feeling of voluptuousness."[16] Literature too gave him enough material to excite his suggestible imagination. But he never responded to his perceptions in a naturalistic manner. They acquired, in his inner laboratory, a truly expressive meaning. That is why his music, with all its suggestive power, never became purely descriptive even when he was depicting a characteristic popular scene or a landscape as, for instance, in his two Rumanian rhapsodies, *Dixtuor* or *Impressions of Childhood.*

The four years spent at the Vienna Musical Academy, from which Enesco graduated with a distinction diploma in 1892, gave the young musician a solid professional basis. Much as he was fascinated by composition, he devoted a great deal of his time to the violin which, in its own way, also led him into the realm of sound.

As a boy, he was trained by teachers who belonged to the Viennese violin school. They still kept alive the traditions of G. Böhm, J. Dont, G. Ernst and Joachim, and did their best to hand them over to the young violinist. In the course of his studies, he was made to work on a very wide repertory containing various masterpieces of the violin literature. S. Bachrich, with whom he had begun his violin studies, and later J. Hellmesberger, both directed him in such a way as to assure a harmonious development of his musical personality. R. Fuchs, who had taught him harmony, counterpoint and composition, had the same aim in mind.

Enesco was an extraordinarily diligent pupil. Working sixteen hours a day, he constantly increased his knowledge. Nothing —neither games, nor any other entertainment of this kind, would distract him from his work. Gradually he developed a special attitude to work which became a natural habit for him, nay, an inner necessity. Later on this attitude, so characteristic of a man committed to his cause like Enesco, will give rise to the following maxim: "rest from work in labor."[17] During his stay in Vienna he acquired, by switching from one kind of work to another, a substantial amount of knowledge which enlarged his artistic horizon. He lost interest in school tasks which seemed to him schematic and too narrow in scope. He was attracted more and more by large-scale works and complicated genres. If before, in his native village, the boy of five called his first compositions "operas", now in Vienna the eleven-year-old composer was writing variations, rondos, sonatas and especially symphonic overtures in Wagner's spirit. That was the outcome of the Vienna period. But that was only a beginning, an accumulation of strength to lay the foundation of a new edifice which was yet to be erected.

Top, facing page:
Georges Enesco during his years at the Vienna Musical Academy.
Bottom, facing page:
The medal of distinction Enesco won at the Vienna Musical Academy.

Enesco at age 19.

Chapter 2

In Paris, Enesco was confronted with an intricate situation full of novelty and contradictions. The golden age of the French opera of the fifties and seventies and later of instrumental music, as well as the upsurge of concert life, helped Paris to regain its former position of authority as a leading musical center of the world. Enesco had a foretaste of its attractive power while still in Vienna, when he was present at the first performance of Massenet's *Werther* in 1892. But by 1894, when he came to Paris, the period of "renouvellement" in French music largely lost its impetus. The French bourgeois art was going through a deep crisis under the impact of the growing contradictions of the imperialist era. In conditions prevailing in the Third Republic, realistic tendencies were losing their social incentive, and progressive artists, who could not put up with the ruthless reality, but had no strength to oppose it, were indulging more and more in a mood of hopeless expectation, reminiscent of Balzac's "Lost Illusions". After the outrage caused by Berlioz's rebellious outburst, which so mercilessly exposed the whole ugliness of the bourgeois idol, it seemed that no one in France could ever again believe seriously in its chaste sanctity. Thanks only to his optimistic conception did Bizet succeed in setting the French opera on a new, dynamic course, but his premature death, like an ill-fated irony of history, seemed to shatter all possible hopes. And yet the best French lyrical operas, well-known for their sincere and straightforward expressive appeal, refreshed the atmosphere still stiffened by conventionalities present even in such otherwise valuable operas as *La Juive, La Muette de Portici* or *Les Huguenots*.

French instrumental music too was not free of conflicting trends. In certain circles it became fashionable for a virtuoso to display his brilliant technique in concert pieces specially written for this purpose, to satisfy public demand. On the other hand, due mainly to Saint-Saëns, Franck, and Lalo, sound, realistic tendencies were beginning to assert themselves more and more clearly. The Franco-Belgian violin school as well as the French piano and organ schools were rapidly gathering strength. By the end of the century, large symphonic and chamber music works had already assumed a prominent place in composers' minds as a result of the desire to find a

Georges Enesco in the first years of his life in Paris.

Jules Massenet, the illustrious French opera composer, who taught composition to the young Georges Enesco at the Paris Conservatoire.

In this letter to Enesco's father, Massenet wrote of his pupil: "Your son is *an exceptional individual*—this is, indeed, the most interesting musical constitution that there can be ... Your son will do you great honor, as well as to our art and his country."

The building of the Paris Conservatoire in the late 19th century.

suitable framework to provide sufficient room for wide-ranging artistic generalizations. But side by side with works of great emotional appeal and imaginative power, there also were compositions in French instrumental music showing a marked preference for a desirable sophisticated design.

So far as the activity of a number of prominent musical figures was concerned, it looked as mixed as ever. Being involved in the Parisian musical life and promoting its most progressive manifestations, they could, at the same time express conservative or even clerical views. There was no unity in the French national musical society either. According to Romain Rolland, it looked like a cathedral divided into separate compartments with different gods in each of them.[18] Such a division of views, which reflected the diversity of life itself, was spreading disunity in the musical world in which various contradictory tendencies were co-existing side by side. Thus, for some musicians, Bach was the most revered composer of all times, while others considered him dull and old-fashioned. Attempts to keep his or Couperin's traditions alive were coupled with innovations of an obviously far-fetched nature; endeavors to assert the national character of French music did not necessarily preclude a servile submission to Wagner's theories.

Such was the situation in musical France when Enesco embarked on a new stage of his career.

The Paris Conservatoire was housed in an old shabby building where, in dark and dusty classrooms, so many world-famous musicians worked. Enesco gained access to the Conservatoire thanks to a letter of introduction from Hellmesberger to Massenet. The latter attracted the youngster both as a man and as a teacher, fascinating him by his charming and friendly manners, his wit and refined musicality. Massenet taught composition at the Conservatoire and, after going through Enesco's works, gave him his blessing as did A. Gedalge, with whom the boy studied counterpoint and fugue. M. Marsick accepted him as his violin pupil. The mere fact of being admitted to the Paris Conservatoire—then one of the highest ranking musical establishments in Western Europe—came as recognition of the young musician's exceptional talent. As the number of contenders was extremely large, the entry standards were very high, especially for foreigners, and only the best among them managed to qualify. Before Enesco, only a few foreign musicians, namely H. Wieniawski, P. Sarasate and F. Kreisler had such an honor bestowed on them. Those who knew Enesco at the time were amazed to see how many-sided was his gift. A. Cortot, who was one of them, after many years, still vividly remembered how struck he was to hear Enesco play equally well the first movement of the *Violin Concerto* by Brahms and Beethoven's piano sonata, *Aurora*.[19]

Although for the first year, Enesco was granted permission to study with Massenet on a voluntary basis only, he continued to compose as intensely as before. The master and the pupil were united in their love for Wagner, the orchestra and polyphony, and this soon established a mutual understanding between them. The elegance of style and purity of writing, in which the author of *Manon* and *Werther* so graciously excelled, helped Enesco to perfect his own language. He especially appreciated Massenet's request to work out the counterpoint technique as much as possible in order to achieve polyphonic skill.[20] Gedalge also encouraged him in this work, paying much attention to the purity of lines in a polyphonic design. His memory was very dear to Enesco who saw in Gedalge a man possessing the secret of how to open new horizons in dealing with students, while maintaining a strict logic of thought.[21]

Thus, from the very start in Paris, Enesco became used to combining his creative impulse with restraint, which made him immune to dogmatic rules and a disorderly way of thinking. Thanks to the contact with Massenet, his lyricism was becoming more delicate. During one year of study with him, Enesco wrote three symphonies, one of which was later performed in Bucharest under the author's direction. These compositions, written in his school days, show, as he himself recalls, a strong influence of Brahms' music while the enhanced quality of their melodic texture reveals the magic touch of the hand of Massenet whom Saint-Saëns so deservedly called "one of the most glittering diamonds in our musical crown."[22]

For the next three years, Enesco continued his studies with G. Fauré, who succeeded Massenet as professor of composition. This was the period of complete maturity in Fauré's art when his music acquired very moving and, at the same time, restrained lyrical undertones while preserving its elegant style. Enesco, who at that

André Gedalge, Enesco's counterpoint and fugue teacher at the Paris Conservatoire.

Above left: The eminent French composer Gabriel Fauré, with whom Enesco studied composition.
Above right: Edouard Colonne, who conducted the premiere of Enesco's first successful work, *The Rumanian Poem*.

point was tending towards such a kind of lyricism, found in the author of *Pénélope* a sympathetic tutor about whom P. Casals had said that "his music hinged on traditions of the great art."[23] Enesco studied Fauré's works not only as a composer, but also as a performer, being a partner in playing together his sonata for violin and piano as well as his two quartets. This common exercise brought them still closer together. Relations with Fauré, who had been struggling against the conservative tendencies of the French right-wing musical circles, contributed to developing in the young Rumanian musician a negative attitude to everything that was outdated or old-fashioned in art. Paying tribute to his master, Enesco had composed *Dedication to Gabriel Fauré* which was performed at the celebrations held in honor of the old maestro in 1922.

During all these years, Enesco continued to work as devotedly and intensely as ever. It is typical of his mentality that even as a teen-age student he wrote music, as he put it, "with all his heart."[24]

His first success came with the *Rumanian Poem* which, at the age of only fifteen he had composed for a symphony orchestra. In this work, performed by E. Colonne in 1898, he wanted to conjure up for the French public the image of his beloved native land which he had cherished since his early childhood. At the beginning of the poem, the music conveys the serene atmosphere of a summer evening. "We are on the eve of a holiday . . . bells are ringing, calling to the evening service; community singing is heard through the open gate of the church. Then night falls . . . the moon rises . . . one can hear a melancholy tune coming from somewhere far off; it's a shepherd playing a doina[25] on his rustic flute. All of a sudden the scene changes, the moon disappears . . . a storm breaks out. When it dies down, a cock is heard. Once again bells are ringing . . . a general dance, and the poem ends with the Rumanian national anthem."[26]

In this way the author wanted to tell the public about his native country in sound pictures, recreating the specific character of its life and landscape. The use of program music for this purpose was not accidental, but came as a result of the type of thinking which Enesco had already acquired in this early period. Hence the freshness and originality of colors which determine the realistic expressive brightness of the *Rumanian Poem*. The vitality of its music lies not only in colorful orchestration, but above all in the introduction of some original Rumanian folk melodies. If we remember, as Rolland says, that towards the end of the century the use of folkloric tunes in French music often resembled "learned theses at the Sorbonne university,"[27] it becomes clear why the *Rumanian Poem* attracted the attention of the contemporary listener.

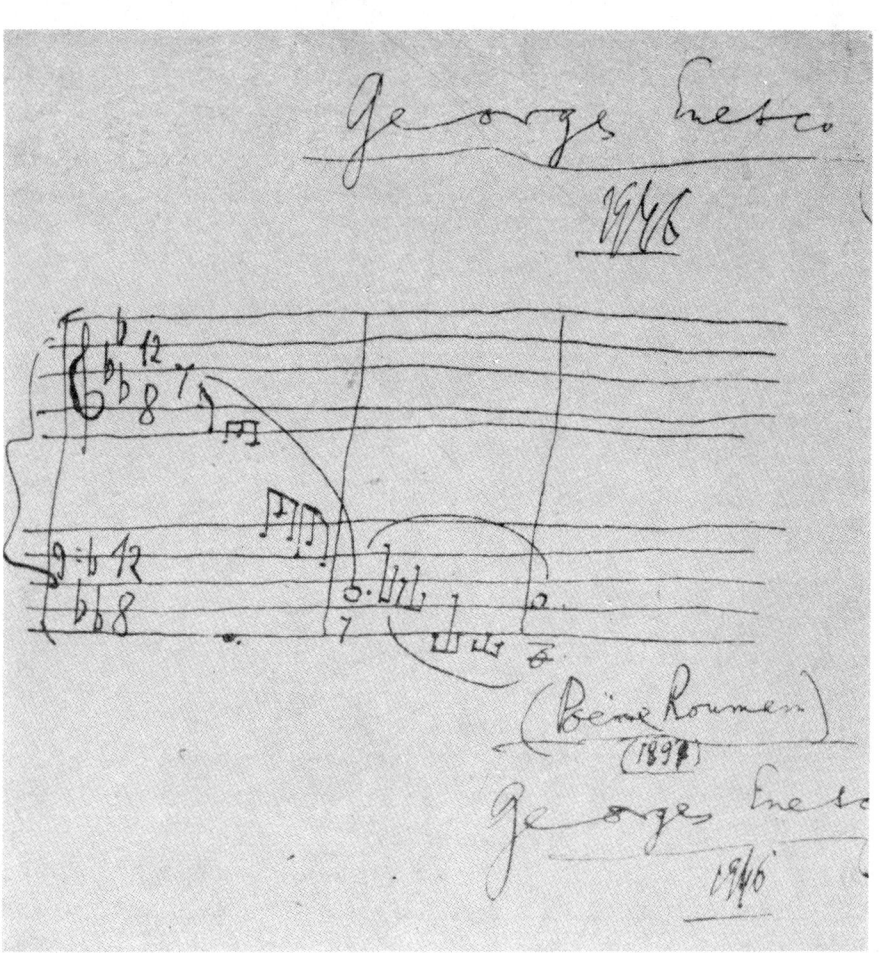

A passage from *The Rumanian Poem*, autographed by Enesco in 1946.

The *Rumanian Poem* marks the beginning of a long path which brought Rumanian music to the international arena. It is very significant of Enesco's patriotic sentiments that in this teen-age composition his imagination was captured by the theme of his motherland. It is true that this theme is as yet treated under its generic and descriptive aspect in the framework of a suite-type composition in which the author used the national anthem of his country, besides popular melodies. Later this theme will be treated in a much more profound and subtle way, free of naïve and official patriotism. This way of treating it reveals a point very important for a true understanding of Enesco's art — its universal essence which rests on a highly developed national basis.

However, the last years of the century were for Enesco but an exploratory period during which he was anxiously seeking his own way in art, accumulating and testing his strength time and time again. By then his interests were already wide-ranging, his aspirations very serious. He was tempted to experiment in various genres, forms and styles. And once again he was attracted, not by refined miniatures or brilliant solo pieces, but by works on a large scale. After the *Rumanian Poem* with its loose structure, he turned to chamber music, piano suite, vocal cycles and orchestral fantasia. He wrote his first sonata for violin and piano, the first piano suite *In the Old Style, Three Melodies* for voice and piano on verses by J. Lemaitre and S. Prudhomme as well as *The Pastoral Fantasia* for orchestra. These works served no doubt as a useful testing-ground for mastering the technique of composition, but they also show greater care in selecting thematic material which becomes potentially more significant as, for instance, in the slow movements from the sonata and the suite. At the same time, they point to the progress in building up large forms and in handling contrapuntal patterns. This may be attributed not only to Enesco's aptitude to think in polyphonic terms, but also to the fact that many of those who influenced him during his Parisian years had themselves grown up as composers in close contact with the organ.

So, in Paris, Enesco's lifelong dream to be a composer had come true, but the violin, though pushed aside by composition, had not been forgotten. His will to preserve and his endurance were as remarkable as ever, but he was not satisfied. Self-conscious and very exigent to himself, Enesco confesses that in his endeavor those days to worship two gods at a time, he sacrificed the violin. The jealous instrument was taking its revenge, and this resulted in Enesco's winning only the second prize at the 1898 examination.[29] This made him think twice; he began to question himself as to whether it was worthwhile to go on with the violin studies. He turned to Saint-Saëns for advice. The old master gave him his moral backing and, encouraged by his authoritative support, Enesco overcame his hesitations. He decided to persevere still harder, and soon the situation changed. In 1899, the young violinist graduated from the Paris

Conservatoire having been unanimously awarded the first prize at the final examination, particularly for his interpretation of the first movement of Saint-Saëns' *B minor concerto*. Enesco expressed his profound gratitude to Saint-Saëns by dedicating to him his first orchestral suite.

Paris, even more than Vienna, helped Enesco to assimilate the artistic culture of the world. In addition, his studies at the Conservatoire to this end contributed to his links with many outstanding musicians. His schoolmates were Maurice Ravel, Roger-Ducasse, Florent Schmitt, Charles Koechlin, Alfred Cortot and Jacques Thibaud. Enesco often played with Eugene Ysaÿe, Pablo Casals and Fritz Kreisler with whom he had studied in Vienna. With many of them, and especially with Roger-Ducasse, Cortot and Casals, calling the latter ". . . the gods of gods, the guide of my thoughts",[29] he maintained a life-long friendship.

Georges Enesco with Pablo Casals in the early years of their lifelong friendship.

A photograph of the violinist Jacques Thibaud, inscribed "to Georges Enesco, with my sincere affection and my profound admiration."

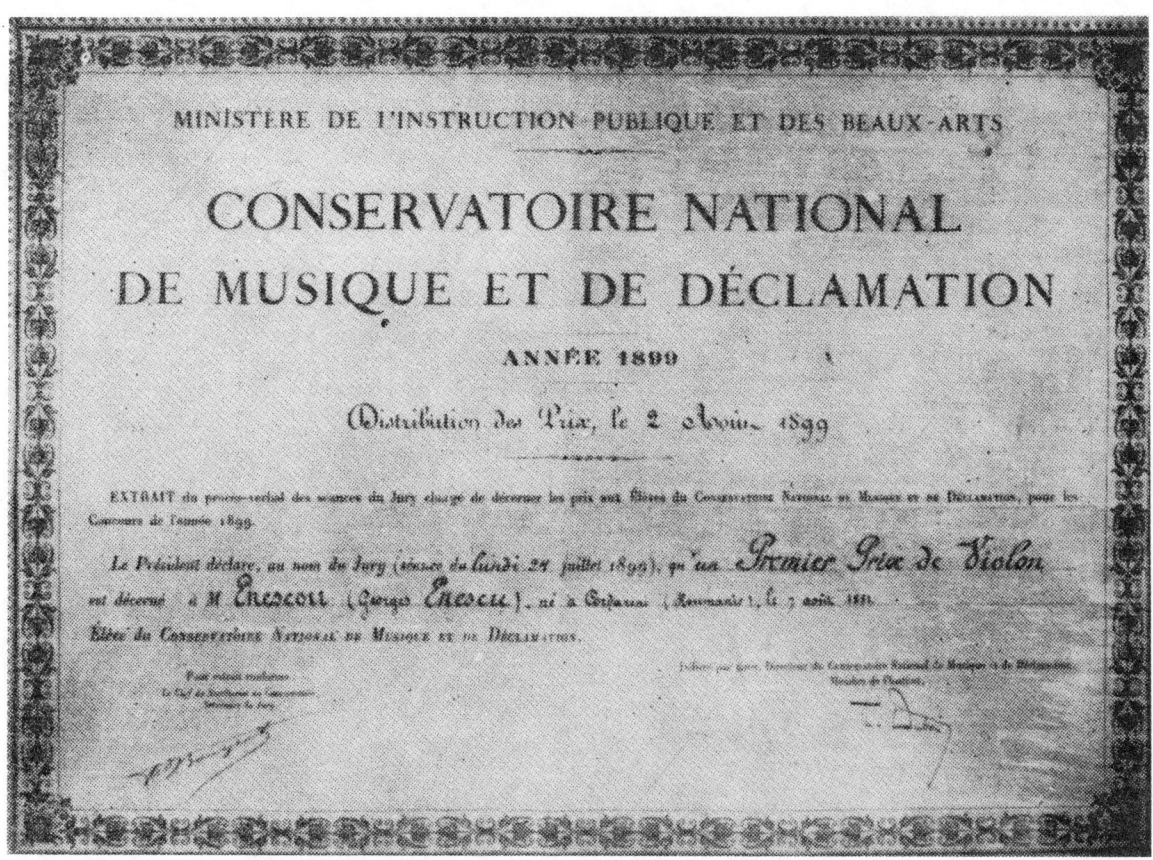

Enesco's Paris Conservatoire diploma for the first prize in violin.

Enesco's school years were coming to an end; but he, who never felt satisfied with what he had achieved, continued to learn as long as he lived. Every new stage of development opened up ever widening horizons, confronted him with new problems which constantly prompted him to go forward in the unceasing search of self-perfection. Any new achievement immediately transformed itself into a new starting point, and one step forward was followed by another. In this way he was advancing on and on, never halting for long to rest; perhaps that is why he never retraced his steps. According to Enesco, he never wrote two similar sonatas or two similar quartets. Only much deeper dedication to a goal can account for so rapid a pace in his development which enabled him to compose, shortly after completing the studies at the Conservatoire, the *Second Sonata for Violin and Piano,* op. 6 (1899) and the *Octet,* op. 7 (1900). It is worth mentioning that in these works he managed to assimilate various influences as well as to affirm his own individuality. Of course, Enesco owed much to his Viennese and Parisian teachers, who had laid the foundation for such swift progress, but it was also due to his own original gift. Casals wrote: "Pupils like Georges Enesco and Florent Schmitt, in whom there had already been a spark of genius, were not shaped by their teacher no matter how outstanding he might have been. A genius is "shaped" by himself, and his teachers, irrespective of their qualities, contribute to his development only in a very modest way."[30]

Enesco wreathing the brows of a diminutive Dinu Lipatti (1921).

Chapter 3

The *Second Sonata for Violin and Piano* is representative of the way Enesco's personality was asserting itself. Unlike the early experiments of many composers, this work shows not only further progress in acquiring technological skill, but also the great emotional power its author already possessed. The sonata reveals in Enesco an artist for whom music is the only means of expressing the secret call of his soul with all its "mysterious fluctuations".[31] Are they not audible enough in the initial lyrical theme of the second movement which captures one's imagination by its touching emotional strain?

What a blend of feelings in the delicate violin melody which carries in it a hidden reproach, as if timidly complaining about something, and yet remains soft, warm, a little sad and somewhat meditative! It seems as though somebody plunged in recollections is narrating a story about something which he dearly loved, but perhaps has lost forever. And because of that, this outwardly calm utterance contains a touch of bitterness mingled with a moving, but restrained emotion:

Enesco in 1903.

This theme has a pronounced national character owing to its structure as well as to specific modal and rhythmic features. Its Aeolian mode, a Phrygian semi-tone which occurs due to the lowered II degree (bar II), changeable duple and triple measurements which betray an affinity with the ancient Slavonic layers of Moldavian musical folklore—all this creates a soft yet intense atmosphere. These features, in a work which Enesco considered to be his first original composition, is very symptomatic of his entire orientation. They emphasize the connection between his way of thinking and the art of his people, and this connection in its various forms will be manifest in his best compositions. It is noteworthy that in his sonata, the seventeen year old composer returned to the popular and national sphere in order to express in generalized terms a deep human feeling. Unlike the *Rumanian Poem*, here he did not follow the easier way of quoting "ready-made" folk tunes, but created an original theme of his own closely linked in its character with popular music.

Enesco's attitude to folklore is exemplified by his following words:
> I believe that popular art is good in itself. To employ it in symphonic works amounts to enfeebling it as if diluting it in water. Every composer must inspire himself by his own means. I know only one exception, and it applies to rhapsodies where folk tunes are fitted to one another and not worked out.
>
> A popular melody can be developed by one means only—by a dynamic progression, by repeating it without alterations, without artificial endings or intercalations . . .
> I wrote my rhapsodies in a purely instinctive way and only later tried to find out what inner requirement had induced me to choose that form.[32]

The character of music determined the means of expression used in the second sonata. Referring to music with no literary plot, Enesco points out that in such music it is ". . . the general feeling that brings into being the sonorous argument."[33] This also applies to certain interpretive effects which in this sonata have much in common with the art of lautars.[34] An example of this kind occurs at the end of the second movement (5 bars before number 16) where Enesco uses a very rapid bow tremolo which in piano-pianissimo makes the violin sound like a cobza (ex. n 3).

Other instances will be found if we examine the recording made by Enesco and Dinu Lipatti.[35] It shows how the violinist uses portamento to stress in a typically lautar-like manner the expressive glissando-effect on the three notes (tonic, dominant and leading note) ending the first movement. No less specific is his vibrato which makes the long note in the finale (bars 8 to 11 of number 21) sound intonationally more acute.

The second sonata also provides many examples of Enesco's monothematic method which very early developed into a leading principle of his musical thinking. This can be illustrated clearly by the fact that the same thematic formations frequently occur in various places throughout the work. Thus, the principal subject of the first movement, cast in a peculiar nine-quavers measurement, reappears in augmentation as the second subject of the finale; the material of the transition section from the first movement is used in the course of further development; the initial theme of the second movement is restated in the finale, but now it sounds brighter than before.

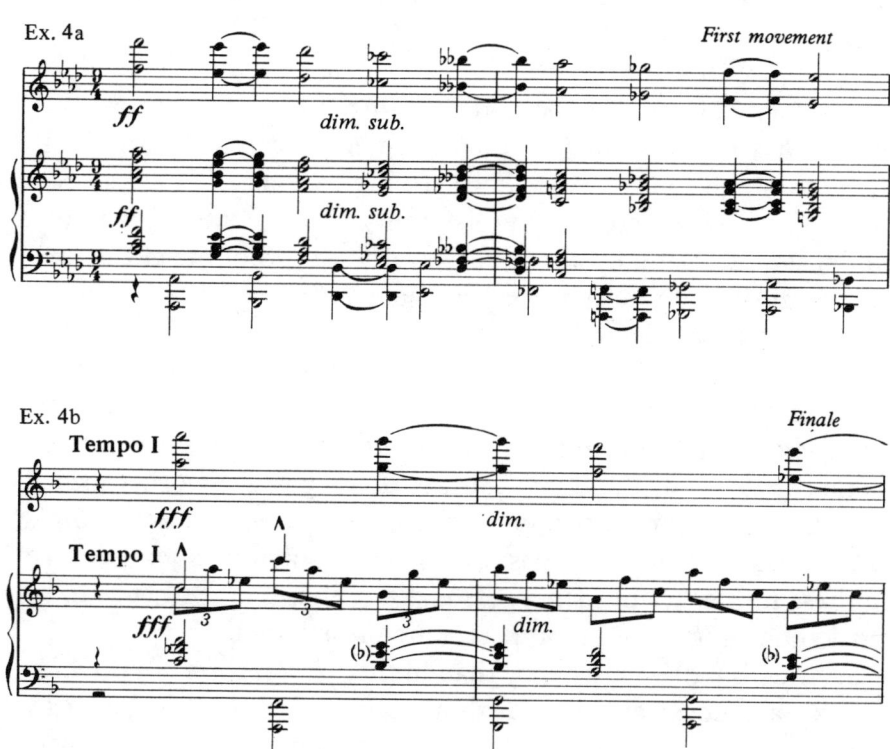

Enesco regarded the act of creation as a conscientious process. This view found its expression in the following words: "To compose one has to restrain oneself."[36]

In accordance with this principle Enesco achieved a high degree of emotional concentration, compressing his feelings to the utmost. Such a condensation of emotion took place especially in the case of an initial theme which, for Enesco, was not a starting point, but represented the outcome of a long preliminary effort.[36] All he had to do was to let its potential possibilities out in the course of ensuing composition. Could any method other than the monothematic one be more suitable for this characteristic quality of his creative process, more fitted to his desire to combine unity with diversity?

The *Second Sonata for Violin and Piano* was written as if in a single drive during a fortnight, but beneath this apparent ease there lay much hard and at times exhausting work. In fact, that work lasted for three years. The period preceding the birth of a new composition Enesco called "the conception phase." This phase was for him a very long one. Compared with it, "the realization phase" took much less time and was much easier. During the "incubation" period various possible solutions were tested and finally selected, and then all that remained to be done was to carry out in earnest what had already existed and matured itself in his mind. Then the work that had been growing within him separated itself from its author like a fully ripened fruit detaches itself from the branch of a tree. "Something is palpitating in my heart without stopping in daytime or at night," said Enesco. It seemed to him that someone from within offered him various solutions, leaving to him the choice of the most appropriate one.[38]

Edvard Grieg.

The habit of scrutinizing and selecting his material thoroughly beforehand explains how different influences could so organically integrate in the sonata with Enesco's individuality. Thus, associations with Franck are clearly distinguishable in the third figures which sound so timidly appealing toward the end of the closing section from the first movement, and again before the piano solo that occurs in the middle of the second movement. The very texture of this piano solo as well as the nature of its polyphonic writing also remind us of Franck. The beginning of the closing section from the first movement points to the *Third Sonata in C-minor* for violin and piano by Grieg, while certain features of the passage-work, especially in the development section of the same movement, are reminiscent of Brahms' violin sonatas. But the Rumanian composer absorbed these influences in such a personal way that their presence in his music does not make his style eclectic or artificial.

Even with more consistency than in the sonata, Enesco's predilection for a concentrated way of thinking revealed itself in his *Octet*. In writing this work, which took him eighteen months to complete, he set for himself a clearly defined task: to write a composition consisting of four interwoven parts which, while preserving their independent function, constitute together the first movement sonata form conceived on a very large scale. Enesco says that, in carrying out this project, he was guided more by consideration of an architectonic nature rather than by a desire to work out an original style.[39] However, the music of the *Octet* is so fresh and original that it contradicts the foregoing words which should not be taken literally.

The composer was so completely absorbed by his chief objective that he simply did not take notice of anything else. The following episode, related by Enesco with his customary good humor, shows how untraditional the *Octet* must have seemed in 1900 when it was written. On hearing it, the son of Edward Colonne exclaimed to his father: "Well, but this awfully beautiful." To this Colonne senior retorted: "Of course, it is more awful than beautiful."[40]

The *Octet*, written for four violins, two violas and two cellos, attracts attention by the significance of its thoughts and the magnitude of its proportions. Compared with the *Second Sonata*, the *Octet* contains a much larger range of lyrical emotions which acquire a considerable dramatic intensity in the course of further development. The main, descending theme of the *Octet*, set out upon the pulsating pedal in the part of the second cello, sounds at first animated, insistent and a little bit alarmed.

Ex. 5

All other themes of the *Octet*, as well as the material for the transition and development sections of the first and other movements, are derived from this initial theme which is subjected to an intense development, in the course of which the theme undergoes several stages of transformation. This applies to the second theme of the first movement which sounds, on the viola, somewhat tired and subdued, and to the threatening beginning of the second movement, and to the opening theme of the third movement with its soft and slightly melancholic sighs, as well as to the exuberant waltz in the last movement (musical examples are given in a schematic outline). Characteristic features potentially present in the main theme are to be felt in the soft outline of the feminine-like melody which appears like a sweet smile towards the end of the first movement, and in the angularly shaped aggressive theme of the fugato. They give rise to the violin melody, which sounds like an excited complaint at the end of the first movement, and to the angry outburst which reaches its dramatic climax at the moment of transition from the third to the last movement.

Ex. 8
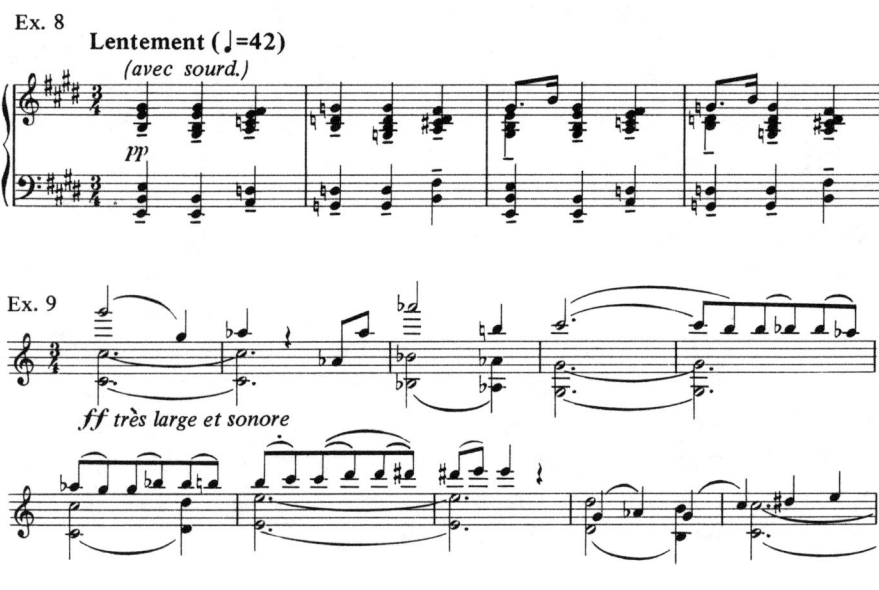

Ex. 9

Ex. 10

Ex. 11

Ex. 12
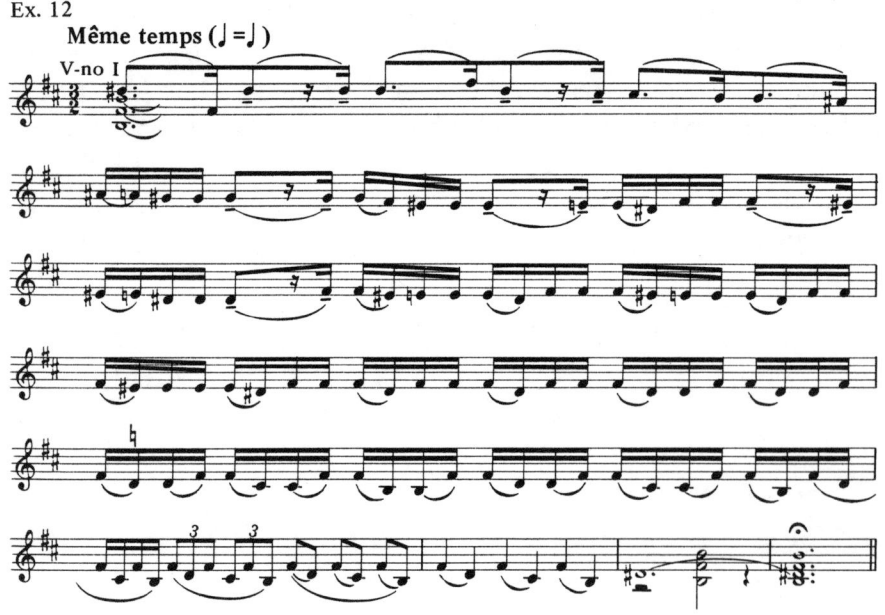

Ex. 13

Instances showing various stages of transformation of thematic material could be multiplied, but those already quoted are sufficient to demonstrate the ingenuity and, above all, the consistency Enesco displayed in applying this principle. Thinking monothematically, he deduced, from characteristic elements of a given structure, new formations which confronted one another, frequently clashing in an uninterrupted process of development. The newly derived theme could differ considerably as compared with its initial source and, acquiring new qualities, transforms itself into its direct opposition. Contrasting forces gradually grow into conflicts which resolve themselves at the final stage of affirmation of the principal idea.

Such a synthesis is reached in the closing section of the last movement where the waltz expresses the triumphant joy of life, and this turns the finale into a force that counteracts the sarcastic grimace of the second movement. It is true that a sudden reminder of it unexpectedly appears like a menacing shadow amidst closing sounds of the finale where a resolutely ascending C-major arpeggio is sharpened by a leap of a diminished fifth towards the lowered second degree.

Ex. 14

With the gloomy, grotesque-like atmosphere of the second movement in his *Octet*, Enesco anticipated the tragically somber dispositions of certain piano pieces by Debussy and Ravel. The second movement of the *Octet* should also be mentioned because the composer turned his attention for the first time to images of a negative character which symbolize the forces of darkness and evil which are hostile to men. Everything in this movement, its aggressive moods, grim excitement, frenzied cries, distorted visions haunting like delirious hallucinations, is reminiscent of Berlioz's gloomy fantastic world with all its demonic paraphernalia. While composing the *Octet*, Enesco wondered how Berlioz would have viewed an instrumental ensemble if only, he adds, one could possibly imagine a man, who in chamber music, had used five orchestras at a time.[41]

There are other things in the *Octet* which make one think of Berlioz. Enesco too chose for this work a large instrumental body capable of ensuring a large volume of sonority; the *Octet* and *The*

Fantastic Symphony by Berlioz are written in the same C-major tonality; and finally, Enesco gives prominence to a theme which has much in common with the Theme of the Beloved from Berlioz's symphony.

Ex. 15a

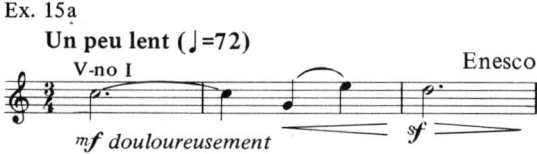

Ex. 15b

It is worth noting that the interval of a major sixth, which is so characteristic of the two themes, occurred in the *Octet* much earlier than the theme itself, foretelling moments of rising emotional tension (viz. examples n. 12 and 13). But if in the French composer's symphony The Theme of the Beloved appears in its purest form in the early stages of the work like an unreal dream only to be completely disfigured later under the impact of ruthless reality, in the *Octet* its fate is absolutely different. Enesco's theme appears in its most elevated version towards the end of the *Octet* as if purified in the course of previous clashes with life. The effect of its appearance there is like that of the sun coming out from behind the clouds, like that of a sigh of relief when a man finally comes out into the open after staggering through a thick and dangerous forest. Despite all the affinities existing between the *Octet* and *The Fantastic Symphony*, the dramaturgical function of their central themes is totally different, and thus stresses the difference in mentality and the ideological conception of the two artists: that of Berlioz, who became deeply disappointed and lost faith in everything, and that of Enesco, who, with all the vigor of youth, believed in life and trusted it.

Besides the high artistic qualities of the *Octet*, one should also mention the technical skill of the young composer. This is illustrated by the masterly way in which he carries out the principle of consecutive development of the main musical idea and its progressive amplification through constant transfiguration. Thus, the triumphant culmination of the finale is already prepared in the third movement where a melodic figure is alluded to, which later gives rise to the exuberant waltz. On a number of occasions, various thematic formations are treated in such a way as to preserve a certain similarity and at the same time constitute a new phase of development, as for instance, in the closing bars of the first and third movements. This technique results in building up thematic arches throughout the work on which its monumental dome rests.

Hector Berlioz, whose music had a great influence on Enesco's work.

Georges Enesco performing at a concert in London (1902).

In many cases in his *Octet* Enesco uses an elaborate polyphonic technique. Besides fugato, he often introduces canon as, for example, in the second theme of the first movement, as well as a variety of other imitational devices. When dealing with a theme, he singles out a characteristic motive or an interval which is later treated in inversion. As a matter of fact, instances of fugal writing occur so frequently in the *Octet* that it is hardly possible to enumerate all of them; but no matter how complicated a polyphonic design might have been, Enesco always tried, in keeping with Gedalge's teaching, to preserve the clarity of melodic lines.

The music of the *Octet* is not as directly connected with the folkloric sphere as that of *The Rumanian Poem* or of the *Second Sonata*; nevertheless, the national background of Enesco's art is to be felt there as well. This is exemplified, for instance, by the fluctuating third at the beginning of the slow movement, and the coexistence of a descending minor scale in the lower tetrachord with the major scale in the upper one in the finale. The major mode of the upper tetrachord does much to enhance the emotional intensity of the musical image.

The national character of Enesco's music revealed itself with great persuasive power in his two *Rumanian Rhapsodies* op. II (1900, 1901) in which he again was inspired by the theme of his native land. The choice of this theme was not accidental. Being a logical consequence of the artist's natural attachment to his homeland, it also reflected his reaction to the circumstances in which he found himself in Paris. From the time the *Octet* had been completed, Enesco, as an artist, felt himself alone. Many of his Parisian friends did not understand this work; nor did they favor his *Concert Symphony for Cello and Orchestra* and the first *Orchestral Suite* which followed, and this made him feel even more uneasy. Paris, which he still admired, gradually began to seem to him much too rational. As for himself, he did not change, remaining (to use his own expression) a delicate and stubborn boy from the far-off Rumanian steppes, "a savage, whom nothing could fully discipline, a staunch adept of independence who accepted no constraint and did not recognize any school."[42] And so he naturally wanted to challenge the refined Paris with something of his own, strictly original and striking.

The interest Enesco had for rhapsody is fully understandable. This interest he felt instinctively as an inner necessity to voice the theme of his native land and this led him to choose the freest and most adequate form which, at that stage of his career, he could best find in a rhapsody.

The two Rumanian rhapsodies were for a number of years far better known and loved by the public than any other work by Enesco. This was due to the originality and freshness of their musical material as well as to the brilliant manner in which it was presented. Both rhapsodies are based on authentic folk tunes, but although the principle of selecting them remains the same, the two works are different in many respects, proving once again that their young author was completely free of standardization or schematism. In fact, in no more than the year that separates the two rhapsodies, Enesco underwent a considerable evolution.

In the first rhapsody, the theme of the native land is presented under its generic aspect on the basis of popular dance music. The rhapsody consists of a series of colorful episodes depicting festive scenes from rural life. Each of them has its own character, but despite their contrasting nature they are united into a single whole, thanks to a brilliantly colorful scoring. In this apotheosis of dance, everything is in motion, generated by a spontaneous impulse. The picturesque atmosphere of the work is sustained throughout so organically that colorfulness does not amount to a sheer display of miscellaneous shades, but grows into a genuinely emotional factor, and this highlights the rhapsody as compared with *The Rumanian Poem*. Sonoristic portrayal technique too is more artistically used in the rhapsody than in the poem. If in the poem onomatopoeic effects had not always been free of naïve naturalistic tendencies, in the rhapsody it already acquired a truly realistic character. This is demonstrated, among other things, by the introduction of the "Ciocarlia" (lark)[43] which incorporates itself quite naturally into the

Program for the first performance of Enesco's *Orchestral Suite* and his *Two Rumanian Rhapsodies*.

general atmosphere of dance and merry-making as an additional means to enhance the intensity of the emotional drive.

Although in his first rhapsody the composer did not intend to develop the folkloric material, he did not restrict himself to its mechanical reproduction, but transformed it to a certain extent. Thanks to his orchestration, harmonization and the use of certain polyphonic devices, folk tunes acquired a new meaning, having been organized by his creative will into an artistically sound whole. But, remaining true to his principle that the folkloric material should be dealt with very discreetly, he achieved his aim by organizing popular melodies rather than by developing them in the proper sense of the word.

The second rhapsody takes us from the atmosphere of general festivity to a totally different world. In this work the theme of his native land is rendered in a dramatic manner. The main musical

A photo of Georges Enesco, inscribed "to my old – although still young – comrade and friend Alfred Casella, as a token of sincere affection. Georges Enesco, Paris, March 1902."

theme of the rhapsody has a severe character inspired by heroic deeds of the past which found their expression in ancient legends and popular ballads. Instead of dance tunes, which predominated in the first rhapsody, here we find ourselves in the realm of song only intermittently interrupted by dance rhythms. Folkloric material too is handled here in a different way; it is not merely exposed, but it undergoes a considerable evolution. It is this that makes the second rhapsody differ in essence from the first, marking a significant shift of opinion in the composer's mind.

The main theme of the rhapsody is potentially very tense. It contains a Phrygian figure which becomes the intonational source of ensuing dramatization. A vigorous development of the theme leads to a point of culmination which was absent in the first rhapsody.

These new features indicate that the composer had departed from the traditional view on rhapsody which in this case acquires certain attributes typical of a poem.

It is known that Enesco intended to write one more rhapsody, but this project was never carried out. Apparently thinking that he had already exhausted all the possibilities of a rhapsodic composition, according to his habit, he decided not to repeat himself. It is characteristic of him that he did not give way to the temptation to follow up the success of the two rhapsodies, but preferred to seek new ways, means and forms more in keeping with his quest for a superior type of development. Assuming that a popular tune can be developed only following the method of "dynamic progression and repetition without any changes"[44] Enesco later no longer quoted folk melodies, composing instead themes of his own based on the idiomatic features of the art of his people. From that point on, the theme of his native land was subjected to a symphonic treatment applied to material that was popular, national and original in character. The material was given a more profound and varied interpretation. Popular and national identity hence was considered not as an attribute of a colorful artistic image, but as a consequence of the esthetic and emotional creed which governs the way of thinking of a musician who realistically reflects the outside world through his feelings and personal emotions.

Thus, realism acquired for Enesco a more and more pronounced psychological meaning, and in the course of this evolution his rhapsodies, particularly the second one, mark a very substantial progress.

In his desire to express a theme of universal humanity in a truthful fashion through the national media, Enesco was guided by the belief that "music is a language which accurately reflects the emotional character of a man and a people."[45]

However, the realistic basis of Enesco's art did not exclude romantic tendencies, already displayed in his first two compositions. In fact, what the Soviet writer Maxim Gorky had said about the complicated nature of an artistic vision could be applied to Enesco. He maintained that "in great artists realism and romanticism are always combined."[46] In a true artist, the coexistence of these two trends is absolutely natural because he cannot create unless closely linked with the art of the people where realism and romanticism live side by side, thus reflecting the dialectical nature of life itself. In the case of Enesco, the presence of this dual phenomenon was brought about by the very background of his creative personality. His realistic orientation was determined not only by the traditions of great classical art; it was also rooted in the art of his people which he had assimilated since childhood. That is why this orientation did not preclude romantic tendencies which, however, had by their nature, nothing to do with the mystic dispositions of the West European post-romanticism.

The same healthy stamina determined Enesco's attitude toward impressionism. He assimilated its achievements, particularly in the field of harmony and timbre, but remained true to himself. The influence of Debussy and early Ravel is obvious. This can be illustrated by numerous examples. One of them, for instance, occurs at the end of the slow movement from the *Second Sonata* for violin and piano. Here Enesco uses two chords forming two perfect

Maurice Ravel.

45

parallel fifths which create the impression of a shadow slowly vanishing in a distant haze.

Ex 16

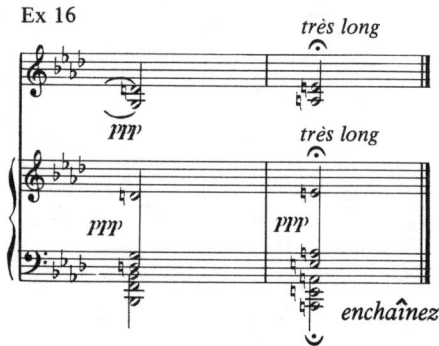

Often he recurred to a succession of perfect parallel fourths as can be seen, for example, in the following fragment Act Two, Scene Two of the opera *Oedipe*.

Ex. 17

Affinities with Debussy and Ravel are particularly evident in the *Second Piano Suite* by Enesco Op. 10 composed in 1903. Like Ravel in his *Pavane pour une infante defunte*, Enesco turned his attention here to the French classical music of the early seventeenth-eighteenth centuries treated in impressionistic spirit. According to the composer, the Pavane and the Bourrée from the aforementioned suite, written in the typical "Ile de France" fashion, are very reminiscent of Debussy.[47]

Speaking of relations between Enesco and Ravel, it is interesting to note that the rhythmic motive of the Toccata from the latter's suite, *Le Tombeau de Couperin* represents an inversion of the second theme of the Toccata from the aforementioned piano work by Enesco. This fact deserves special notice because this suite had been written before Ravel's.

Ex. 18a

Ex. 18b

In 1904, Enesco received the first prize for a piano suite in a competition sponsored by *Musica* magazine. Here, we see his picture along with those of the other winners, including the celebrated harpsichordist Wanda Landowska.

While highly appreciating the achievements of Debussy and Ravel, Enesco nevertheless did not share the esthetics of impressionism. He longed for far-reaching generalizations which presupposed a much wider realistic basis. His dynamic character simply would not let him revel in savoring his own perceptions, no matter how refined they were. Action—not aimless wandering through his inner world—was the main thing for him in music. His attitude toward impressionism was well expressed by Casals who recalled how Enesco, speaking about the charm of Debussy and Ravel, had said that he would like to have not only a charming music, but a more significant and all-embracing one.[48]

A sketch of Georges Enesco by Iser
(1912).

Chapter 4

The search for "a more significant" and "all-embracing" music brought Enesco to symphonic art. He turned his attention to it only when he felt he could stand up to this challenge. It took him considerable time until he fully realized that to write a symphony had become for him an imperative necessity brought about by the desire to express a great idea—to speak on behalf of an artist inspired by the progressive tendencies of his epoch. The optimistic spirit and wide scope of his symphonic conception make it differ from those of Gustav Mahler and Richard Strauss, characterized by tragic thought and subject individualism respectively.

Enesco's positive approach to life revealed itself in his *E-flat major Symphony Number One*, Op. 13 (1905). This work carries a message full of belief in the final triumph of a noble cause over the difficulties that arise before it. The choice of such a theme and its optimistic treatment speak of the progressive aspirations of a mature Enesco whose artistic vision detected the rise of new social forces in the period preceding the first Russian revolution of 1905 and the peasant unrest which swept over Rumania in 1905-1907. The optimistic spirit of the symphony also reflected the vitality of the 24-year-old musician encouraged by the successes of his concert career.

By its orientation, the *E-flat major Symphony* occupies a special place among other West European symphonic works of the beginning of the century. Taking up a theme of an important civil implication, Enesco revived the best traditions of the great symphonic art of the 19th century. Moreover, he revaluated those traditions in the light of his own time. His ideals triumph, not through the death of a heroic personality as they did in Beethoven's music, but through the act of self-affirmation of a man who, in the process of development, becomes aware of his moral strength. That is why in Enesco's symphony there are neither tragic nor heroic elements as Beethoven saw them. From the start of his symphony, the Rumanian composer creates a feeling of an intense emotional drive in which romantic impulsiveness acquires a heroic character.

Ex. 19

This amalgamation of a romantic impetus with heroic undertones makes one think of Schubert's *C-major Symphony* or of Schumann's *Manfred* overture. But Enesco's music is completely free of the psychological split and torment of a romantic personality. His hero does not hesitate when pursuing a noble aim; he is certain as to the outcome, and knows that the aim shall be attained. He is convinced that the path to victory lies through the development of the high ethic qualities of men which will in future enable Oedipus to challenge fate with so much audacity.

Of the three movements that make up the *E-flat major Symphony*, the first in the dramaturgic layout of the work is the most important, representing a complete phase in the development of its idea.

This idea carries such weight that all other elements supplement rather than oppose it. Hence the tightening up of the main sections of sonata from the tendency to obliterate the formal demarcating lines between the exposition, development section and the recapitulation which, together with the coda, constitute an uninterrupted and fast flowing stream. The slow movement with its poetic dispositions introduces a moment of relaxation and contrast into the symphony. However, this does not bring pacification or complete serenity; the slow movement denotes an emotional balance which at times does not exclude sad recollections. As to the finale, its gay atmosphere makes it sound as a logical outcome of the entire work, the end of which turns into an outburst of joy forming an element of life itself.

In 1919 Enesco finished his third, *C-major Symphony,* Op. 21.[49] This work, which took him three years to complete, came as a result of sustained reflections; as a progressive artist he had been staggered by witnessing the sufferings of mankind during the First World War. He returned home from abroad when the war broke out, for he wanted to be with his people in those years of hardship. As a patriot he chose to share the fate of his fellow countrymen and their difficulties although he could easily have found a safe refuge in any part of the world.[50] This was not a hypocritical gesture, nor was it a rash decision taken for publicity reasons. As usual he turned his sympathy to action. He gave concerts for the wounded, prisoners of war and students, performing as soloist and conducting the symphony orchestra he had formed in the town of Iasi. The proceeds from these concerts went to charities. He saw all the misery and distress the war had brought to men and women; this made him revolt against the forces of destruction, against the absurdity of war, and as an artist he condemned it in his *Third Symphony*.

Above left:
A bill of the première of Enesco's Symphony No. 3 in C major, conducted by the composer.

Above right:
A program of Enesco's concert in Washington.

Center right:
Georges Enesco among the wounded in an army hospital.

Below right:
The hotel in Bucharest where Enesco lived during World War I.

It is a monumental work, consisting of three large movements, written for orchestra chorus (singing without words), organ and piano. The central theme of this symphony may be described as a struggle between good and evil, between creative and destructive forces. This theme is treated not in an abstract manner but in a generalized philosophical way which determines the dramatic intensity of the music, the presence of striking contrasts and acute, grandiose culminations. It seems that the hero, who in the first symphony was only becoming aware of his strength, is now fighting with all his might against his cruel foe. His noble image has acquired courageous and lyrical features and this transformation of his personality becomes a source of sharp contrasts in comparison with the dark forces of destruction. The finale of the *Third Symphony* leaves no doubt as to the outcome of this duel: the music acclaims the triumph of life over all obstacles.

An intense but restrained mysterious feeling emanates from the main theme of the first movement. By its nature this theme is very contrasting and contains, as is often in Enesco's music, elements of different emotional strain. They vary from stoic detachment to deep anxiety, but the theme appears to be an integrated whole despite its internal contrasts.

From the very start, a steady feeling of restraint is created here by the use of large rhythmic values which, owing to a moderate tempo in compound measurement (six quavers), seem to be of a particularly extended length. This impression is also emphasized by the sustained flowing motion of the descending figure which, in spite of piano, sounds very massive, thanks to a compact doubling of the melodic voice. The feeling of anxiety is rooted in the following nucleus of the theme (viz. second bracket of the example 20), which is much more rapid and angular, terminating abruptly with an ascending diminished fifth.

At the beginning of the theme, kettle-drums, by their regular pulsation on the tonic, mark every beat of the bar, accentuating still further the length of the long notes in the melodic voice. In all this there is an obvious analogy with the beginning of Brahms' *First Symphony* witnessing once again his influence on the Rumanian composer. It seems that here, as in Brahms' symphony, man is plunged in painful reflections. But the analogy does not amount to a mechanical reproduction of Brahms. Far from simply copying him,

Bill of the Enesco festival in December 1909.

Enesco keeps his own personality intact and gives his music an individual touch which reveals the national background of his art. Unlike Brahms, Enesco uses here not C-minor, but C-Mixolydian intensified by the heightened fourth degree as it often is in Rumanian folk-music. The appearance of the Mixolydian seventh introduces mysterious and disturbing undertones into the first nucleus. Its intonational tension is also enhanced by the altered subdominant which enters as if to prevent it from descending any further. This occurrence makes the second nucleus sound more alarmed and this later turns it into an important source of dramatization.

The third nucleus of the main theme (viz. the third bracket of example 20) which also will be playing a substantial role in future development, introduces yet another contrast. By its steady steps (a perfect and then diminished descending fifth from the notes separated by a major third) it brings into the theme a shade of sadness and at the same time, resolve, as if man recovering from his recent ordeal finally has determined to fight it out.

Taken as a whole, the three nuclei make up the complex image of the first movement's principal subject. Its basic material is subjected to active development from the start of the exposition which in general is typical of the mature composer's style (viz. for example the principal subject of the first movement from his *Sonata Number Three* for violin and piano). Now he is more and more tempted to employ in sonata form free and wide-stretching structures rather than regular, symmetrical and closed ones of the type of a perfect period or ternary model. Such free structures consist of a series of laconic links which grow one from another, transforming themselves in the course of intense development. This technique constitutes a characteristic feature of Enesco's way of thinking.

No less characteristic is his approach to the sonata form in which the first movement of the *Third Symphony* is cast. His treatment of this form is very carefully thought out and applied with great consistency, but is not at all schematic. Therefore, such terms of the sonata-allegro form as a given subject or the chief sections, which according to the established rules of the said form, have for Enesco but a very relative meaning and can be applied to him only in the widest possible sense of the word. In this respect the first movement of the *Third Symphony* provides a very convincing example.

Thus, the aforementioned nuclei, exposed and developed at the same time, grow eventually into a large and freely cast structure that, from a formal point of view, looks like a slow introduction to the first movement, but in reality represents the principal subject of the first movement. After a brief pause that interrupts further expansion, this structure leads to a new phase in the dramaturgical set-up of the movement. This phase signals a change of mood which now becomes one of agitation and alarm. This change of mood is brought about as a result of transformation of the principal subject's third nucleus. Its altered intonations sound now with an insistent vigor like a threatening warning. This is a warning of the coming offensive forces whose onslaught is forecast by the music's resolute pace. A more rapid motion, staccato notes and a rigid sonority all contribute to create this tension. It spreads also to the principal subject's second nucleus which, as if stepped up by the approaching danger, gets more active and more dramatic, exerting in its turn an influence upon the first nucleus. At first its even descending flow still keeps its former outlook, sounding serenely in the middle pitch of the horn. But this attempt to use something gentle as a means to quell vile passions fails against overwhelming odds. As a result of this failure, the formerly gentle figure becomes itself disquiet too, succumbing to general nervousness. In so doing it passes to the upper voices of the orchestra where it becomes entangled in a variety of contrapuntal lines. At this point it seems as if one more effort

In 1906, Enesco's picture appeared on the cover of *Musica* magazine.

would make the victory of aggressive forces complete. But apparently exhausted in previous clashes, they begin a temporary retreat; the music that characterizes them is gradually dying down, and from beneath its fading outline there appears—at first timidly and then more and more clearly—the smooth initial figure of the first nucleus. Its diatonic basis and relaxed motion do much to diffuse the tension when it is taken up by the upper woodwinds and particularly by the hautboy, whose lean melodic phrases foretell the appearance of the second subject. Starting from the end of the principal subject, this long stretch of music traditionally should be termed a transition but in fact it is so worked out and expanded that it looks like a real development section. Yet again, the technique used by Enesco to develop his material contains many details reminiscent of Brahms, especially of his typical way in building up certain transition passages in the orchestral scores of his *Violin Concerto* and the *Double Concerto for Violin and Cello*.

Thanks to the preceding preparation, the second subject logically continues the line of previous development. At the same time it marks a new stage in setting out the dramaturgical plan of the symphony when lyrical emotions of the highest and most poetic nature become prominent.

Nothing remains here of the clash that ended just a moment ago. Conflicts have disappeared, taking with them suspicion and anxiety. They are succeeded now by a boundless joy of existence which seems all the more powerful after the recent upheaval, but although discomfort has given way to tranquillity this does not lead to stagnation.

From the very first sounds of the solo violin there comes a feeling of touching animation; however, the musical material of the melodic line is not new. As usual, Enesco draws it from some previous formations. In this case it is evolved from the third intervals of the second nucleus from the principal subject. Now their former character is completely altered owing to the use of several devices, such as the introduction of long rhythmic values, groups of legato notes slurred in pairs in which the short sound leans on the long one situated on the strong beat, and finally the solo manner of interpretation. In their present form, they are breeding languor and not anxiety as before. The former angularity of lines has given way to the neat melodic pattern of the solo violin part; it looks as if the violin were embroidering undulating designs on the transparent tissue of the orchestral score. It constitutes a clear background against which this melodic embroidery is projected like flowers on a meadow. Although here there are no illustrative effects, the very atmosphere itself evokes an association with a sunlit meadow in full blossom. This association is so real that it creates the impression of a splendid summer day with all its beauty and wonderful fragrance. Therefore, the ideal world, which in the symphony is symbolized by the second subject, appears not as a vague ideal dream or a symbol of unobtainable happiness, but as an ideal dream that has already become a reality.

The second subject, like the principal one, takes its final shape in the course of development of previous formations originating in the first two nuclei from the principal subject's theme. Here the composer makes extensive use of the descending figure from the first nucleus as well as of the third interval of the second one. They are subjected to an intense polyphonic treatment in which they acquire an increasingly languid character. This is accompanied by a gradual smoothing out of their melodic lines leading to a new and very passionate theme:

Ex. 21

Autograph of Georges Enesco's 1915 work for piano and voice, "Le Silence Musicien."

The tuneful sound of the horn, joined by the hautboy and presently by the violins, as well as the soft tonality of E-flat-minor enhance the emotional qualities of this melodious theme which becomes so profoundly expressive that it seems to echo a triumphant song acclaiming the everlasting joy of life.

This feeling, strong as it is, continues to grow in intensity. It reaches its climax in the closing section whose lucid G-major and light texture make it attain an even higher degree of impulsiveness. At this stage, the theme of the closing section acquires a new expressive element; there appear dance rhythms adding a fresh generic flavor to its melodious features.

Both the second subject and the closing section are completely free of any folkloric quotation, nor is there in them the slightest hint of an ethnographic stereotype, and yet their animated emotional sphere makes them reminiscent of the Rumanian national music. This effect is strengthened in the parts of the violins by the use of certain specific features taken from the lautar interpretative art which Enesco knew so well. This refers particularly to a special kind

57

of tenuto and vibrato which, combined together, make the sound acquire a very special passionate expression.

Suddenly an intrusion interrupts this emotional trend: there appears a disquieting fast-moving melodic figure which is rapidly gaining ground. It engulfs both the descending semi-tone and the ascending third, that is to say, all the attributes of discomfort that the first two nuclei carried in themselves. This enables it to put an abrupt end to the feeling of sublime enjoyment that prevailed throughout the second subject and the closing section. To signal the end of exposition and at the same time the beginning of the development section, there come two extended passages rolling down like two huge, threatening waves across the entire range of the orchestra. This precipitated rush of triplet figures, massively doubled by the strings and the woodwinds, creates a feeling of nervousness and

A 1910 picture of Enesco with his autograph.

suspense before an imminent clash.

This time it is a clash of a nature different from that which preceded the appearance of the second subject. There the initiative came from the dark forces; they were what launched the offensive, and their thrust carried in itself something ruthlessly aggressive. The balance of forces between the opposing sides has changed now. From the very beginning of the development section, it becomes clear that the positive forces have the upper hand in the struggle. This points out the special significance of the development section as a basically new stage in disclosing the main idea of the symphony. The superiority of the positive forces comes here as a result of the intensive build-up of a vital factor which took place during the evolution of the second subject.

The start of the battle is signaled by the appearance of the third nucleus of the principal subject now transformed into a challenging call. In its present version, this nucleus no longer contains any trace of its former retrospective elements: two massive chords of the strings forte, emphatic staccato and a quickened tempo, as well as the inversion of the intially descending fifth into ascending fourth contribute to make this change effective. Now the music sounds resolutely, but without harshness. This touch of softness is due to G-minor—a legacy of the former minor dominate in C-Mixolydian. Thus, audacity mingled with a warm feeling stresses the humanitarian character of that force which has risen to counter the power of destruction.

The battle call uttered by the two chords at the beginning of the development section is answered softly by the flute which takes up the smooth descending figure from the first nucleus of the principal subject. Now this figure too is no longer strained as before, but keeps the more relaxed form it acquired in the second subject. This transformation implies once again that the forces involved in the struggle are not equal. Their inequality is underlined still further when this figure passes to the horn and then to the solo violin which almost recreates the lucid atmosphere of the second subject. This provokes an angry reaction from the opposing side; the disquieting elements belonging to the second nucleus, which have not yet lost their hostility, are trying to disrupt this atmosphere, but their attempt remains in vain. They are unable to alter the situation, and their feverish exertion amounts to no more than convulsions of a would-be giant, and the thunder, roaring away in the distance, serves only as a remainder of the frightening past. For only a short while during a brief culmination in this phase of the development section do the adverse forces manage to advance, but they are again halted by the appearance of the second subject's elements embodied once more in the part of the solo violin. This solo now sounds even brighter than before, thanks to figurations of an improvised character. Now their return reiterates even stronger than before the deterrent role they have played earlier in the course of transformation of the disquieting elements from the second nucleus of the principal subject.

The leading role of positive forces gains new momentum in the second phase of the development section as a result of preceding evolution. It begins with the aforementioned chords played by the strings. They sound now even more compact in the key of D-minor a fourth lower than before, but this time there is not the slightest attempt to oppose them. As if stimulated by their lead, the well-known figure from the first nucleus is revitalized; however this is by no means the only change. An ever-growing emphasis is laid on an upward moving figure, originated during the previous phase, which actually represents an inversion of the initial nucleus from the principal subject. Its second nucleus too acquires a new character. Henceforth this new thematic formation, united with the previous one by a single drive, becomes a spearhead of the force that shall defeat the power of darkness. But one more effort is needed to bring the victory about, and eventually the last battle gets under way.

It begins with an animated phrase audaciously making a thrust forward. Sounded by horns and trumpets with the massive support of the orchestra, it evokes an association with the noble figure of a knight in full, glittering armor. This association is so vivid that it conjures up the legend of Lohengrin who came down to earth to crush injustice. Here the music assumes grandiose proportions in a true Wagner-like fashion. This heroic music is inspired by the enthusiasm provoked by a just struggle—a struggle whose victorious end is already in sight.

This moment marks the turning point from which the third phase of the development section begins. Several woodwind and string instruments restate the smooth, descending motive from the first nucleus completely deprived now of its former tension. But this is only a temporary lull. It is broken by the same motive, this time taken up by the brass in its inverted form. It resolutely assumes an ascending course. This leads to a return of G-minor bringing a sense of relief by establishing a tonal unity between the beginning and the end of the development section. A new transformation of the ascending motive occurs: it is reduced now to three notes only forming the interval of a minor third. This changes its character, making it similar to a passionate oration.

The development section concludes with an E flat-major episode. Its music is full of jubilation reflecting the triumph of that noble ideal which inspired the creative will of man. There appear new motives, based on the sounds of the E flat-major triad, which mount in continuous succession as if pushed upward by one another. They are founded upon elements taken from several thematic formations. These include a transformed version of the final element of the second nucleus intermingled with the inverted figure from the first nucleus. It is interesting to note that all the ingredients making up this new amalgamation are used in the form

Enesco in 1918.

they first assumed during the third phase of the development section. Considering the special significance of the episode as the point of culmination of the entire development section, their merger here is dramaturgically in line with Enesco's conception and reveals the main characteristic feature of his monothematic principle. At this moment of the highest climax marking the victory, he felt the necessity to integrate all the elements which in both nuclei constituted the potential that made this victory possible. Thus, the ideological synthesis determined the synthesis of thematic material as well.

Just as there was no break between the closing section and the episode, there is none between it and the recapitulation. The latter has its particularities conditioned by the conception of the work.

According to this dynamic conception, the recapitulation had to represent a new stage in the general build-up of the symphony, and therefore a mere reproduction of the principal subject in its initial form was ruled out. From an artistic and dramaturgical point of view, it would have meant a step backward, considering the intense development that took place in the preceding portion and especially after the clear-cut victory of noble forces achieved in the episode. To avoid this, Enesco chose an original way to solve his problem in accordance with his impulsive nature which so characteristically prompted him to develop a musical idea in the course of a continuous expansion.

The fact that the episode and the second subject belonged to a similar emotional sphere made it logical to use the latter as the first theme of the recapitulation. But while this device was in general sufficient to assure continuity so far as the recapitulation and the development section were concerned, its application in this particular case would not be enough to make the evolutionary process follow an ever-mounting course. In order to avoid a decline in the emotional build-up of the music, the composer had to introduce new dynamism into the recapitulation. To achieve this he used his favorite means which will also later be met in his *Sonata number three for violin and piano*. However, in the two works, it is applied in different ways. In this sonata, the emotional interdependence of the principal and second subjects will lead to the revaluation of the musical material of one theme under the imaginative influence of the other, whereas in the symphony it leads to an integration of the two themes during which the first is transformed. In both cases the recapitulation contains one theme only, and this fact alone makes it differ from the exposition.

The interconnection of the principal and second subjects in the first movement of the symphony goes far beyond their simple addition. Merging organically with the second subject and forming with it an inseparable whole, the first theme not only changes its outlook, but also exerts an influence over the other. There remains nothing now of its former tension owing to the serene atmosphere of the C-major key and a transparent, evenly flowing figuration in the harp accompaniment (ex. n 22).

Ex. 22

It has freed itself from all its potentially disturbing attributes, such as the tense Mixolydian seventh, the massive doubling of orchestral voices with its mysterious effect and the ostinato pulsation of the kettledrum. Played by the first violins, it sounds frank and serene, and it seems that its former angularity has been flattened down in the contact with the warmth of the second subject theme. The music is very calm now.

This metamorphosis is very important to comprehend the future destiny of this theme which, transforming itself, will produce a number of subsidiary thematic structures that will play a substantial role from a dramaturgical point of view. As the conception of the symphony unfolds, they will move farther apart from one another though preserving intonational links with the above theme. Thus, it will provide the basis both for the sarcastically devilish theme of the scherzo and for the theme of the purest beauty in the finale.

Georges Enesco with members of the Rose Quartet.

But having absorbed the principal theme, the second subject in its turn did not remain outside its sphere of influence. As a result, the second theme now acquired a greater degree of intensity mainly due to a higher pitch and to a still more freely cast figuration of an improvisational nature in the solo violin part than was the case in the exposition. Now it reached such a degree of emotional build-up that its animation grew into a romantic ecstasy. The potential expansiveness of the second theme induced it to develop even wider and more freely than before, and this development attained so high a level of impulsiveness that it engulfed the closing section, leaving intact only its last strain of melody.

Viewing the recapitulation as a synthesis of the two subjects of the exposition, made possible by the whole preceding development, Enesco gave the recapitulation a special meaning, stressing its significance as a new and a higher phase of dramaturgical development in accordance with the central idea of the work. This enabled him to carry the development throughout the recapitulation along a mounting course to reach its peak in the coda.

After the upsurge of lyrical emotions, which took place in the recapitulation, the coda sounds like a hymn celebrating the victory of mankind. The music, with its apotheosis-like grandeur, suggests a scene picturing the triumphant entry of a liberator into a freed city anticipating the future heroic feat of Enesco's Oedipus; but despite the brilliant setting of this majestic scene, there is no trace of pomp in it. True to himself, the composer creates here the sense of grandeur not by artificial effects, but through the expression of inner strength. A regular succession of clear-cut harmonic figures, founded on arpeggiated chords of the brass instruments, creates an impression of a majestic procession slowly advancing amid general acclamation. The air of festivity is sustained by the use, in the upper voices of the orchestra, of a rapid figuration imitating the ringing of bells. This atmosphere of frantic jubilation is accentuated by the reiteration of the C-major tonic chord as well as by the use of a massive scoring like the one so often practiced by Wagner. It is interesting to note that the aforementioned figuration, though representing but a small detail in the general context of music, plays a substantial part in creating this atmosphere, for it at once attracts attention by its dynamic qualities. At first glance it seems to be a new element, but in reality, it represents another modification of a short motive which occurred initially in a scarcely noticeable way soon after the beginning of the development section. In its turn, that motive originates in a contrapuntal voice from the third nucleus of the principal subject.

Ex. 23a

Ex. 23b

Ex. 23c

This is not the only reminiscence found in the coda. It inherits from the principal subject a reminder of the Mixolydian seventh and the heightened fourth degree, both of which add an element of tension to the festive atmosphere of the coda; this is no more than the last small cloud darkening the horizon only for a very short while. It instantly disappears as if driven away by a challenging call of the horn.

However, the composer did not imagine that the struggle was over. He knew the reality too well to indulge in complacency. A peaceful state of mind and appeasement were for him quite different things. Living in a world of harsh realities and not of sweet illu-

A sketch of Georges Enesco.

sions, he could acclaim the triumph of reason over the madness of war, succumbing neither to a naïve admiration nor to an endless despair at the thought that the evil is virulent and still exists.

A stern reminder of this comes with the second movement of the symphony. It is a sinister scherzo in which somber visions fully predominate. Its poisonous atmosphere provokes an outburst of demonic sarcasm resembling the devilish orgy that takes place in the Scherzo from the *Octet*. If anything, the onslaught of aggressive elements has become even more furious now, as if they had gained confidence in their destructive power. The music in its frenzy creates a scene of pandemonium resuscitating horrible visions, infernal yelling and moans. All this devilish scene is punctuated by an ostinato rhythmic figure which, with its insistent repetition, symbolizes an automatic device in action or, perhaps, the regular noise of stamping army boots which do not care a bit what they are trampling on—newly ploughed fields, flowers or living human bodies. Only at the very end of the movement does the general mood change: there appears a major third as a signal that the orgy of death and destruction is over.

The threatening element of the Scherzo is centered on a march-like motive which is at the same time despotic and ingratiating, demonically malicious and somberly foreboding.

Ex. 24

Its elastic rhythm and a light staccato of the string instruments give it a touch of stealthily disguised perfidy. It is easy to see that it represents a completely modified version of the formerly noble motive which has first occurred in the recapitulation of the previous movement.

The nervous mood of the Scherzo is largely due to the versatility of the initial motive.

Ex. 25

Because of its distorted outline it seems rather convulsive, and a short but rigorous crescendo coupled with a strong accent on its second D-flat makes it sound like the cry of a bird of prey, frightened, and threatening at the same time.

There is yet another factor which plays a substantial part in creating the aggressive atmosphere of the Scherzo. It consists of a figure made up of three consecutive descending fourths which persistently occur in various voices of the orchestra.

Ex. 26

Appearing here and there, like gusts of cold wind, they throw a dim light over the morbid scene of devastation and misery caused by the war.

Among other motives from the Scherzo, two more should be pointed out:

The first of them creates a frenzied feeling mainly because of a swift upward thrust which gives it an air of utter concentration. The second consists of a succession of descending chromatic semi-tones. "Creeping" down like a snake, it underlines the fatal character of the music.

But at long last dawn has broken over the mutilated earth, announcing a new day in the life of mankind. The triumph of reason, in which Enesco believed so much, has finally come; the creative forces have overcome the power of annihilation, and the nightmare of war with its fearful shadows has given way to the long awaited day of peace. The sun has begun to beam its rays from a clear sky, bringing to life frustrated nature. And, as if to greet the rising day, two horns have begun a song of welcome depicting, almost in idyllic colors, a picture of the resurrected world.

Oscillating the music between the serene C-major tonality and the soft A-minor key against the background of an evenly balanced figuration in the harp accompaniment, Enesco gives the introduction to the third movement of the symphony a particularly warm and tender expression. The introduction, becoming more and more transparent, ends with a long drawn out fifth (A E) slowly fading away in the highest pitch of the violins. In keeping with the serene atmosphere of the introduction, there appears a melodic figure in it, played by the first horn in the first octave; it represents an inverted version of the initial nucleus from the principal subject of the first movement so familiar by now. Here this strain of melody sounds like a motto conveying a feeling of tranquillity.

The finale begins with a theme of immaculate beauty and purest emotional inspiration which unfolds itself through profound meditations coming, as it were, from the most secret shrine of the soul. This theme is made up of six expressive motives and represents a remarkable specimen of the mature melodic style of the Rumanian master.

Ex. 29

This is a deeply humane ode to the resuscitated life and happiness achieved in spite of difficulties. Yet again this theme, new as it is from the point of view of its emotional nature, contains a number of elements used several times before. In this respect special notice should be taken of its last but one motive as it finalizes a long process of modification. Being founded upon the first nucleus of the principal subject in the form it took during the recapitulation of the first movement, it reproduces exactly the intervallic structure of the demonically sarcastic motive of the Scherzo. Thus, using the same intonational embryo, Enesco deduced from it two motives absolutely different in character. One symbolizes the negative, vile and ferocious forces while the other, the positive and ideal ones.

This characterizes the humanistic nature of Enesco's philosophical approach to life, the genuinely optimistic sense of his conception. Facing life as a realist, he saw its positive and negative sides, and had no doubt as to the outcome of their struggle. That outcome determined the happiness of mankind, and he firmly believed that only the conscious will of men, as the antithesis of a beastly destructive force, could lead this struggle to a victory. This belief made him identify that will with creative power, giving it vigor and vitality which grew stronger, provided man's heart was pure.

That is how he viewed the way to true happiness, and there is no wonder that Enesco acclaimed the victory of his favorite hero — Oedipus — over evil by saying: "Happy is he whose soul is pure." And though a man is mortal, the creative will he carries in himself lives forever. This determines his advantage over death, which becomes but an episode of life, for the immortal is not the man who never dies, but he whose deeds are immortal, he who is helping others to go "forward on the way to the better." That is why Oedipus, in spite of death, becomes immortal, because his memory helps Athens to attain happiness.

The *Third Symphony* by its philosophical conception anticipates the opera *Oedipe*. In addition, both works are connected one with the other by intonational links. As will be shown later, the symphony, together with the first piano sonata, marks an important stage in shaping the theme of destiny from the opera.

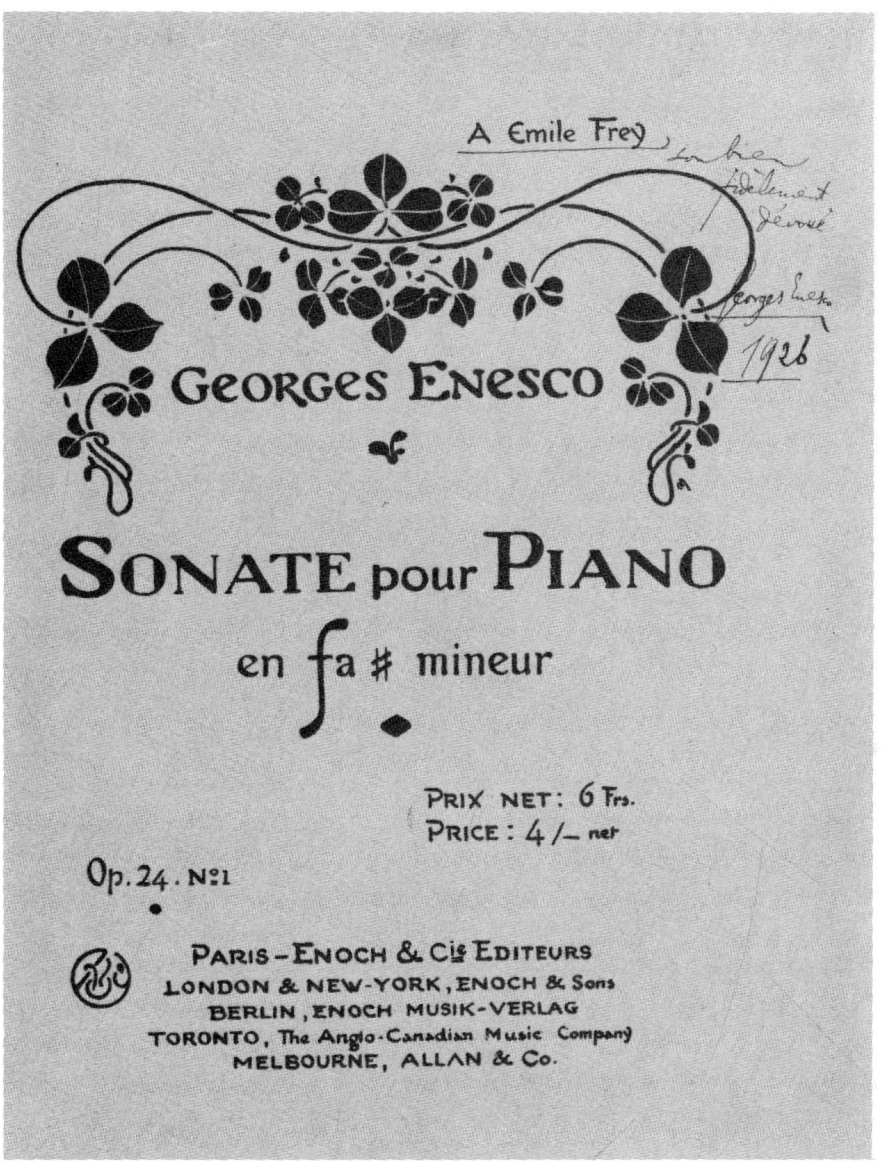

The title page of Sonata no. 3 in F minor, with a dedication and inscription to Emile Frey, "from his most faithfully devoted Georges Enesco."

Turning back to the finale of the symphony, it is interesting to note that it is cast, like the scherzo, in a free form. But while the scherzo is reminiscent of the old toccato so far as its type of motion and liberty of structure are concerned, the finale, with its sections freely strung together, is close to the unusual, classical symphonic music pattern used by Beethoven for the finale of his *Ninth Symphony*. Enesco's finale, made up of five large sections including coda, proceeds freely along the dramaturgical line of the work, constantly developing the main, noble idea of the symphony. This development carries the intense feeling of the music to a remarkable height, thanks not only to vigorous intonational modifications of thematic material, but also to the use of a mighty orchestra coupled with a chorus singing without words. The chorus is introduced in the second section and starts off with a phrase already met before (viz. bars 6 and 7 in the example 28). Sung now by female voices, this phrase acquires a particularly soft expression. Its emotional qualities turn it into a leading theme of the finale in the course of which it will be taken up by various voices of the choir and the orchestra.

The choral part does much to enrich the color of the music, but the orchestra too contributes to that effect. This is especially so in the coda where the composer introduces a tamtam and many other percussion instruments. The introduction of the tamtam could give rise to an analogy with the last movement of the *Symphonie Fantastique* by Berlioz, but the two composers use this instrument for quite different aims. Berlioz uses it as an additional means to stress the delirious atmosphere of an infernal nightmare, while in Enesco's symphony it has no sinister meaning whatsoever; its sounds, gaily projected against the background of a transparent orchestration, serve to announce the triumph of daylight over darkness. This seemingly small detail again points out the basic difference of conceptions that characterize the two symphonies, one which reflects the pessimistic view of a deeply disappointed artist while the other demonstrates the optimistic approach to life of a musician who trusted it.

The concrete way of thinking that characterizes the *Third Symphony* brings it close to programme music despite the fact that it has no plot in the ordinary sense of the word. This is due to the imaginative power of its content. Enesco understood programme music in a very wide sense. He shaped an image on the basis of his personal associations, conveying in a realistic way, their poetic idea. Such an approach to programme music became his guiding princi-

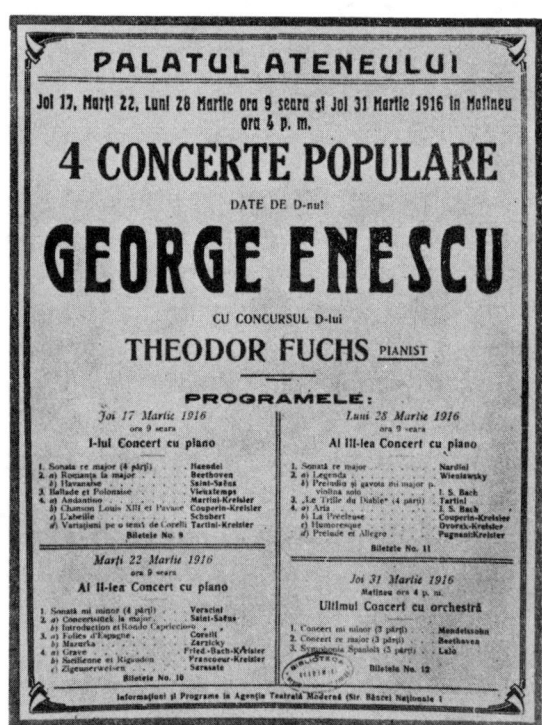

This bill of four concerts Enesco gave in March 1916 gives one an idea of the great variety of his performing repertoire.

Florizel von Reuther's rare photo of Enesco playing for Elizabeth, Queen of Rumania, and the ladies of her court.

ple during the period of maturity. This principle unites the *Third Symphony* with his other important works, such as the *Sonata Number Three* and the suite *Impressions of Childhood*, both written for violin and piano, as well as the orchestral *Rural* suite. In this respect they are also related to his opera, the *Second Cello Sonata* and two piano sonatas in which he reached the height of dramatic expression and philosophical thought. Each of them in its own manner is inspired by the idea symbolizing life itself, the idea of man's struggle against the adverse forces personified by fatal destiny which is finally conquered despite all its ferocity.

A portrait of Georges Enesco.

Chapter 5

As before, the theme of his native land continued to excite and inspire his imagination. Several of his mature works are, in various ways, connected with this theme which, as time went on, was receiving a multi-faceted and profound treatment. As his art progressed, it became for him the highest symbol of the human spirit.

Aiming at grand artistic generalizations, Enesco as a composer and as an interpreter did not envisage music outside its emotional and national allegiance. In this respect his *Third Sonata for Violin and Piano* Op. 25, 1926 is fully representative. This work, subtitled by the author "In the Rumanian popular character," is a remarkable example of how a popular atmosphere, painted in national color, is brought about as a result of a creative re-evaluation of the idiomatic intonational features of Rumanian music. The composer here does not quote folkloric melodies as he did, for instance, in his *Rumanian Poem* or in both rhapsodies. The direct link with popular music is noticeable not only where melody is concerned, but also in the field of harmony whose original character becomes particularly pronounced when the harmony is evolved from the very structure of melody.[51]

The emotional content of the sonata is specifically national in character and at the same time has a profound universally human meaning. This determines the significance of the poetic idea embodied in the thematic material of the sonata. That material, being fully original and of a genuinely national character, is cast and developed in popular style.

Naturally, it took Enesco a great deal of time to achieve so perfect a synthesis of development technique with thematic material of this particular kind. The way to it lay from the *Second Rhapsody* to the Dixtuor for two flutes, oboe, English horn, two clarinets, two bassoons and two horns (Op. 14, 1906).

This work was inspired entirely by the theme of his native land expressed in elegiac tone through a pastoral atmosphere. It serves as a background for a series of colorful scenes of a popular character echoing rhythms of folk dances; as in the *Second Rhapsody*, they are here superseded by tuneful melodies. The *Dixtuor* makes one think of a finely painted landscape whose delicate design resembles the skillfully cut woodwork which embellishes Rumanian and Moldavian village huts, or the national ornaments on a peasant carpet.

The *Dixtuor* also attracts attention by the fact that it is scored for ten wind instruments—a combination that was at the time quite unusual in chamber music.[52] In this work, unlike the *Octet*, Enesco sought the softness of sound and not monumental acoustic effects and in so doing, he revealed himself to be a fine master who knew how to exploit the variety of the color and expressive possibilities of woodwind and brass instruments.

Like many other large-scale compositions written previously by Enesco, the *Dixtuor* contains a number of musical themes but this time he did not choose the free framework of a poem, rhapsody or suite, preferring a three-part composition and the sonata form. Preference given to this type of form over a free rhapsodic structure testifies to the evolution of Enesco for whom the sonata form already represented the embodiment of the highest principle of thematic organization. In this respect, the *Dixtuor* marks an important step on the way that led Enesco to the *Third Sonata for Violin and Piano*.

This sonata shows very convincingly how musical material of a national character can be treated in accordance with the sonata principle. Its three movements not only contrast one with the other, but also each of them consists of contrasting sections developed from a single source.

The first movement provides a very good example of that technique. Its principal subject is made up of several contrasting nuclei, the most important of which are the following four:

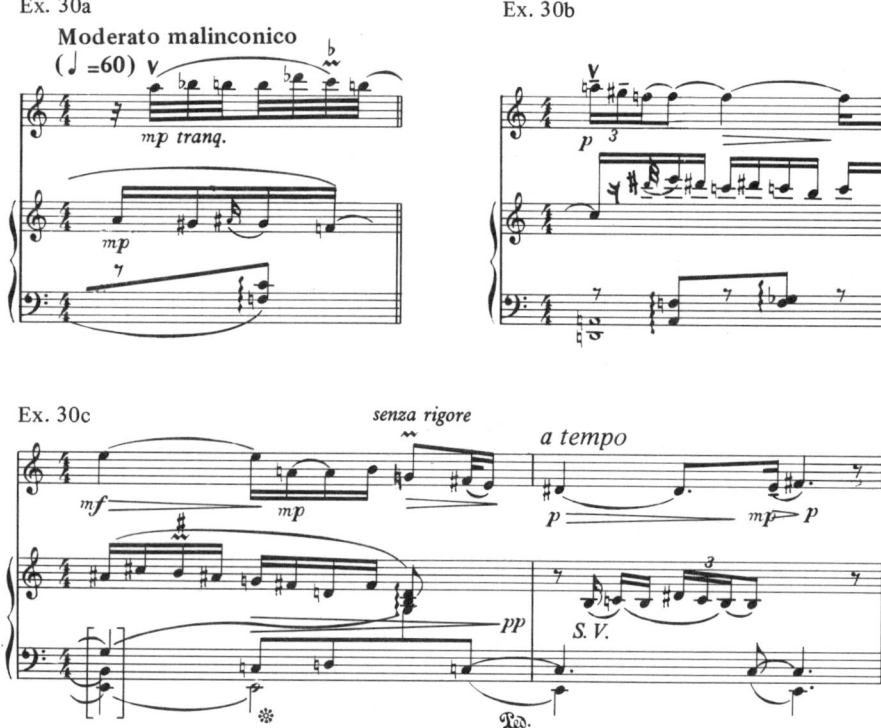

Ex. 30d

The first of them has, so to speak, something of a painful reproach in it, the second is rather categorically exacting, while the third carries an expression of considerable inner power; it has a wider melodic range which includes the Dorian sixth, giving the music a touch of dignified uprightness. The fourth nucleus introduces an animated, noble feeling which inflames the whole theme. These distinct nuclei or motives represent various phases of the same process governing the development of the main poetic idea of the work. They all sound against a common background characterized by a steady "streaming" figuration in the piano part which establishes itself from the beginning of the sonata. Thus, the exposition of the principal subject, involving a rapid succession of contrasting thoughts, already represents a stage in its development.

The second subject with its rollicking, devil-may-care mood and dashing dance rhythms introduces a new contrasting element.

Ex. 31

This theme is so swift that it scarcely has time to materialize in full; no sooner does it appear than it yields place to the closing section which sounds as a passionate love song. It provides another example showing how the thematic material is subjected to a continuous transformation so typical of the composer's style. The closing section with its well defined new character nevertheless preserves evident intonational links with certain elements of the principal and second subjects.

Ex. 32

An allusion to the initial thought in the parts of piano and violin marks the start of the development section. This portion of the work is not large, but very concentrated. The composer here makes extensive use of the disquieting elements of the principal subject which appear now and then with an increasing dramatic insistence. Gradually they become more and more somber, especially when they are taken up by the piano bass. At this point there appears a new, ascending strain of melody in the violin part. This new element adds a stern and passionate feeling to the already very animated music. This is due to the somber color of the Dorian G-sharp minor which predominates in the first part of the development section. But the growing tension unexpectedly subsides; this sudden change of mood is brought about by the appearance of a long C-sharp major chord which sounds all the more brightly after the somber atmosphere of the previous bars. By using the G-sharp-minor and the C-sharp major chords side by side, Enesco reproduces one of the characteristic features of his people's music, namely the specific emotional effect caused by a major subdominant in a minor mode like the Dorian.

In the second phase of the development section, the emotional build-up is taken to a new height. This is achieved by exploiting even more dramatically than before the most active elements of the principal subject. They succeed one another with an ever increasing pace, leading to a point of culmination. To heighten the pressure still further, Enesco returns, as is usual for him in similar cases, to acutely dissonant harmonies involving frequent use of unresolved second which produce a strong "friction" effect. The tension rises to a point when an explosion seems inevitable. When it eventually comes, Enesco emphasizes its dramatic effect by making the strained harmonies resolve in G-major, but not simultaneously in the parts of the two instruments. As a result, this new key sets in first in the violin part and then, almost two beats later, in that of the piano, thus making the tonic and dominant harmonies "overlap".

This violent eruption marks a sudden turning point: it seems man, having exhausted himself by this tremendous effort, now remains completely worn out.

The recapitulation begins with a new theme in which the principal and the second subjects of the exposition are combined, the first being represented by its intonational elements and the second by its rhythmic design (ex. n 33). Here again, as in the recapitulation from the first movement of the *Third Symphony*, Enesco uses one theme only, for its represents a synthesis of the two subjects from the exposition.

Ex. 33

Enesco in 1929.

Another deviation from the generally established scheme is the introduction of an episode which compensates for the lack of the second subject in the recapitulation

Ex. 34

The episode represents an important contrasting factor in the recapitulation. It is preceded by a stretch of music founded upon the idea of the second nucleus of the principal subject vigorously developed by means of imitative counterpoint in the piano part. A change of measurement (12 crochets instead of 4 quavers) and a far quicker tempo also contribute to add new momentum to the music. Coming as a contrast after this new wave of development, the episode does not, however, defuse the atmosphere, but merely alters its previous mood. This is due to the complex nature of the episode consisting of a very expressive melodic line in the violin part emphatically accentuated by repeated staccato chords of the piano.

These chords reproduce the rhythmic figure of the second subject and have a strictly coloristic function. They are made up of the root note struck together with its fifth and an augmented fourth, thus representing a vertical version of a figure used horizontally by lautars mainly in rapid dance music where it consists of a swift succession of the tonic and dominant, the latter being preceded by achromatic, ascending appoggiatura.[53] To make the coloristic effect of this chord even more pronounced, Enesco adds new notes.

The episode leads directly into the closing section which preserves its former emotional character. Calming down, it passes into a short coda in which the violin carries the main thought of the sonata upward from one octave to another until it fades away completely.

Coming from somewhere far off, a dreary song is heard over the sullen steppe. It seems that a shepherd, plunged in bitter thoughts, is complaining about his unhappy life. This is the immediate impression one gets from the outset of the second movement. It is due to a very sad and seemingly simple melody played by the violin against the background of a single note monotonously repeated by the piano (ex. n 35). This ostinato background gives it a touch of weariness and, at the same time, disquiet. The rustic character of this melody comes from the use of "bleak" violin harmonies which imitate the sound of a fluer.[54] Combined with a slow tempo (Andante sostenuto e misterioso), all this creates a sense of frustration.

Ex. 35

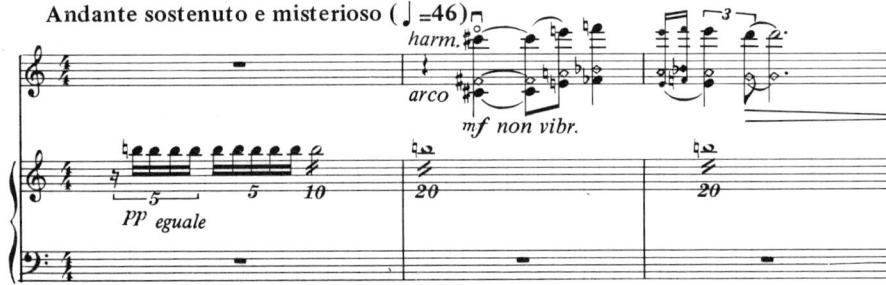

But quite unexpectedly the scenery changes: timidly at first and then more brightly, the sun beams over the horizon, a gust of wind sweeps across the steppe, and the shepherd pulls himself together. Passing now through a brief glimpse of hope and then through mounting indignation, his sad complaint eventually grows into an outburst of violent anger (ex. n 36).

Ex. 36

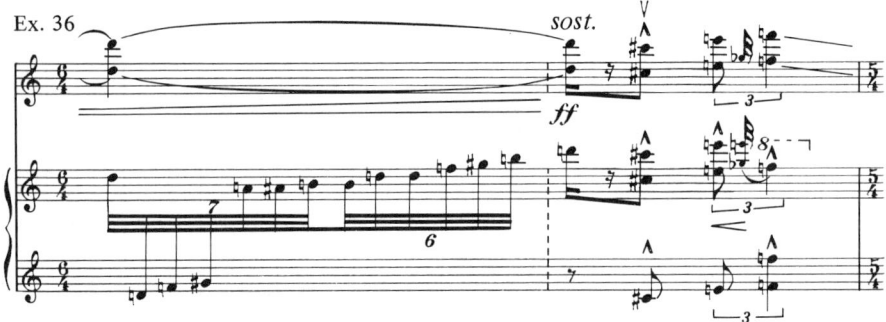

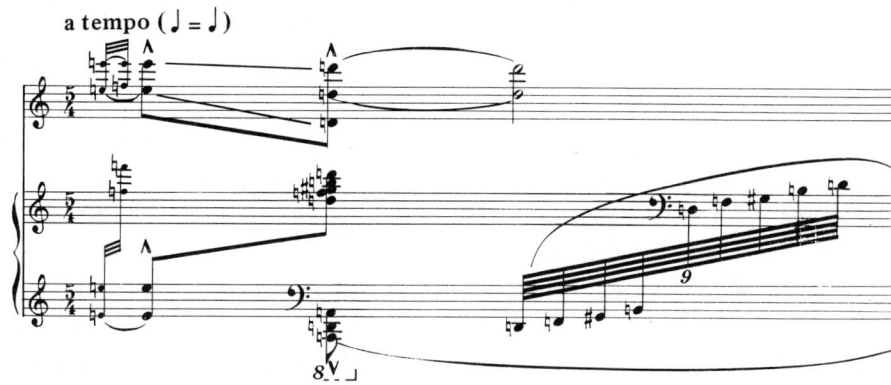

This example represents a new and dramatized version of the initial phrase from the second movement which itself was derived from the second nucleus of the principal subject. Such modifications show once again how Enesco transforms a given motive through his monothematic method which enables him to produce a seemingly unlimited number of tributary musical ideas.

The second movement also contains some moments of relief. Brief as they are, they play an important part, from the point of view of the general conception of the sonata. One of them, and perhaps the most elevated one, comes in the wake of the previous angry outburst which is what makes it especially striking (ex. n 37). By its lucidity and calm character, it is reminiscent of the most serene dispositions of Franck.[55]

Ex. 37

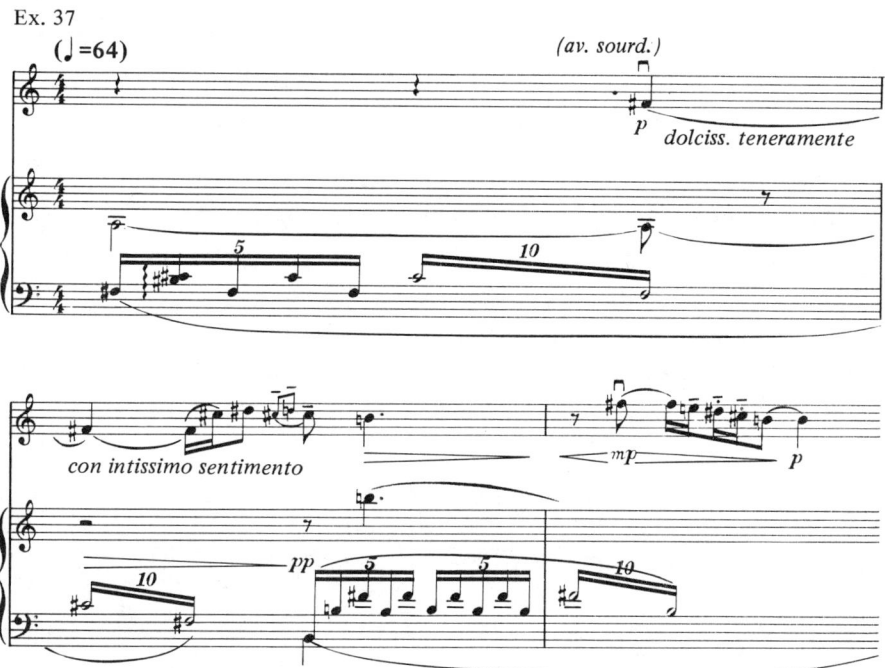

However, this moment of relief was not meant to last for long, and when despondency reappears, it seems to be all the more painful. This provokes again, but only for a brief while, a mounting uproar, only to die down in the indifferent wilderness of the dismal steppe—that forlorn land which for centuries has been the silent witness of so much human misfortune.

With its rapid and frequent shift of mood and improvisational character, the second movement of this sonata is close to the free framework of a poem-fantasia. Incidentally, with regard to its poetic content, this movement is a fascinating poem of hardship and suffering endured by the people, with which the composer had firsthand experience during the war years. This led him to a deeper and more dramatic understanding of the theme of his native land, to the identification of the stricken motherland with the suffering of mankind. This in turn gave a profound psychological meaning to the descriptive effects and made the coloristic devices grow into a factor of great emotional power.

The last movement comes as a conclusion of the whole sonata, generalizing its chief poetic idea. In spite of its almost rhapsodically loose framework, the finale represents a well-knit pattern, thanks to its main theme, which, from the intonational point of view, has much in common with other themes of the sonata. This is especially so if we compare it with the initial melodic figure of the Andante, but of course the main theme of the finale has an altogether different character (ex. n 38).

Ex. 38

This is also true with regard to a passage in the piano part accompanying the theme, which represents yet a new version of the "streaming" figuration that opened the sonata.

A remarkable example of the same technique is provided by the episode which occurs in the finale. Emotionally it is a new theme

Ex. 39

(ex. n 39); by its passionate drive and charming languor, it exceeds any previous thematic formation, but so far as its intonational basis is concerned, it is "welded" together from several elements that have already been used before and particularly from those which made up the episode in the first movement. The affinity between the two episodes is underlined by the use of the same staccato coloristic harmonies. Similarities of one kind or another abound in almost every succeeding portion of the finale. They are subjected to a very intense development which carries the dramatic build-up to a climax. At this critical point a completely new theme appears, representing an outstanding specimen of intonational generalization (ex. n 40).

Ex. 40

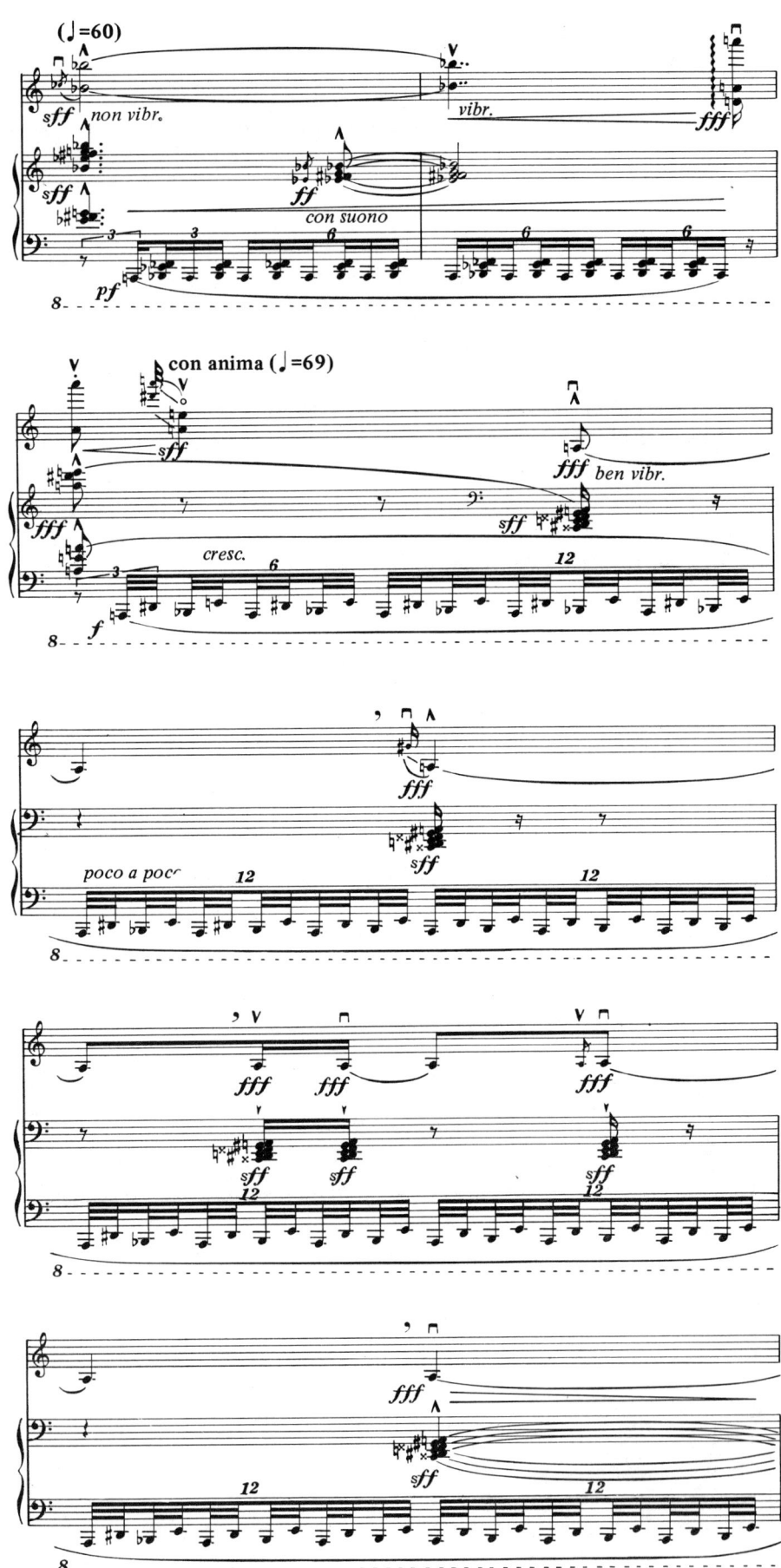

This final theme comes as a reply to the question which remained unanswered at the undecided end of the Andante. A tremolo fortissimo, thundered out with terrific force in the bass, forms a roaring background against which is heard an inspired melody of the violin proudly floating high up in the air like a bird over a whirling sea. It is a song of wrath and regret, of joy and sorrow, of challenge and victory. It seems as if over the horizon, through the smoke and flames of a blazing fire, there rises a giant figure of a man who cast off his chains. Whoever he is, Prometheus or Oedipus, his daring challenge echoes the prophetic cry of the stormy petrel from Maxim Gorky's poem who already knows ". . . that clouds shall not hide the sun, they never shall!"[56]

Enesco was working on this sonata with devotion for a long time, carefully selecting his musical material and polishing up every detail. The same care is seen in the way he sorted out the interpretative means which to a large extent reproduce the specific technique of lautars' art.[57] That is why the sonata abounds in chromaticisms and all sorts of ornaments combined with the sharp bow strokes so typical of the lautar way of playing (viz. ex. n31). There are many cases in the sonata when the violin and piano imitate the sound of popular instruments, such as, for instance, fluer (viz. ex. n 35) and tcimbal (viz. ex. n 36). It is very interesting to see how Enesco uses the two instruments, for which the sonata is written, in the style of a popular orchestra—taraf (ex. n 41). By the way, this extract from the finale represents an entirely new version of the melodic strain of the second nucleus of the principal subject re-stated here in the form it assumed in the opening bars of the Andante.

Ex. 41

The composer's knowledge of his people's music enables him to make the violin imitate the sound of plucked instruments in a masterly manner.

Ex. 42

[musical example: Tempo I (♩=132)]

Benno Rabinoff.

In his sonata, Enesco as an expert violinist with fine artistic taste and great ingenuity, also makes extensive use of other characteristic features of the popular interpretative tradition, such as placing the bow in various sections of a string, an expressive portamento, notes without vibrato and, finally, an increase of intonational intensity as a result of a given note being heightened or lowered in accordance with the modal structure of the music.[58]

There is something else, too, in the sonata, something much wider and much more far-reaching than an ingenious display of amazing idiomatic curiosities. It is the very mentality of a typical folk-musician that Enesco managed to convey through his music. In this connection it would be interesting to see how he himself understood his own work. Luckily, this can be done by quoting the fine American violinist, Benno Rabinoff, who studied the *Third Sonata* with the master. Before playing this work at an evening musical party given in 1972 a few years before his death, Rabinoff recalled that "the sonata had been analyzed for him by the composer as a fantasy on the life and soul of the gypsy fiddler, the kind of musical vagabond who roamed about Europe in the old days, playing at campfires, imitating not only the sounds of nature but also the techniques and stunts of other gypsy players."[59]

From the point of view of national character there is an evident similarity between the sonata and three other works by Enesco: the third *Rustic Suite for Orchestra*, Op. 27, 1938, the suite *Impressions of Childhood* Op. 28, 1940 and the orchestral *Concert Overture on Rumanian Popular Themes* Op. 32, 1948. But they all differ in

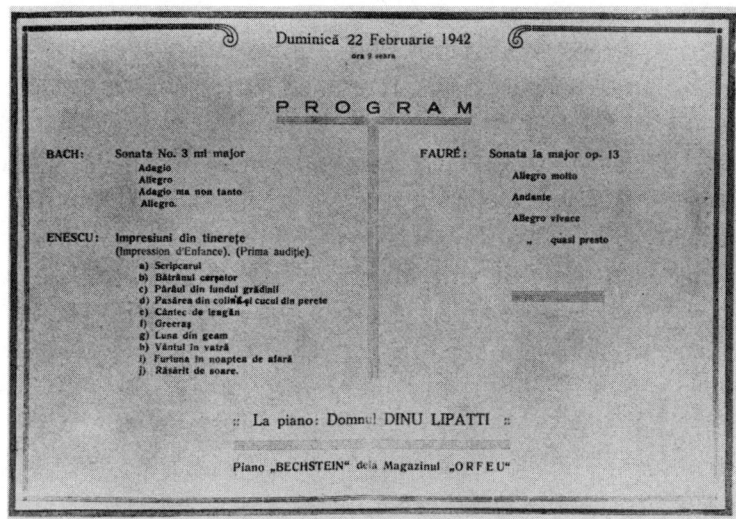

Program of the 1942 première of Enesco's *Impressions of Childhood*, with Dinu Lipatti at the piano.

character so far as their conception, genre and form are concerned.

The *Rustic Suite*[60] is a piece of programme music. Each of its five parts bears a special subtitle which, as is usual in Schumann's music, evokes concrete associations in a listener's imagination. Its programme resembles that of the *Rumanian Poem*, but this programme is conveyed in psychological and not in descriptive terms. There is nothing conventional in otherwise very suggestive subtitles, such as "The nature awakening in spring", "A moonlit stream", "A village dance", "Migrant birds at nightfall" and "The native house." The world of nature is portrayed here not directly, but through poetic perceptions of people dwelling in the countryside. There are many colorful characters among them, including, of course, the traditional figure of a lautar. All of them are perceived not in a subjective manner but, on the contrary, through a generalization of poetic ideas as was the case in the *Third Sonata for Violin and Piano*.

The same generalized approach is also to be met in the suite *Impressions of Childhood*. From a formal standpoint, this work represents a suite consisting of separate episodes, but in reality it is more like a poem whose sections form a single artistic whole.

The free framework of such compositions like suite or poem appealed to Enesco very much. Leaving much room for a free display of imagination, such a framework enabled him flexibly to combine spontaneous expression with a logical way of thinking; both of them were inherent in his character which would accept no limitation imposed by a generally established structural design. This must have been the cause that made him choose the framework of a poem for his first large-scale symphonic composition. As years passed, his interest for free cast forms did not dwindle and this is shown by the number of suites written by him, including the three orchestral ones.

With maturity, Enesco fully mastered the ability to integrate freedom of expression with self-restraint, and this is clearly seen in *Impressions of Childhood*. Here he completely succeeded in avoiding the kaleidoscopic structure of a suite pattern, and this allowed him to express what he wanted in ten miniatures in a laconic and yet fully comprehensive manner. And here again, as in the *Rustic Suite*, his preference for recollections did not signify a desire to escape from reality, just as the admiration he had for nature or the nostalgic attraction of his native land did not lead him into the subjective sphere of personal reminiscences. On the contrary, his individual associations, highlighted by a great humanitarian idea, acquired an objective, universal meaning to such an extent that they transformed themselves into generalizations of a remarkable psychological and realistic power. The programmatic content of the work disclosed by the author also contributes to this effect. Its suggestive precision gives the music an almost tangible reality which, however, does not curtail the freedom of inspiration.

First of all, Enesco portrays a lautar with all his specific features, but there is nothing conventionally exotic in his appearance. He sees him as an international character, as a simple creature who expresses the everyday life, joys and sorrows of people.[61] His mood is as changeable as the weather. He can be exorbitantly cheerful and then suddenly sad and thoughtful, mischievously provoking or full of passionate love. This makes his playing fancifully capricious. It is full of rapidly changing impulsive figurations which follow one another in a seemingly unpredictable way. He is a master of improvisation in the course of which he freely uses all sorts of specific devices. His improvisation involves melody, rhythm and interpretative techniques. This is to be felt in so many ways that it is quite impossible to enumerate all of them, but perhaps he is at his best in the use of asymmetrical melodic patterns, swiftly changing motion, stirring rhythms and strongly articulated bow strokes.

The improvisational character of this portrait miniature is made still more obvious by the absence of piano accompaniment. This is in keeping with the popular tradition according to which a lautar improvises solo. Here Enesco uses the same practice as Ravel in his concert rhapsody *Tsigane* which also begins in the style of a solo improvisation. In keeping with common popular practice, Enesco's lautar starts his improvisation with a loud "cry" which at once attracts attention.

Ex. 43   Allegro deciso non mosso (♩=96)

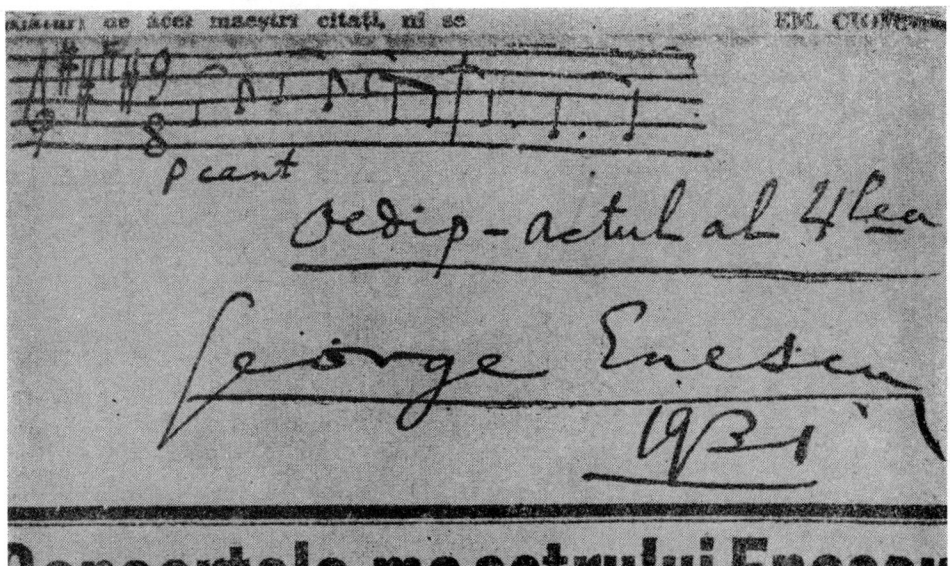

A passage from Act 4 of *Oedipe*, autographed by Enesco in 1931.

Enesco in his souvenirs says that he wanted to portray a lautar "without any allusion to folklore."[62] Therefore he used no folkloric melody in this miniature, but here his musicial ideas are truly popular in spirit and character. Moreover, the idiomatic nature of his "Lautar" is so specific that it left no doubt as to his nationality, although the composer did not intend to cast the image in local colors, considering him to be "an international character". Intonational roots of the composer's music are so national by their very essence that they manifest themselves even when he has no intention to be national. This is clearly illustrated by the following two extracts.

The Rumanian character of the miniature is due not only to the presence of certain modal idioms, such as, for instance, the emphatic reiteration of B as the second degree of A major (viz. the beginning of the piece, ex. n 43). In many cases, it is also due to the employment of technical devices taken from the practical experience of lautars. Besides all the aforementioned sharply articulated bow strokes, they include a specific portamento used in combination with an intensified vibrato, swift appoggiaturas, short, fast trills as well as a frequent recurrence of open strings, especially in fifths, which add a touch of harshness to the violin sound. Among other factors that help to create the popular atmosphere of this piece, one should also mention a figuration in typical taraf style.

Ex. 45

After the exuberant "Lautar", the next miniature produces a very contrasting effect. The music here is no longer temperamental and colorful as before, but dreary, bleak and somber. Enesco called this miniature "An Old Beggar"; he portrayed him with very sober means in the best traditions of *The Winter Journey* by Schubert. The old man—says Enesco—mutters: "misery, misery . . . To convey his image I had in mind a cheerless and stifled sonority."[63] To this aim the composer uses special timbre effects, casting his music in dark, monotonous shades. A slow tempo, a muffled sonority in the middle piano register, tied texture and an inert type of figuration create an impression of rigidity and stagnation.

The melancholic mood of the music is aggravated by the lack of tonal stability. This is felt from the very opening of the piece where Enesco repeats twice a succession of a 6/4 D-minor chord with the last inversion of the chord of ninth, based upon the second degree of the Dorian mode and containing an augmented fourth. The sense of instability becomes still more acute because Enesco leaves this strongly dissonant chord unresolved. This laconic chord progression, left in permanent suspense, provokes a feeling of utter despair.

Ex. 46

Enesco's villa, "Luminis de la Sinaia."

This is answered by the violin which, as if speaking for the beggar, takes up his cheerless muttering in a harsh and rigid voice. Thus the two instruments begin a slow dialogue interrupted by meaningful pauses. The uniform character of their parts makes the despair and frustration so profound as to extinguish the slightest glimpse of hope.

But quite unexpectedly, the slow, narrative pace of the music changes: all of a sudden the old man bursts into anger as if rebuking his fate. A short but swift culmination takes this outburst to a dramatic focal point, but after a few striking staccato notes in the deep bass it dies down, yielding place to the original feeling of apathy.

The next miniature is of a quite different type. This is a landscape in music entitled *A Little Stream in the Back of a Garden*. "I can see it even now," says the author. "It is a tiny stream which murmured softly in the back of our garden,[64] sometimes forming a small pond clear as a looking glass."[65] Following immediately after the previous miniature, this piece catches one's imagination by its transparent aquatic colors. Instead of the dark, dull shades and dim sonority used to depict the appearance of an old beggar, Enesco sees here everything in a light and exquisitely fluctuating coloring.

This miniature virtually amounts to a "tone-picture" showing that Enesco in his fifties could, as easily as in his childhood, interchange his visual and auditive perceptions. That is why in this work there are so many markings whose origin is typically visual, as for example "chiaro" (transparently), "luminoso" (brightly), "estinto" (a fading light), "glauco" (with a blue-greenish shade) or "con una sonorità acquatica" (with an acquarelle sonority). The color-sensibility of Enesco, who in this respect resembles Scriabin, accounts for an extensive use of such indications as "en resonance sans frapper l'accord"[66] (obtaining an echo without striking the chord), "fluido" (fluently), "molto flautato" (very undulatory) and "flessible" (flexibly). Compared with these mostly unorthodox remarks such indications in the violin part as, for instance, "mettez vite la sourdine" (put on quickly the sourdine) or "senza vibrato" (without vibrato) already seem quite traditional.

This miniature, just as the others, is also rich in all sorts of dynamic and agogic indications which Enesco uses with surprising accuracy.[67] According to its poetic content, the composer returns here to certain coloristic effects characteristic of the impressionist palette. Using a fragile, fluctuating texture in the violin and piano parts, maintained mainly in their upper and transparent compasses, he creates here from the very start a sense of fluidity. The thinly sketched outlines of the music are rendered still frailer by the pale sound of harmonics, played on the violin without any vibrato, which seem like water-colors.

No less descriptive by nature are short passages which appear now and then running up and down like thin water currents. By the manner of writing they are similar to those used by Szymanowski in his myth *La Fontaine d'Arethuse*, but here their function is not to recreate the fantastic atmosphere which surrounds a nymph, but to convey concrete associations evoked by the real world. Among them, those suggested by the zig-zagging silvery ribbon of the little stream are no less concrete and at the same time very poetic indeed. They resulted in fragmentation of the melodic line whose undulated design is meant to imitate the turns of the tiny stream. But this elaborate descriptive technique with all its coloristic effects does not result in superficial illustration. On the contrary, it is subordinated to an artistic task aimed at bringing about a happy feeling through a refined poetic setting of a landscape. Although a landscape is viewed here in the narrow sense of a spot cherished since childhood, it acquires, in Enesco's mind, a meaning of something much more significant, symbolizing the idea of his native land as a whole, an idea to which he, as an artist patriot, was so deeply attached. So, his individual associations did not remain in the sphere of subjective recollections, but assumed the meaning of a wide-ranging objective generalization.

"As Bird in a Cage and a Cuckoo Clock" opens up a new group of miniatures in the cycle *Impressions of Childhood*. Unlike the previous piece, which belonged to a pastoral sphere, this one represents an episode taken from family life. The shift from one poetical sphere to another brings a new contrasting factor into the interchange of miniatures, and in this respect the choice of an everyday life atmosphere by Enesco reminds one of that by Schumann in his *Carnaval*. But the chief preoccupation of Enesco was not to make it underline other episodes as Schumann did with "German Waltz" placing it on either side of "Paganini", but to use it as an independent link in the chain formed by other episodes.

In this miniature, Enesco confronted two images of distinctly different nature, two favorite attributes of his early childhood; a living bird and a dead cuckoo. Here they figure not as worn-out, abstract symbols of the old-fashioned family way of life, but as real things allegorically representing two opposite worlds—the turmoil of an undaunted captured bird and the imperturbable punctuality of a mechanical cuckoo.

The little bird is twittering repeatedly in a shrill voice imitated by the violin in its highest pitch. Using a quick repetition of acute staccato notes, extracted by the bow very close to the ridge of the instrument, Enesco makes its twittery sound in a peculiarly stringent manner (ex. n 47). He is not tempted to make the bird indulge in brilliant trills or sweet and cheerful singing as might have been expected in a piece of such onomatopeic character. He employs instead a very rapid astringent staccato stressing his intentions by the following indications: "un poco staccato, non spiccato" and "pesitando", thanks to which it seems that the bird is not only twittering, but at the same time is gouging the bars of the cage with its beak. Immediately it becomes clear that he has in mind not a cheerful little bird singing happily on a branch of a tree, but a secluded, lonely creature. There is a touch of sadness, perplexity and uneasy expectation in its twittering. The bird is restless and worried, and because of this, it finds no enjoyment in life. So Enesco does not paint an idyllic pastoral picture, but conveys a dramatic allegory full of psychological significance. In so doing, he injects a new meaning into the old tradition of imitating the singing of birds which has been practiced very widely in music, especially since Vivaldi. In this case it ceases to be an attribute of a happy state of mind and emotional harmony, brought about by man's communion with nature, and becomes a symbol of solitude, non-acceptance of the media that surrounds him and of protest against it.

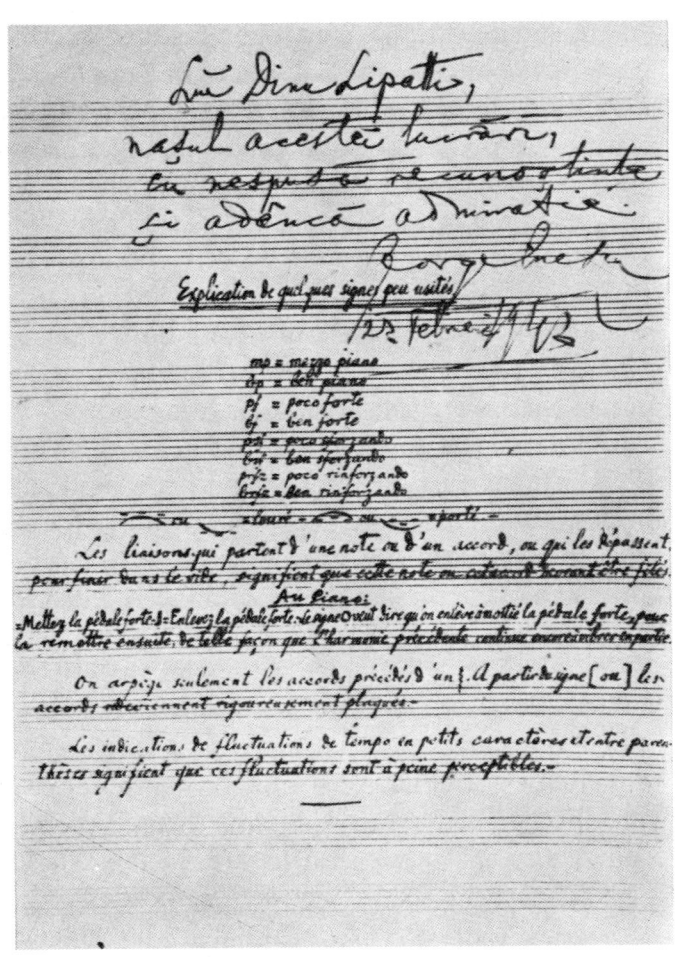

(avec sourd.) nostalgico non troppo un poco staccato, non spiccato   poco

An autograph manuscript of *The Impressions of Childhood*, inscribed to Dinu Lipatti.

That is, no doubt, how the artist himself must have felt remaining in his country on the eve of the catastrophe to which Rumania had been pushed by the fascism he hated so much. In his memoirs, Enesco recalls the circumstances that prompted him to write "*The Impressions of Childhood*": he was offered the post of senator by the pro-fascist government headed by A. Antonesco which he indignantly rejected.[68] Thus denying the reactionary regime the possibility of taking advantage of his worldwide authority, Enesco expressed his negative attitude to it in a refined artistic form. Far from trying to take refuge in the world of remembrance to get away from the unpleasant reality, the artist-democrat, even on the threshold of his seventh decade, did not lose the necessity to be active; he did not seek oblivion through idealization of childhood, but expressed his quest for action by protesting against the present. That is why the feeling of loneliness, symbolized by a bird shut in a cage, has nothing to do with the frustration that had once befallen the old beggar. In the present miniature, loneliness is equated neither with hopelessness, nor with apathy, but is seen as active resistance, and that gives this piece a special meaning, assuring its importance among other miniatures of the cycle.

The feeling of loneliness is here made more acute by the fact that at first the violin plays alone. Even when it is joined by the piano, this feeling does not alter, for the music in the piano part has a character of its own, not supporting but rather opposing that of the violin. While the latter is used to imitate a living bird, the piano part portrays the mechanical cuckoo. It is rendered by a short, abruptly cut figure in the upper, "cold" register with an automatic insistence. This is made even more obvious by the rigid rhythm of the lifeless cuckoo contrasting so much with the loose rhythmic organization of the "living" bird. The two opposite spheres, the heartless and the animated one, at first alternate and then confront each other, sounding together only to stress their antagonistic nature. Here, as in "The Old Beggar", Enesco counts on the effect resulting from the alternative use of his two instruments; but in that miniature, the piano and violin parts belonged to a single emotional sphere, and therefore by alternating them, the composer made them complete one another, while here the same method serves to show how fundamentally apart they actually are. In the course of this confrontation, the violin part is always associated with the image of a tormented bird, and that of the piano is associated with the clockwork. The sound factor too is playing its role in underlining the contrasting role of the two instruments; the thin, shrill voice of the bird on one hand, and the hollow, metallic chimes of the clock on the other. The two instrumental parts coincide in character only then, when they are made to imitate the cuckooing of the mechanical bird (ex. n 48). With stubborn insistence, the cuckoo strikes seven o'clock. This was the signal, recalls Enesco, for the bird and the boy to go to bed.

Ex. 48

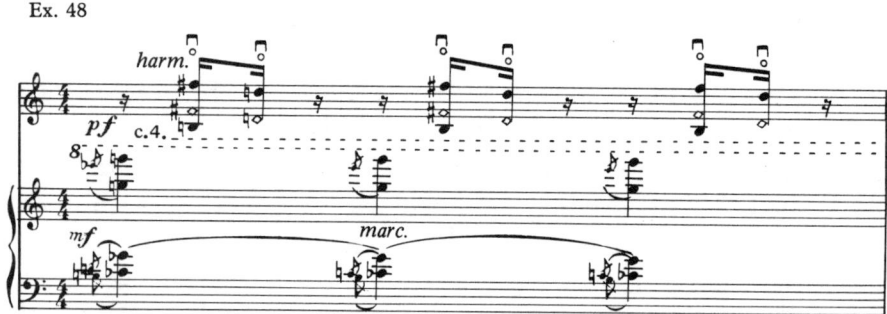

The psychological connection between this miniature and "The Old Beggar" affected their thematic material. When after the rough intrusion of the cuckoo, the bird becomes silent, the piano takes up a short motive from that miniature. An automatic device silences, for

In this prospectus of the 1936-1937 season at Carnegie Hall, Georges Enesco is introduced as "Rumania's musical ambassador-at-large."

the time being, the tormented voice of a living creature: "The time came," said Enesco, "to impose a curfew on the bird."[69]

The meaning Enesco gave to this miniature radically changed the character of the technique used in it. The living bird and the cuckoo clock are depicted by effects of a typically descriptive nature. And yet, despite this, their use did not transform it into a naturalistic exercise because they were made to acquire the power of artistic generalization of an important poetic idea.

There is one more thing which makes this miniature very interesting, for it shows convincingly how the technique developed by folk musicians can enrich the concert interpretative style. As in a number of his other works, and particularly in the first *Rumanian Rhapsody* and the *Third Sonata for Violin and Piano*, Enesco here made extensive use of the art of the popular fiddlers he loved so much. This refers to the manner in which he imitates the singing of birds so frequently reproduced by lautars in their concert fantasies known as "Ciocarlia." Placing the bow in different sectors of the string, changing the angle it forms with the string and making the stick of the bow lean towards the head of the violin, as well as altering the frequency and amplitude of vibrato thanks to a flatter position of a given finger on the string, Enesco managed to enrich the violin sound with a variety of timbral effects. The age-old popular practice helped him to turn coloristic devices into expressive means of the highest order.

The "Cradle Song" occupies the central place in the cycle. It marks a new phase in the unfolding of the entire work. This determines its special role and function. If the previous miniatures, programmatic as they are, were not bound together by a common plot, all the pieces that follow the "Cradle Song" represent various episodes of a single story. This, however, does not mean that the first four miniatures have nothing to do with the rest. They served to establish an atmosphere which, from the emotional viewpoint, was necessary to make the programme of the work as a whole sound and convincing. Without them, the story of a child who was frightened by a night storm and then calmed down in the morning might have looked naîve and trivial.

The special position of the "Cradle Song" is highlighted by the fact that it also marks the starting point from which the humanistic idea of the entire work is beginning to materialize. In light of the allegoric programme chosen by the author, this idea could be translated as the victory of a rising day over nightfall. Besides, judging from an artistic point of view, the "Cradle Song" represents one of the best specimens of the composer's art (ex. n 49).

A middle-aged Enesco with his dog.

Following the signal given by the cuckoo, the nurse puts the child to bed. To lull him to sleep she is telling him tales: "You will be big and strong, you will be . . . you will be . . ." he can hear her say.[70] But soon he is no longer able to catch the sense of her words; a sweet drowsiness overtakes the child, and he sinks into that kind of unruffled serenity which children feel when they fall asleep in the lap of their mothers or old nurses. Now he can hear only the voice so familiar and dear to him. It goes on and on: the nurse is continuing her tale in a steady manner, and there is a touch of epic grandeur of an old ballad in her narration as well as that of a moving intimate lyrical song. The music here evokes comfort mingled with secret nostalgic yearning. Everything here seems surprisingly simple and at the same time very exciting.

Although the "Cradle Song" bears no dedication, it is no doubt the artist's tribute to the memory of his dear, old nurse. It is impossible to say whether Enesco was here inspired by the Russian poet A.S. Pushkin, but his music, by its warm and poetic atmosphere, calls the lines full of kindness the latter had addressed to his old nanny:

"Dear doting sweetheart of my childhood,
Companion of my austere fate!
In the lone house deep in the wild wood
How passionately for me you wait."[71]

That is, perhaps, why the music here conjures up the image of the nanny who had told the poet in his childhood about

". . . Deeds of days passed long ago,
Legends cast in ancient times."[72]

The manner in which the music is rendered here seems also to have an association with the image of the old nanny. As a matter of fact, the theme of the "Cradle Song" is at first rendered entirely in a monodic way. It is played in unison by the two instruments which causes the melody to sound archaic, resembling the voice of an old person. Because of the unison texture, it also resembles a popular tune as was the case with the *Second Sonata for Violin and Piano* or with the prelude from the first orchestral suite.

Another interesting feature of this theme is its national character which gives it a particular flavor. Here, as in the slow movement of the *Second Sonata*, Enesco uses the Aeolian mode and a changeable measurement of duple and triple time. These features, rooted in the ancient layers of Rumanian folklore, bring the music close to the Slavonic sphere and simultaneously underline its archaic character. It sounds very, very gently with a shade of soft sadness in the E-Aeolian mode invigorated by a modulation into the C-Mixolydian which leads it into A-minor. It is interesting that Enesco, in accordance with popular tradition, paves the way for the C-Mixolydian by using beforehand a descending group of notes in the key of C-minor. The subtle beauty of this method of approach to tonal relationship contributes much to enhance the expressive qualities of the piece.

Soothed by the lullaby, the child eventually falls asleep. A cricket, Enesco says, is heard. The moon is shining through the window throwing trembling, silvery glimpses across the room. Suddenly a storm breaks out; the wind is howling in the chimney, awakening the child. He is frightened and hides his head under the pillow. This is, roughly speaking, the content of the three following miniatures which constitute the last but one phase of the work. Representing different episodes of a single plot, these miniatures follow one another without interruption continuing the main line initiated by "A Bird in a Cage and the Cuckoo-clock."

Here again descriptive means play a decisive role in conveying the poetic idea, but they are applied in a different manner according to the character of a given episode. In "The Cricket" and "The Storm" this role is closer to pure illustration than in "The Moonlight", for the very nature of things to be described requires onomatopoeic means. But even so, the onomatopoeic technique is used not merely for the sake of illustration. In the last of the three episodes, the composer imitates the storm and the wind howling in the chimney in order to convey the feelings of a child frightened by a tempest. Thus, ponticello in double stopping (ex. n 50), which creates an almost concrete sound effect, conveys the fear of a disturbed child. Here a typical timbral device, operating as a descriptive factor, is meant to achieve a psychological effect.

Ex. 50

By the way, this fragment, played by the violin as a cadenza without accompaniment, shows how Enesco uses the coloristic resources of his instrument. Developing the ponticello technique applied by Ysaÿe, for instance, in his first and second sonatas for violin solo, Enesco showed, even to a greater degree than his famous Belgian colleague, that coloristic devices can be used on the violin not only to obtain picturesque effects, but also as an essential artistic means of a true psychological power.

"The Moonlight" is distinct from the neighboring miniatures also because it has thematic links with the previous section of the work. This link results from the fact that the main thematic material of "The Cradle Song" reappears in the said miniature towards the end of which it is re-stated in diminution. It acquires now a new and very dynamic character thanks to a quicker motion, a new, more active piano texture and motive development. This transformation has affected the character of the sound as well. It is "sung" now by the violin not in the "blank", low amplitude voice of an elderly person as before, but in a full, bright voice which reverberates even louder against the background of transparent figurations in the piano part clearly associated with glimpses of moonlight. The music assumes now a fantastic character. If earlier it was a tale lulling a child to sleep, now it is a fantastic dream. Owing to a thematic link between

Facsimile of the manuscript of Enesco's acceptance speech at the Academia Romana.

the two miniatures and this transformation in the latter, "The Moonlight" does not produce the impression of an isolated episode. On the contrary, it comes as a consequence of "The Cradle Song," and this strengthens the unity of the entire work which puts it outside the formal limits of a suite.

The last section of the work is even more nontraditional for a suite-type composition. It is, in the full sense of the word, a finale in which all the lines of previous dramaturgic development converge, a finale where the central idea of *Impressions of Childhood* is generalized in true symphonic manner; according to Enesco, the nightmare is over and the sun has risen. When the child wakes up in the morning, the sun is already shining brightly. Birds are singing, but their voices no longer echo the torment of a captive bird or the tough pedantism of the mechanical cuckoo. The child is breathing freely;

he is happy, he passed unharmed through the night and the storm. That is how the artist discloses the idea of his work to which he, as a humanist, was so deeply attached. Through ordeal to the triumph of light over darkness—that is what he really wanted to imply by his *Impressions of Childhood.*

Enesco called the closing section of this work "The Sunrise", but despite the suggestive character of this programmatic title, it would be wrong to assume that he had in mind merely a sunlit landscape. The sunrise is viewed here in an allegoric sense as a symbol of great artistic and ethical significance. Therefore, here too coloristic effects acquire a generalizing and psychological function. That function is underlined by the fact that several themes from preceding miniatures recur in this finale, transformed in such a way as to stress their optimistic potential. As Enesco says: "The themes, associated with the sun and shadow, reappear, but now sound placid and peaceful because of a shift from a minor to a major key."[73]

One example of such a transformation is given at the beginning of the finale (ex. n 51). Thanks to the high crystalline violin harmonics, this short phrase sounds now very fresh, as if purified by transparent morning dew. It seems to carry with it that invigorating freshness of a crisp, chilly dawn which foretells a bright summer day. And yet, despite the changed and now sparkling texture of the violin and piano parts, one can easily recognize it as a new version of the opening theme from "The Cradle Song". There is also a change of mood in the motive which was previously associated with the old beggar, but his frustration has now completely vanished. It has lost its familiar apathy, acquiring an instant and cheerful drive.

Ex. 51

Vaux-le-Pénil,
ce 4 9bre 1910 —

Mon cher Monsieur Enoch,

J'ai été si navré d'apprendre que vous aviez été souffrant tout dernièrement que je viens vous dire bien vite combien je vous souhaite un prompt et très complet rétablissement —

Je ne rentre définitivement à Paris que vers la fin du mois, et alors j'irai vous voir, et compte vous trouver plus gaillard et plus épatant que jamais !

Mille et mille choses affectueuses, en attendant, cher Monsieur Enoch !

Georges Enesco

Enesco's letter to Enoch, his Parisian publisher.

The lautar too is among those taking part in the finale. His colorful figure appears here and there, generating fluidity which adds dynamism to the whole tissue. His impulsiveness makes, as it were, even the old beggar seem younger. Under the impetus of his active intonations, the emotional build-up gradually gains momentum; extensive virtuoso figurations flash across the piano part resembling the whirling "bravura" passages from the coda of the last movement of the *Third Violin and Piano Sonata*. The intensity also grows, thanks to the frequent use of double stopping, various chords and open strings in the violin part which make that instrument sound more ample and crisp. Among other factors which contribute most effectively to bring this drive to its climax, one should single out the following: an active melodic line often torn apart by jumps over large intervals, timbral and pitch contrasts, as well as heavy accents thundered out fortissimo, polyrhythmic and polymelodic structures which lead to the formation of polytonal chords. And finally, all this "apotheosis of light" ends in insistently reiterated D-major key which sounds as powerful and triumphant as the force that achieved victory over darkness.

In one way or another, this idea inspired many works of Enesco, taking shape in the *C-major Symphony*, gaining momentum in the finale of his *Third Violin and Piano Sonata* to reach its focal point in the opera *Oedipe*. Its affirmation in the *Impressions of Childhood*, written in 1940, stresses the unfailing optimism of the composer who perceived the rising sun through clouds of war which had once more been gathering over Europe. Moreover, the idea of this work involves not merely a condemnation of destructive forces, but above all a constructive opposition capable of overcoming them.

The fact that this positive idea is expressed in subtle lyrical and psychological terms in a work of chamber music type reveals the extent to which that humanitarian idea became a part of the very being of the artist.

Autographed excerpt from the
Sonata no. 3 for Piano and Violin.

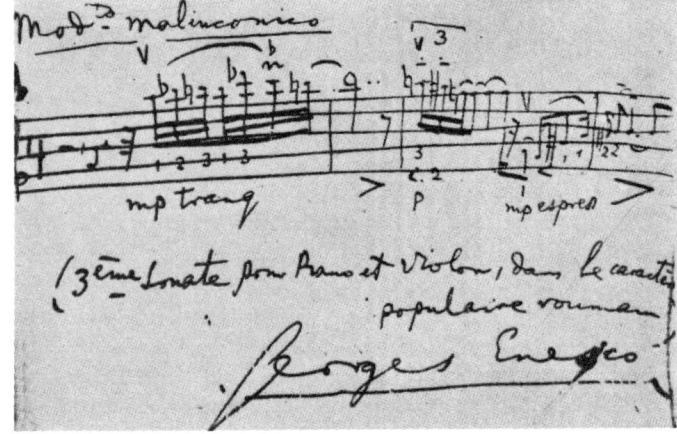

The Concert Overture on Popular Rumanian Themes shows the variety of forms in which this idea could be expressed. By staying abroad, Enesco missed his country very much—this is the feeling the work conveys with great dramatic emphasis. Intimately linked with his people, he took to heart their hardships and as a composer and concert player was always eager to help those in need. He often took part in charity concerts, as for instance, twice in March 1947 when he played in New York to raise money for children of drought-struck Moldova who suffered from malnutrition.

The *Rustic Suite*, the *Impressions of Childhood* and *The Concert Overture* follow the line of the *Third Violin and Piano Sonata* also so far as the crystallization of the composer's national style is concerned. It is not a result of the quotation of folkloric tunes, nor is it a consequence of some magic technical formula, but it represents a genuine reflection of the soul of the Rumanian people, a reflection of its emotional and psychological background.

That is why national idioms became for him a form suitable for expressing universally human ideas. These included the belief that life and the creative impulse of men shall triumph over the forces of evil and darkness. Hence his interest in such themes as the antique myth of Oedipus whose will proved to be stronger than fate.

Cover of the program of the première of *Oedipe* in Paris, March 13, 1936.

Chapter 6

It took Enesco a long time before he finally decided to choose the story of Oedipus for his opera. The desire to write an opera came to him as early as 1906. By this time he felt himself artistically mature enough to tackle such a venture; it attracted him more and more as he realized what a powerful influence opera could have on a large audience, and this represented a special point of interest for an artist as educationally minded as he. But he could not find a suitable plot. He sought something that would inspire significant ideas, and he declined many offers made to him by French authors whose libretti resembled trivial stories from newspapers.

Finally, in 1910, he happened to see "Oedipus-Rex" by Sophocles at the "Comedie Française" featuring the well-known French actor J. Mounet-Sully. Deeply moved by his acting, Enesco made his choice. This opera took him about a quarter of a century to complete, encompassing ten years of persistent labor.

That is how *Oedipe* came into being, representing a work which Enesco considered the main preoccupation of his life, the purpose of his existence, a work praised by Casals as "an absolutely original opera of a tremendous dramatic power."[75]

There is a marked divergence of view as to when the opera was finished. Judging by the note on the last page of the score in Enesco's handwriting, he completed *Oedipe* in his summer countryhouse at Tuscany on April 27, 1931, but some Rumanian authors, especially in their earlier works, maintain that the opera was finished in 1932. However, recent research carried out in the USSR brought to life a hitherto unknown fact which throws new light on the circumstances and place of completion of the opera.

As a matter of fact, Enesco, in his speech at a banquet given in November 1937 to mark his concerts in the town of Akkerman (at present Belgorod-Dnestrovski in the Ukraine), said that he was particularly fond of this city, for it was here that he had finished the opera *Oedipe* into which he had put all his soul.[76] The speech is reported in a dispatch sent from Akkerman in November 1937 to the Bucharest newspaper "Universul" and was found by the author of this book in the Central State Archives of the Moldavian Soviet

The house in Tuscany where on April 27, 1931, the opera *Oedipe* was completed.

Socialist Republic. Reporting this event, the Akkerman correspondent does not specify exactly when it took place, merely saying that it happened some years ago. As it is known, before 1937 Enesco visited the town only twice: in May 1931 and also in May 1932. Assuming that his third and last visit should be discounted — it came a year after the first performance of *Oedipe* in Paris — Enesco must have meant either the first or the second visit.

How can one explain the divergence between the statement, made at the banquet, and the footnote at the end of the score? It must be assumed that apparently he found it necessary to revise once again the version completed in Tuscany and that he did it, as he says, in Akkerman, without altering the date in the footnote. Such an assumption is all the more plausible as there are certain other divergences of date concerning the opera.[77]

The main point of interest in the aforementioned dispatch is not so much that it reveals one more chronological detail, but that it indicates the place where the opera actually was completed. As a matter of fact the correspondent emphasizes that in putting the finishing touches to his work, the composer was inspired by the glorious past of the antique city of Akkerman. Its ruins could have conjured up in his imagination the figure of the sphinx whose ominous shadow seemed to haunt these ancient places. They might have reminded him of so many invaders who mercilessly ravaged them throughout the ages, including Greeks, Romans, Scythians, Polovitsians and Turks to cite but a few unwelcome guests. Like a

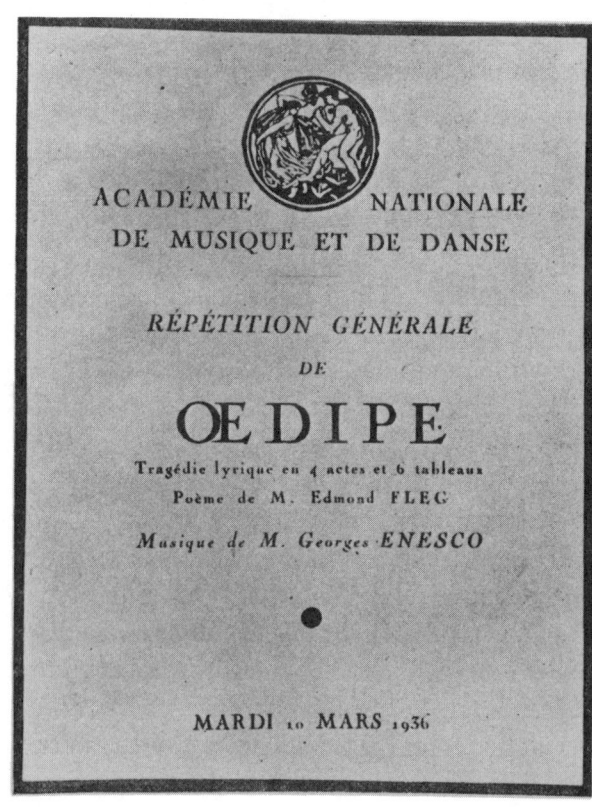

Bill for the dress rehearsal of *Oedipe* at the Paris Opera.

dauntless guardian of dark memories of those times, there stood on the top of a huge rock a massive fortress, its 26 towers still looking formidable with their narrow embrasures projected in all directions. Contrasting with this stern relic of the past, nearby, as a symbol of purity and human dignity, there murmured placidly a fountain nicknamed Paroskivia after a girl who, according to a legend, had drowned herself here to escape dishonor in a Turkish harem and was transformed into a crystal clear spring. At the opposite shore of the Black Sea, as if close at hand though miles away, one could distinguish the faint silhouette of the city of Ovidiopol where Ovid is said to have been exiled because of his rebellion against the abuse of power by Roman rulers. Under the influence of this bizarre, epico-legendary atmosphere, Enesco could have found a new stimulus to revise the end of his *Oedipe*.[78]

The opera *Oedipe* (Op. 23) is a lyric tragedy in four acts (six scenes) the first of which may be considered to be a prologue and the last act the epilogue of the whole drama. It was first performed in Paris on March 10, 1936 in the Grande Opera Theatre, the official gala-premiere taking place three days later.[79] Thus came into being an opera of great artistic value deeply realistic in its humane implication. This was the merit not only of Enesco, but also of Edmond Fleg who wrote the libretto.[80] The presentation of this opera in the mid-thirties, when the struggle between the progressive and reactionary forces reached a high degree of intensity, marked an outstanding event in the history of western music.

Enesco's interest in the tragic fate of Oedipus is closely linked with the philosophical orientation of his art as a whole. He was attracted by the tragedy of a man who rebelled against injustice and who triumphed over it, thanks to his courage and conscious willpower. He felt something in common with Oedipus, saying that the latter symbolized his own fate. But it would be wrong to explain the choice of such a plot for his opera solely on considerations of autobiographical order. This choice was due to far more important causes.

One consequence of these trends is a marked renewal of interest in antiquity which has been, for centuries, long a source of inspiration for so many artists. This upsurge of interest became especially noticeable since the end of the nineteenth and the beginning of the twentieth century. Dissatisfied with the reality of their time and seeing no prospect in the present, many an artist turned his attention to antiquity in the hope of finding in it a way out of the impasse. As a result, there appeared a large number of works inspired by antique or biblical themes, such as *Oresteia* by Taneev, *Salome, Elektra* and *Daphne* by Strauss, *Promethee* and *Penelope* by Fauré, *Socrate* by Satie, *L'Orestie d'Eschyle* and *Médée* by Milhaud, *Le Roi David* and *Antigone* by Honegger, *Oedipus Rex* by Stravinski, *Oedipe* by Enesco, *Antigonae, Trionfo di Afrodite* and *Oedipus der Tyrann,* by Orff, and many others. But artists differed in their approach to antiquity in accordance with their individuality, seeing in it, like in a mirror, their own reflection. For some of them, antiquity entailed a departure from reality or a critical attitude to it, while for others antiquity provided a means of getting nearer to reality and of fostering its positive side.

In their *Elektra*, Richard Strauss and Hugo von Hoffmannsthal glorified not the highest ideals of antiquity, not its humane values, nobleness, faithfulness, purity in love, self-sacrifice for the sake of a grand cause or heroic ventures, but ruthless vengeance of almost inhuman ferocity. The same applies to *Salome* in which R. Strauss and Oscar Wilde expressed strong, but negative, passions. In a masterly way, they transformed the heroine of this biblical legend into a symbol of repugnant sensuality. The fact that bloodthirsty vengeance of beastly sexual instincts are presented in so luxurious a manner does by no means imply that the artists in question intended to condone or, still less, to glorify them. Far from it. Here is the case where surface beauty makes moral ugliness even more disgusting, and therefore this way of presenting it serves a positive purpose, apparently referring to the reality the artists had to cope with. That is how, despite the so-called decadent conception of an ancient theme, the artists revealed their negative reaction to the moral disarray of their time, just as Shakespeare exposed vices of his own epoch in his antique plays. Thus, a true work of art, in which artistic and progressive qualities are inseparable from one another, objectively carries a progressive implication, for its author, thanks to the intuition of a humanitarian artist, reacts to the positive tendencies of social development even if he reflects them through a negative approach.

Another interesting work on an antique theme is the opera-oratoria *Oedipus Rex* by Stravinsky, written for soloists, chorus and orchestra. Its libretto, based on Sophocles' tragedy bearing the same title, was written by J. Cocteau in collaboration with the composer and translated into Latin by J. Daniélou. Considering that the plot of his work belonged to a universal heritage, Stravinsky stripped it of any national or individual features; hence the choice of Latin – a universal language belonging to all countries and all epochs. The composer's desire to emphasize the "supernational" and "superindividual" character of his work determined the use of traditions of the old mass and oratorio viewed in the light of classicist tendencies so far as the style, forms and genre were concerned. The strict metrical organization of the Latin text, traditional repetitions of certain words and phrases, the use of the old contrapuntal technique turns this work into a masterly substitute for an ancient style. But despite all the ingenuity Stravinsky displays, the cosmopolitan character of the work and its archaic features reduce its vitality and humaneness, that is to say, just those qualities without which the greatness of antiquity becomes nothing more than obsolete grandeur. A similar approach to antiquity, especially towards the end of the second decade of our century when social contradictions

Composers Igor Stravinsky (left) and Richard Strauss (right), among many others, based stage works on ancient Greek subjects.

were becoming more and more acute, could only mean a departure from reality, an utter neglect of the most pressing problems of the day.

As to Enesco, his attitude to antiquity was motivated by considerations of a quite different nature. It can be summed up by the following quotation from the well-known nineteenth century Russian writer, A.I. Ghertsen: "Antiquity's power of attraction lies in its humaneness . . . it helped to work out a new approach to many things." Enesco wanted his Oedipus to be not a god, but a real living man. "If," says the composer, "somebody is moved by certain feeling I gave him, this is because people, I believe, find in his complaint something common to themselves."[81] It is just the link with the everyday reality of our time that gave the theme of Oedipus a burning contemporary sense, deepened its meaning and widened its implication, thanks to Enesco and Fleg. By freeing this theme from fatalism so characteristic of the ancient way of thinking, they created not a pessimistic drama, but an optimistic tragedy.

It is necessary to stress the part Fleg played in the work on the opera thanks to which the humanitarian character of Enesco's esthetics became even more defined. The collaboration of the two artists contributed also to make its democratic features more pronounced. Having portrayed Creon as an insidious, cruel person fond of power, the composer and the librettist emphasized in this way the contrast between the two different conceptions of power symbolized by him and by Oedipus. The former embodies the autocratic notion of power, while the latter stands for its democratic nature. So, Creon's outlook reflects his part as a historical figure which represents the despotic force capable of putting an end to the feudal strife that was hampering the unification of ancient Greece. In the light of Creon's despotic character, the personality of Oedipus acquires additional weight. This is illustrated by the famous sentence ascribed to Oedipus who considers it his duty, at a terrible cost to himself, to save the people of the city of Thebes from the disaster which had befallen them:

"Because each of you is preoccupied with himself,
But I must care for you all, for the city and myself."[82]

The fact that Oedipus as its leader is fully aware of his responsibility to the people makes his selfless achievement assume a true civic sense, the democratic meaning acquires a special importance during the years preceding the Second World War.

The democratic views held by Enesco and Fleg also affected their approach to chorus symbolizing the people as an active force. By restoring the active role of the chorus, they, unlike a number of their recent predecessors, not merely revived one of the best traditions of the mature antique tragedy, which reflected the democratic social structure of ancient Greece, but gave it new meaning in light of the growing struggle of democratic forces against reaction.

It must be added to their credit that they also freed Oedipus from certain weaknesses, without any attempt to idealize him. Thus, their hero is not at all a rash, ill-tempered, irritable man as portrayed by some other authors. It is true that Sophocles gave a clue to such an explanation of Oedipus' behavior, but Voltaire, for instance, focused his attention on it in his play bearing the hero's name. The same tendency manifests itself in a number of plays connected with Oedipus, belonging to several authors of the eighteenth and early nineteenth centuries. As to Voltaire, he did not hesitate to make his hero haughty and disdainful which was what, in his opinion, provoked the fatal clash with his father.

Having rejected the moralizing tendency in dealing with Oedipus, Enesco and Fleg gave a more sound motivation to that scene in conformity with their ethical and esthetic position. According to them, his behavior was motivated neither by his arrogance, nor by hot temper, but came as a result of indignation provoked by an insult. By the way, thanks to Fleg and Enesco, the Oedipus dilemmas lose the meaning attributed to them by the representatives of the classicist school. Unlike Corneille for instance, they saw the implication of Oedipus' tragedy not in the fact that blames a man for his attempt to understand the enigma of destiny, but in something quite different: a man, as a reasonable being, inspired by a noble ideal, can master the secret of fate, subordinating it to a humanitarian goal.

And finally, the composer together with the librettist eliminated the apparent contradiction in the character of Oedipus which

A sketch for Oedipus' costume.

Sophocles deliberately introduced in his second tragedy. According to the ancient dramatist, who reflected the social and historic layout of ancient Greece, the presence of the body of Oedipus in the city of Colon becomes a guarantee of universal happiness; since this happiness is symbolized by the safety and welfare of Athens, his remains must at the same time represent a deterrent to the enemies of the Greek capital. Hence his menacing utterance:

"Then my cold dust lying in the coffin
Shall be sucked with their hot blood!"[83]

Enesco and Fleg realized that these words must not be attributed to the bloodthirstiness of Oedipus. They knew that in Sophocles' tragedy too this utterance did not contradict the humane nature of his hero, but was only a peculiar form used by him to express his intention to insure the security of Athens. As this city led the struggle for the unification of all of Greece, Oedipus, in whom Sophocles

111

saw a symbol of Athens' prosperity, logically had to become a threat to the city's enemies, to all those who had been hindering the fulfillment of its progressive social and political mission. Having transformed the dying Oedipus into a symbol of human happiness, Enesco and Fleg, thanks to their nondogmatic approach preserved the unity of his outlook, and without distorting the historical truth, carried his image beyond the range of a historically limited epoch.

The two artists conceived their hero as a man devoted to justice whose uncompromising spirit incited him to revolt against the arbitrary will of Fate. When at the crossing point of three routes, Oedipus lifts his club against destiny, he behaves not as a helpless victim of a fatal force, but as a relentless fighter who accuses the immortal gods of injustice. Once Oedipus realizes that he is innocent, he takes the offensive, and this shift from self-scrutiny to militant action is shown with great dynamic power and psychological accuracy. Oedipus receives one blow after another, but he continues to fight. This bitter struggle grows in intensity leading him to victory over the Sphinx which symbolized the almighty Fate. The authors of the opera replaced the naïve riddle (with which the Sphinx, according to the legend, had been terrorizing people) by a question: "Is there in the world anything or anybody more powerful than Fate?" By doing so, they have the proud answer of Oedipus, a profoundly symbolic implication. This is emphasized by the fact that in accomplishing his heroic deed, Oedipus was motivated, not by selfish considerations, but by the desire to save the city of Thebes from the tyranny of the Sphinx. In this way they made Oedipus' outlook more noble, purifying it from defects which, as the ancient Greeks thought, a man must have to justify his misfortunes. It must be said again that this conception of Oedipus' character was due not to an idealization of a man, but to a realistic approach to the nature of his drama which takes place in adverse circumstances.

But this phase of the opera, dramatically intense and psychologically accurate as it is, does not yet constitute its focal point which will be reached only after even more tragic events take

A passage, in Enesco's hand, from *Oedipe*.

Facing page:
Fascimile of the first page of the manuscript of the score of *Oedipe*.

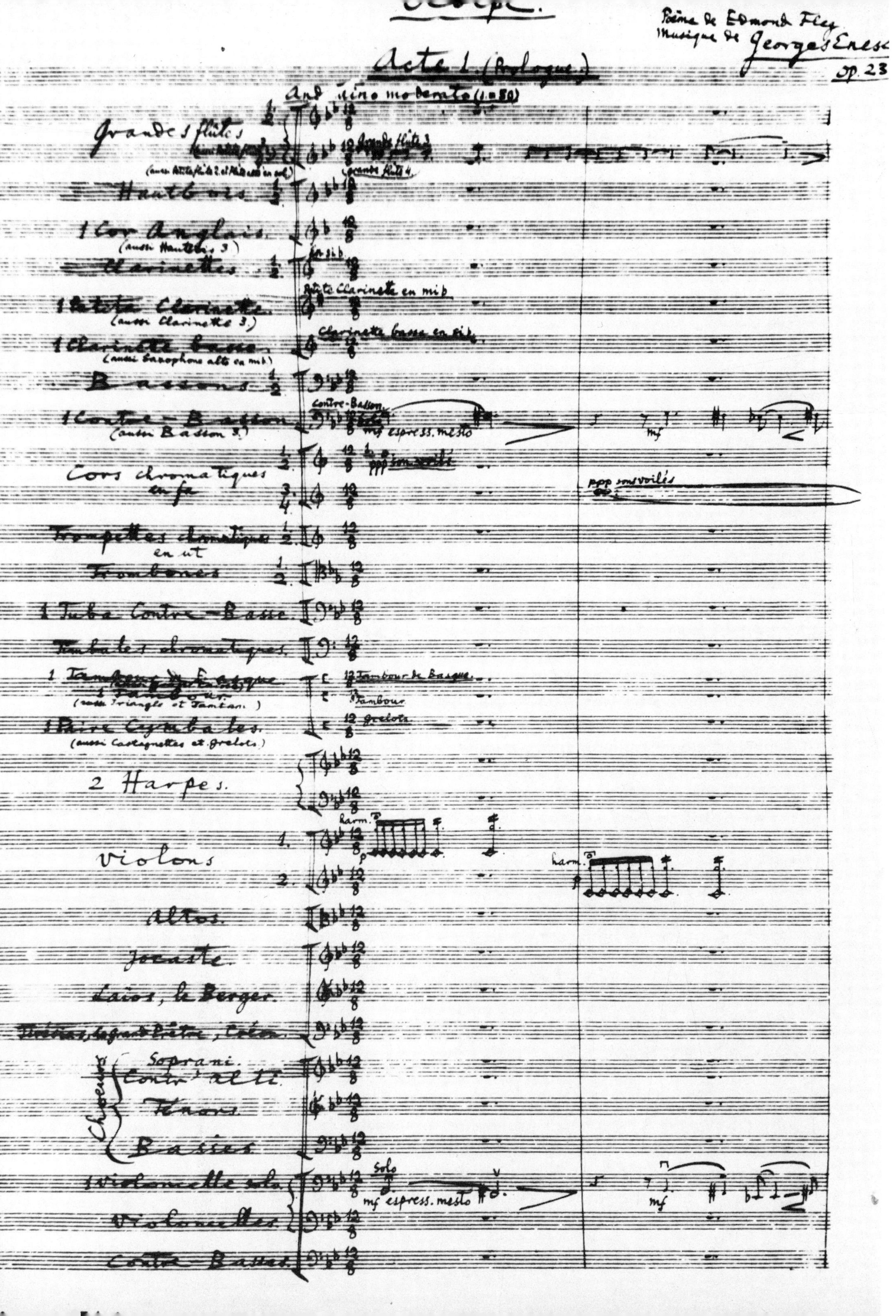

Poème de Edmond Fleg
Musique de Georges Enesco
Op. 23
Acte I. (Prologue)
Andantino moderato
Grandes flûtes
Grandes flûtes 3
Grandes flûtes 4
Hautbois
1 Cor Anglais
(aussi Hautbois 3)
Clarinettes
en si b
Petite Clarinette en mi b
1 Petite Clarinette
(aussi Clarinette 3)
Clarinette basse en si b
1 Clarinette basse
(aussi Saxophone alto en mi b)
Bassons
Contre-Basson
1 Contre-Basson
(aussi Basson 3)
mf espress. mesto
ppp sons voilé
Cors chromatiques en fa
ppp sons voilés
Trompettes chromatiques en ut
Trombones
1 Tuba Contre-Basse
Timbales chromatiques
Tambour de Basque
Tambour
(aussi Triangle et Tamtam)
1 Paire Cymbales
(aussi Castagnettes et Grelots)
Grelots
2 Harpes
harm.
Violons
Altos
Jocaste
Laïos, le Berger
Soprani
Contr'alti
Ténors
Basses
Choeurs
Solo
1 Violoncelle solo
Violoncelles
Contre-Basses

place in the third act. There Oedipus learns that despite all his efforts to avoid it, he involuntarily perpetrated all the abominable crimes he had been doomed to commit, even before his birth. This fatal blasphemy was ruthlessly pursuing him, and the very course of events it determined led him mercilessly to do what he wanted to avoid at all cost. Eventually he is faced with a cruel moral dilemma: he could have not disclosed his criminal mystery; he could have escaped to Corinth following the call of his adoptive parents. But this would have meant admitting the defeat inflicted on him by Fate and also that the city he once had saved from the Sphinx would not be freed until the criminal was punished. The first he cannot accept as a man convinced of his innocence, the second—as a citizen, as a leader conscious of his supreme duty to the people who are relying on him.

He finds a way out of this dilemma not by rejecting his responsibility, but through acceptance of punishment for the crimes he has involuntarily committed, the punishment to which he is doomed by a new malediction of Fate. Oedipus is free to make his choice; he chooses, according to his own will, not the easy way out, but a thorny path in the face of an ungrateful mob, which chases him away, and this choice points to his outspoken protest, to his dauntless spirit nourished by an unfailing belief in his moral purity and in the forthcoming victory of justice. Thus, the acceptance of self-inflicted suffering represents here an active step. He was morally encouraged to take this decision by the positive attitude of his daughter, Antigone, the only creature who did not turn away from him in this hour of distress. Her unselfish confidence and humaneness held a promise of the forthcoming redemption.

To comprehend the philosophical conception of the opera *Oedipe,* it is necessary to bear in mind that from this moment, its hero for the first time becomes the master of his destiny instead of being its instrument as before. Now he knows where the path of suffering is leading him; he is convinced now that it shall lead him to victory, and that his determination shall prevail over injustice. Thus, the idea of morality through self-imposed suffering from injustice (Oedipus' self-inflicted blindness), did not result here in humility, but acquired a new meaning: Fate can be vanquished only by defeating it completely.

This meaning is disclosed in philosophical, symbolic terms in the last act, forming the epilogue of the opera. Fortunately, the authors of the opera preferred not to turn the final act into a brilliant apotheosis full of pompous effects. They chose instead to express the synthesis of the drama in a symbolic way and they succeeded in doing it without conventional rhetoric or oratorical gestures. The maxim that "Happy is he whose soul is pure" is rendered here in moderated tones of lucid lyricism against the background of a springtime landscape, and that is why it does not sound like an abstract saying, but stands out as an aphorism full of wise, humane implication. Although Enesco speaks of "supreme reconciliation", the death of Oedipus, who has regained his sight, represents not a passive and mystic symbol, but an active and optimistic outcome, because his moral purity and determination are made to serve the happiness of mankind. They are immortal, since he is transformed from a man who needed a guide into a guide leading people "forward on the way to the better."

Oedipus' victory over the pitiless Fate ceased to be an abstract symbol, becoming a concrete allegory full of a strong moral and social sense. The struggle with Fate identified itself with the fight against tyranny, subjugation and injustice for freedom of human personality.

During the period of growing reaction in Western Europe, when the brown plague of Hitlerism was already threatening to engulf the whole world, such an interpretation of an antique myth assumed a politically defined character reflecting the progressive tendencies of our epoch. So, the Oedipus theme of all ages became, in a new historic reality, a form of expression of the best humanitarian aspirations of progressive men and women everywhere.

The same aspirations lie at the root of a number of statements, made by Enesco on several occasions, which leave no doubt as to where the sympathies of this democratically minded artist lay in the conflict. Seeing how economic crises were hampering the development of art, he wrote: "... it is impossible to speak about 'the recovery' of beauty while people have nothing to eat."[84] The following words show how emphatic he was in his condemnation of fascism: "Germany of today, so much impoverished from the artistic point of view, bears no resemblance whatsoever to the true nobility of that people. In today's Germany I can see no trace of that greatness which the masters of the past have brought to mankind."[85]

Knowing how detrimental to the progress of humanity the forces of reaction are, Enesco, as a man and an artist, could not remain indifferent in the face of the struggle for democracy. In this respect, his attitude to the formation of the Popular Front in France is very characteristic. He made it known in a statement published by the Rumanian democratic antifascist newspaper in Paris in 1936 – the year when the première of the opera *Oedipe* took place. Welcoming the setting up of the Popular Front, he said: "It is desirable that the example of France, where the forces of democracy achieved a victory, should be followed by our country too. I welcome enthusiastically such an action. Tell everyone that I stand for the triumph of reason over those forces which are trying to keep our country in darkness and ignorance."[86]

Turning back to the opera, it would be appropriate now to outline briefly its plot according to Enesco:

Scene I (prologue): in the palace of Laios and Jocaste, the people of Thebes are celebrating the birth of the heir to the throne. Shepherds bring wreaths and garlands of flowers, women – purple

Opening page of the first edition of
the piano vocal score of *Oedipe*,
with an inscription to Gustave Bret.

The murder of Laios, Act II,
scene 3.

tissues, warriors—gilded bows and arrows. Jocaste and the high priest are choosing a name for the newborn child, but old Teresias, who had been blinded by the wrath of the goddess Héra, predicts that Oedipus is doomed to become the murderer of his father and the husband of his mother, and to prolong his cursed species—the father of his own brothers and sisters. People disperse in dismay. Laios hands over the baby to a shepherd ordering him to kill it in the mountain wilds.

Scene II (act II): in Corinth a young man, standing by a column, is meditating in the light of the setting sun. This is Oedipus. The shepherd did not carry out Laios' order, but gave the baby to another shepherd who in turn handed it over to the Corinthian King Polibos and his wife Merope. They adopted Oedipus and brought him up. Having learned by chance that he had been doomed to kill his father and to marry his own mother, he decides to leave Polibos and Merope whom he believes to be his real parents. Refusing to become a criminal, he struggles against his fate.

Scene III: after wandering across the country, Oedipus finds himself at the crossing point of three routes. Which of them has he to choose to avoid the fatal curse? Tired of his endless wanderings, he wants to go back to sunny Corinth, but a bolt of lightning bars his way. In a burst of indignation he angrily accuses the gods of injustice, raising his club against his destiny. Suddenly a carriage carrying Laios appears from behind a corner, moving fast towards him. The driver strikes him with his whip. "Away, you slave!" Laios shouts at him threatening Oedipus with his sceptre. The club, lifted against Fate, comes down on Laios' head. Oedipus has killed his father; Fate has scored its first victory.

Scene IV: the Sphinx is slumbering at the gates of the city of Thebes, its huge silvery wings pulled close together. Under the starlit sky, a sentry is singing his dismal song. Oedipus appears. He learns from the sentry that the Sphinx is terrorizing the town, killing everyone who dares to approach it. He who defeats the monster shall free the city and be awarded the royal crown and the hand of Jocaste. Oedipus wakes the Sphinx. The latter asks him a question: "Who is stronger than Fate?" Stating the truth, Oedipus replies: "Man!" Fatally hurt, the Sphinx bursts into tears and demonic laughter. 'The future," she says vanishing, "shall show whether I am deploring my defeat or laughing at yours." Amazed, Oedipus repeats these words. The day is breaking. Thebans come out to greet their deliverer who vanquished the Sphinx. Oedipus, crowned with the golden crown, sees Jocaste who is advancing towards him. Their hands touch one another, foretelling their future relations.

Scene V (act III): the city of Thebes is ravaged by plague. Teresias demands the punishment of Laios' murderer; otherwise the plague will continue. Oedipus wants to find and to punish the criminal. Teresias foretells that before nightfall he will find the guilty man and lose his sight. Suspecting the terrible truth, Oedipus wants to

Sketch by André Boll of *mise-en-scène* for Act IV of *Oedipe*.

check the events beyond any possible doubt. Messengers from Corinth ask him to return to the aged Polibos and Merope. Oedipus declines this invitation; taking advantage of the presence among the messengers of the shepherd, who saved him as a baby, Oedipus makes him reveal the secret of his birth, parricide and incest. The people demand that he be exiled. Learning that Jocaste has committed suicide, Oedipus in despair blinds himself. He bemoans the fate of his four children appealing in vain to the crowd for compassion, because as he says, he has already been punished enough. Being chased away, he leaves the city leaning on the shoulder of Antigone. Before parting, he curses the ungrateful Thebans and predicts his victory.[87]

Scene VI (act IV – epilogue): being innocent, Oedipus is not a criminal, but a victim. He has been overpowered by Fate, but he is not guilty because he did his best to avoid the crimes he had been doomed to perpetrate. He is a martyr of redemption. His body, buried in the soil of Greece, will protect its people and assure its victory.

The realization of such a plot on a musical stage was not an easy task. The authors' intention was not to restore the traditional features of an antique tragedy or to retell the events taken from it, but to create a dynamic and swiftly developing drama. Enesco maintained that a lyrical tragedy must have an intriguing plot and intelligible literary text, for, as he said, people go to the opera not only to hear the music, but also to understand what the acting is about. This was all the more important in a work whose implication was so profoundly philosophical and symbolic. Another thing they had to reckon with was the absence of a love intrigue and the comic episodes the public expects to see in an opera. Considering all that, the authors had to look for new forms and means of expression.

On the other hand, Enesco had no intention whatever to ignore the experience of his predecessors. He never felt the slightest desire to be original merely for the sake of originality. Although, as he recalls, it seemed to him, while writing *Oedipus*, that he could see looming over his shoulder the shadows of dauntless Siegfried and gentle Pelleas, he did not copy Wagner or Debussy[89] nor did he imitate Beethovens's *Fidelio*.

The opera consists of a number of large scenes freely merging one into another in the course of intense continuous development. Instead of arias, ariosos and ensembles of a traditional type, the composer makes in it extensive use of dramatic monologues and dialogues of a pronounced narrative and declamatory character. Recitatives in opera are very flexible, ranging from a semi-spoken to a semi-sung narrative. Scenes in opera are extremely varied, their forms and expressive means being determined not by a ready-made scheme, but by the feelings and actions of characters taking part in them. Much in these scenes depends on chorus which functions as an active character. Chorus reacts promptly to all events, exchanges cues with the characters on the stage, qualifies their actions and situations. The choral score is meant for a very large choir capable, if necessary, of staging together with ballet-dancers a mass scene as, for instance, in the finale of the second act. The dramatic tension of this scene and its large-scale proportions make it stand out as one of the most striking and fully developed examples of its class in the whole range of opera literature.[89] Choruses are differentiated according to dramaturgical requirements, as for example, female choruses (Corinthian women), male choruses (warriors and old men) and mixed choruses. Choruses have a descriptive or a dramatic function always aiming at a psychological effect in accordance with dramaturgical requirements.

The part played by the orchestra is extremely important, highlighted by the masterly scoring we know from the symphonic works of Enesco. The orchestra provides the means for individual characterizations and creates the atmosphere of a given situation. It carries the principal burden so far as the development of the entire drama is concerned. Using instruments either separately or in groups including massive orchestral tuttis, the composer not only conveys the atmosphere, images and feelings of his heroes, but anticipates the events to come in a truly symphonic manner. The well-known French music critic, E. Vuillermoz wrote in the "Excelsior": "There is no common criterion to go by in discussing the orchestration of *Oedipe*. Instruments are speaking here in an unusual way using a straightforward, inspired and meaningful language which has nothing to do with the traditional polyphony. This language is for the most time very discreet. It is modest and does not go beyond whispering even at the most impressive moments. In the first scene

E. Vuillermoz's review of the première of *Oedipe* in the *Excelsior*.

the orchestra provides a running commentary on the events, but does it in a 'low voice.' It accepts them with some kind of trembling passivity. It is shivering, full of awful expectation. Its reaction amounts to brief painful reflexes; it does not bother about structural logic or symphonic rhetoric. The events taking place on the stage are reflected in the orchestra like in a mirror whose surface gets brighter or darker according to changing circumstances. It seems that the orchestra symbolizes humanity terrorized by gods. In the last act this agonizing torment gives way to an intense, but thoroughly controlled, lyrical sentiment glorifying the superiority of human values over fatality and reminding one that Enesco was a pupil of the author of "Penelope."[90]

The compositional framework of the opera contains a number of very interesting features. Taken as a whole, it represents a monumental structure in which unity and diversity are organically combined. Everything in it, from the general outline to the slightest detail, is subordinated to a single creative goal. In this masterpiece, inspiration and meticulous planning are so harmoniously combined that it could be compared in this respect to the best creations of Bach and Beethoven, Wagner or Brahms.

The opera represents a very large three-part composition without recapitulation, or more exactly a sonata form, in which the main idea of the entire work is summed up in its coda. It is interesting to point out that there is an analogy between the general framework of the opera and that of the first and last movements of the *Third Violin and Piano Sonata*, namely: the polythematic structure of the exposition as well as the omission of recapitulation whose usual function is overtaken by a very developed coda.

The exposition in the opera occupies the whole of the first act at the same time fulfilling the function of a prologue. Here are introduced all the themes of the work, here are set out the principal events of the forthcoming drama which, according to Enesco, must unfold swiftly in an intriguing manner. The development section is very large indeed, occupying the second and the third acts. The last act, serving as an epilogue, has the function of a coda, thanks to which the compositional structure of the entire work becomes well balanced.

The middle section, characterized by an uninterrupted flow of intensely dramatic episodes, passes through two phases of development (acts II and III) marking two lines along which the composer discloses the main idea of the opera. The first phase involves a series of events playing a decisive part in the development of the plot. Chief among them are: the voluntary exile from Corinth (scene II), the parricide (scene III) and the victory over the Sphinx (scene IV).

Starting from the second scene, the development becomes ever more rapid and active. Here man's will clashes in an open and fierce conflict with his destiny as a result of a direct and active struggle. The first phase of this titanic struggle ends with the parricide and the second with the defeat of the Sphinx. Enesco succeeded in building up an emotional climax of tremendous dramatic power. He achieved it by using an uninterrupted chain of interdependent episodes displaying in a sharply contrasting way contradictions potentially embodied in this scene. The culmination of the second phase is put in evidence by the superiority of man over the monstrous Fate. Here the dramatic impact of the first part of the development section reaches its highest point. An active struggle of a human being against an adverse force, symbolized by destiny, is shown in its utmost severity.

Enesco recollects that he had great difficulty finding appropriate means to depict the moment when Oedipus scored his victory over the Sphinx, for, as he said, he had to build up an almost unbearable tension, to express by music something that went beyond the ex-

Facing page:
Enesco's orchestral depiction of the death of the Sphinx.

pressive power of words. To describe the howling of the Sphinx, he had "to imagine something unimaginable." "When I finished that scene," recalls the composer, "it seemed to me that I was going mad."[91] And yet the extraordinary high degree of emotional tension is achieved here, just as elsewhere in Enesco's music, without any affectation. He was always against artificial pathos and seemingly impressive pauses. He did not want his music to "make speeches"; he abhorred empty phrases and false pretensions, preferring to create an impression using, so to speak, not superficial gestures, but a restrained and strictly disciplined language expressing a strong inner feeling. This quality, which adds much to the composer's credit, drew an interesting comment from Vuillermoz, who said that his music ". . . represents the subconscience of drama."[92]

All the phases of the first part of the development section are characterized by the fact that Oedipus remains but a pawn in the game played by Fate although he is struggling hard against it, for he fulfills the lot assigned to him. His victory is only the reverse side of the Fate's victory, and therefore this part of the development section is dominated by negative factors. Actually just those factors constitute the lever in this drama, determining in advance the results of Oedipus' heroic endeavor.

From this point of view the second line of development, beginning with the fifth scene (act III) is basically distinct from the first. It is here, in the second part of the development section, that we see the outcome of the last phase of the plot leading to the highest climax which marks the turning point of the work. It is here that the man, as has been said before, preserving his liberty of action, decides for himself what to do. He takes the initiative into his own hands becoming the master of his destiny. That is why Enesco was right to consider this phase to be the peak of the drama. The new aspect of the problem conditioned a new character of development followed by the second line. From this moment onward, the development takes place not so much so far as the change of events is concerned, but rather in the sphere of inner struggle which leads, with increasing vigor, to the final triumph of free will and high ethical values. This line reaches its logical conclusion in the coda which represents a synthesis not only of the opera *Oedipe*, but of the entire philosophical and ethical concept of this humanitarian artist.

The dramaturgical conception of the opera from a musical standpoint represents an excellent example of diversity and unity combined together. This comes as a result of the basic principles of Enesco's way of thinking which have been dealt with before. Thanks to them, both diversity and unity can co-exist on an equal footing, preserving their individual identity throughout the course of a continued intense development, during which the meaning and the situation of the drama are brought home to the listener in a series of ever more contrasting episodes. Various themes of the opera, acting as leitmotivs, constitute transformations of a single thematic struc-

Sketch by André Boll of the *mise-en-scène* for Act III of *Oedipe*.

ture in the majority of cases. Developing its nuclei, Enesco deducts from them different motives which assume a pronounced individual character while keeping inner links with the initial theme. In the course of complex modifications, the theme releases its potential which in turn gives rise to new formations. Monothematic thinking and leitmotiv technique here go hand in hand as in the symphonic music of Berlioz and Liszt.

The four main leitmotivs of the opera are: that of the Fate, of parricide, of the victory of man and of Jocaste. It is interesting to point out that Jocaste is the only character in this opera to have her own personal leitmotiv. Other characters, including Oedipus, are depicted mainly by means derived from one or another motive which change in accordance with a given situation. The fact that Oedipus has no leitmotiv of his own is not accidental. His part serves to reveal the central idea of the work and therefore absorbs various elements that emerge at different stages of this dialectical process. In this respect, one may say that the image of Oedipus is conceived on a wider basis than, for example, that of Siegfried. He is called to be not a symbol of certain definite features predetermined for him from the very outset, but first of all an embodiment of the essence of the drama and, as such, is characterized not by a permanent leitmotiv, or a set of leitmotivs, but by the whole complex of forces taking part in the struggle. This determined the basic difference of Enesco's approach to leitmotivs as compared with that of Wagner's, despite his attachment to that master. In his music, leitmotivs do not amount to a strict system of pre-established musical symbols, but represent a means of firmly demonstrating a poetic idea in its symphonic development.

Ominously enough, like a warning of forthcoming misfortunes, the symphonic prelude to the opera starts with the leitmotiv of Fate. Somber as it is, it becomes bleaker still, thanks to the harsh, muffled sound of the counter-basson.

Ex. 52

[Musical score: Andantino moderato (♩=50)]

Richard Wagner.

Played against the background of a single insistently repeated note on the violins, this leitmotiv breeds menace and obsession. A large space that separates it from the middle orchestral voice creates the impression of a frightening vacuum. Here, as at the beginning of the slow movement from the *Third Violin and Piano Sonata*, the feeling of stagnation is expressed by a combination of two opposite factors: motion versus immobility.

This leitmotiv, by its internal qualities, is potentially very intense. Its inner tension becomes a source of conflicts that lie ahead. The leitmotiv represents an absolutely asymmetrical structure consisting of seven bars and ending with a half-cadence in tonic key (G-minor). As usual in Enesco's works, such complex themes are characterized not only by an odd number of bars, but also by a complete lack of symmetry so far as dislocation, grouping and inner structure of motive are concerned. They differ both in the size and in the weight they carry in the phrase. With the exception of the first motive, which occupies one bar, all the others cover two bars each. But this happens in different ways: a motive may end on a strong or a weak beat, at the beginning or in the middle of a bar, with a short note or a long one which is sometimes syncopated. In one case, a motive begins from the second beat after a rest while in another, it ends with a rest. The motives are not uniform as to the time-value of notes, nor are they similar from the point of view of melodic direction. The latter is very unstable: an even flowing motion, asymmetrical up and down leaps, etc. Even then, when there is a certain analogy of melodic design between two motives, (viz. bars 4 and 5), they are substantially distinct from one another. This difference is felt in many respects: the first of them has a range of a perfect fourth and the second, that of a diminished fifth; the first contains a figure formed by descending crochets which begins on the second beat of the bar and is interrupted by a rest on its relative strong pulse while in the second motive, the figure in question starts on the first beat of the bar and is made up of unequal rhythmic values and terminates with a syncope.

The only unifying rhythmic factor in the leitmotiv of Fate is the regular repetition of the upper voice; otherwise this leitmotiv has no clear-cut rhythmic organization which emphasizes the sensation of instability. As a contributory factor to this effect, the composer also uses other devices. For instance, he skillfully disguises the limits of bars and beats especially, by rests and syncopes that provoke a displacement of metro-rhythmic accents.

Intonationally speaking, the leitmotiv of Fate is not at all stable either. As a matter of fact, it contains all notes of a chromatic scale except the natural seventh. The picture is further complicated because certain altered notes are susceptible to acquire at a given moment the function of a modal resting-point. Although the initial and the ultimate notes of this leitmotiv belong to the tonal sphere of G-minor, such deviations lead to strongly felt modal changeability which seems to be all the more contradictory compared with the tonic pedal in the upper voices. This is especially true with regard to the emphatic role of the lowered second and the heightened fourth degrees whose alteration, by the way, frequently occurs also in Rumanian folk music. The stress laid upon A flat (viz. bar 3) produces a particularly expressive effect following the lower leading note instead of the tonic. One should mention yet another thing which adds an extra element of tension, namely that the leading note is preceded by an augmented second so obviously tending toward the tonic. Augmented intervals and especially seconds and fourths have for Enesco a particular significance, as can be seen in a number of his works, for example the *First* and *Third Sonatas for Violin and Piano*. But their presence in *Oedipe* assume an unparalleled importance. They can be met with in a variety of forms, including enharmonic and inverted versions, occurring in various leitmotivs especially at moments of great dramatic tension. The same applies to the semi-tone first occurring in the initial bar of the leitmotiv of Fate. And finally, to the intonational intensity of that leitmotiv is contributed a figure (viz. bars 5 to 7) consisting of a series of full tones. Passing in large rhythmic values, this figure becomes associated with the ominous character of the leitmotiv.

The elements potentially contained in the first leitmotiv will be subjected later to an intense process of development and modification giving rise to all the other leitmotivs of the opera. A theme of such a nature is very typical of Enesco's way of thinking. In his view, as has already been said, a theme was not a starting point, but an anticipated result of the whole forthcoming development. He was of the opinion that a true composer in his theme must be able to generalize the entire work he was about to write, just as an architect had to see in his mind's eye the edifice in all its beauty and grandeur before starting to erect it. Everything a theme carries in itself in an embryonic form must, at an appropriate moment, come into the open prompted by an intense development. A constant metamorphosis of thematic nuclei, modification of one motive into another: that was the favorite method of the Rumanian composer reflecting the monothematic nature of his art.

The leitmotiv of Fate is the result of prolonged preliminary work. Destined to convey a great philosophical idea, it was gradually taking shape in the author's imagination. It took a long time for this process to mature, stage by stage, passing through two previous works which had played a very important part in framing the outlook of the composer. The first of them is the *Third Symphony* at the beginning of which, as we already know, there comes a slow-moving descending figure, massively doubled by a number of orchestral voices, containing a characteristic interval of a diminished fifth (viz. ex. n 24).[93] The second stage in the process of crystallization of the leitmotiv of Fate is afforded by the principal subject from the first movement of the *First Pianoforte Sonata* (Op. 24, 1924).

Franz Liszt.

Ex. 53

Here too we have a theme which, from an intonational and rhythmic standpoint, is even more dramatic than the previous one. The new theme has a number of attributes possessed by the latter, such as a wide ranging doubling, predominantly descending motion and the interval of a diminished fifth. Apart from them it has already some features foretelling the leitmotiv of Fate: for instance, augmented seconds, syncopes as well as if it were unsteady, "tottering" moves whose instability is fraught with an ominous anxiety. Passing through various metamorphoses, the theme underwent a considerable evolution over a period of about fifteen years and as a result, it finally transformed itself into that dark and formidable force liable to be defeated only by Oedipus as an embodiment of the best humanitarian aspirations which Enesco cherished both as an artist and as a man.

The theme from the first pianoforte sonata, representing an important step in the formation of the leitmotiv of Fate, can throw a light on the origin of intonational and coloristic characteristics of that leitmotiv. That theme in many respects evokes associations with the second phrase from the introduction to Liszt's *B-minor sonata* (ex. n 54). In turn this phrase has basically much in common with a number of themes frequently met with in nineteenth century romantic music (viz., for example, the beginning of the fourth movement of Berlioz's *Symphonie Fantastique*, the leitmotiv of Wotan's spear from Wagner's tetralogy or Weber's opera *Freischütz*).

Ex. 55b

Ex. 55c

But this theme, which had become for the romantic composers of the past century a symbol of destiny in its fatal aspect, gave Enesco only its characteristic attributes which he needed to create a theme of a quite different kind. As an optimistic artist who did not question the ultimate triumph of noble ideals in the real world, he saw in problems caused by Fate not an invincible force, but only an obstacle that had to be and should be overcome no matter how hard and dangerous it was—overcome in a struggle inspired by a great idea leading mankind forward on the way to the better. Thus, in the light of new artistic requirements, there took place a reappraisal of the traditional romantic means and effects to make them serve a new realistic purpose.

The leitmotiv of Fate could be subdivided into five assymmetrical characteristic nuclei each of which supplies intonations, rhythms and coloring to produce new thematic formations.

Thus, the augmented second from the first nucleus together with the dynamic pattern of the fifth nucleus gives rise to the aggressive leitmotiv of parricide (ex. n 56). There is something of a nuisance in this pricking rattle-like motive repeating itself with obstinate insistence. Played on the bassoon it sounds very harsh, breeding a nasty feeling of ominous instability. This feeling is made worse by the fact that it comes immediately after a chord of diminished 7th (without third) thundered out fortissimo in the upper register of the orchestra. Leaving this chord unresolved, Enesco borrows its fundamental to which he adds a minor ninth, thus forming the leitmotiv of parricide.

Ex. 56

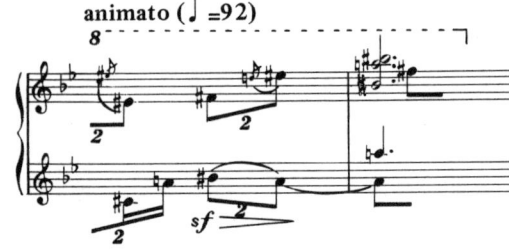

It is characterized by acute intonational tension resulting from the successive alternation of a minor sixth and an augmented second which, when put together, form an interval of a major seventh (C sharp-B sharp).[94] All along, the upper note is stressed by a strong accent. As this figure, repeating itself, starts a crochet later, the accent too is shifted from the second crochet to the third (in a measure of twelve crochets). Dotted rhythm and syncopes make this leitmotiv look still more grotesque and obsessive.

This feeling is further increased by the use of stretto, thanks to which the characteristic figure of this leitmotiv is imitated one crochet later than at the first presentation. This imitative device imparts a sense of uneasiness stressing the repulsive character of the leitmotiv.

Symbolizing a heartless, obsessive force, this virulent leitmotiv appears at the most crucial moments of the drama focusing their ominous nature. It furnishes the intonational material for the characterization of Teresias who stands out as a living embodiment of fatality. It literally permeates the entire scene at the crossing point of three routes, reaching its highest focal point at the moment of parricide. It personifies that ruthless Fate against which the rebellious Oedipus is waging war during the first phase of development of the dramatic idea countering the irrational oppressive power of destiny with the self-conscious force of a human being. The morbid attributes of this skeleton-like motive are once again used to portray the very dramatic scene in the third act when Oedipus discovers the truth about the crimes committed by him against his will.

Another instance of musical transfiguration is afforded by the leitmotiv of the victory of man (ex. n 57). Formed on the basis of the third nucleus of the leitmotiv of Fate, this optimistic motive symbolizes the triumph of positive forces asserting the greatness of human spirit.

Ex. 57

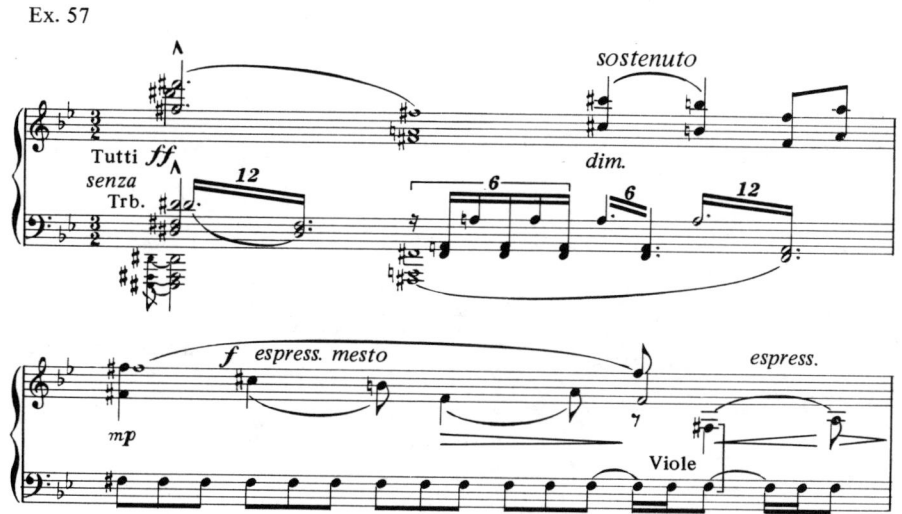

This leitmotiv originates upon the submediant of the F-sharp Dorian as a result of an intense sequential development of the main musical idea of the leitmotiv of Fate. Restated twice almost by the whole orchestra the new leitmotiv sounds like a daring challenge.

Countering the morbid effect produced by the leitmotiv of parricide, this motive marks the most important stages in the realization of the composer's main idea as well as in the formation of Oedipus' image. It is heard in a modified version when Laios is handing over the baby to the shepherd (scene I) as if foretelling that force which shall finally overcome Fate. When Oedipus proclaims for the first time that he shall defeat Fate which even gods fear (scene II), his assertion is emphasized by the leitmotiv in question. It has here an all-the-more prophetic meaning as this challenging statement accompanies his decision to leave Corinth—a decision he was in fact made to take in accordance with the fatal curse. The psychological significance of this crucial moment is borne out by the fact that the leitmotiv of the victory of man sounds here in its original version. This helps us to grasp the full meaning of that leitmotiv which, remaining akin through its intervallic structure both to the first nucleus of the leitmotiv of Fate and to the leitmotiv of parricide, acts from now on as their irreconcilable antagonist.

This meaning becomes even clearer at the opening of the third act when Oedipus is faced with a new danger. The outbreak of plague makes it imperative to expose the murderer of Laios. But now it signifies a step leading towards the liberation of a man from the tyranny of Fate and not towards his enslavement by it as before. That is why the threatening factor is embodied no longer in the leitmotiv of parricide, as it hitherto was, but in that of the victory of man which, in a modified version, sounds like a menace in the bass parts of the orchestra (ex. n 58). To use this phrase as a threatening factor—the phrase that actually carries the promise of salvation—represents a very subtle artistic device.

Ex. 58

Enesco's imitation of the Comédie Française actor Mounet-Sully as King Oedipus.

The thought that a man henceforth asserts his superiority over Fate is emphasized by the fact that the victory leitmotiv will sound now, as if it were in spite of the merciless Fate. Thus, we will hear it twice in the orchestra: the first time when Oedipus, having blinded himself, appears in front of the awe-stricken crowd, and the second time when he, full of desperation, complains about the injustice of Fate (ex. n 59 "a" and 59 "b"). The very special significance this leitmotiv assumes from that turning point of the drama is further underlined by its use at the end of act III. In this way, Enesco indicates his firm belief that the path to victory lies through struggle and not through suffering, forgiveness or reconciliation.

The triumph of Oedipus is rendered in a no less subtle manner when he passionately exclaims: "I defeated Fate!" (the closing scene of Act IV). Symbolizing this triumph, the leitmotiv of the victory of man takes in certain elements belonging to different nuclei from the leitmotiv of Fate, and having assimilated them, becomes still more optimistic (ex. n 60).

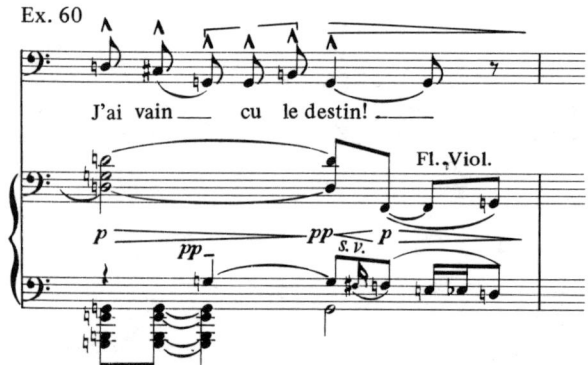

Every time the leitmotiv of the victory of man appears, the composer changes its profile in accordance with the situation. In the third act, under the influence of unhappy events, it becomes more dramatic owing to many means of expression applied by the composer with much ingenuity. This refers to various harmonic, polyphonic, rhythmic and other means which contrive to serve a given dramaturgical purpose. Among many instances let us draw attention to one example where the leitmotiv of the victory of man and that of Jocaste are polyphonically interwoven against the background of descending glissando lamentation (from fortissimo to pianissimo) of the chorus in whose part there is no indication as to the precise intonational or rhythmic value of sounds (viz. ex. n 59 "a").

But whatever combination Enesco chooses to make the leitmotiv of the victory of man assert its rights, he does it in a profound psychological way, avoiding any superficial would-be-grandiloquent effects. Thus, its transformed elements are present both in the orchestra and in the vocal part throughout the very moving scene when Oedipus takes leave of Antigone before his death.

With much artistic taste and technical skill, the composer handles the last nucleus of the leitmotiv of Fate treating it in accordance with the requirements of the plot. Here are a few examples. Having just learned about the terrible curse and told about it to his adoptive mother Merope, Oedipus reflects on hardships that lay ahead for him away from his native home and sunny Corinth. This lyrical monologue, whose tenderness contrasts so much with the previous dramatic episode, is accompanied by a very expressive phrase derived from the last nucleus of the leitmotiv of Fate (ex. n 61). Having been modified again, the same source provides the material for the leitmotiv of the Sphinx (ex. n 62).

Ex. 61

Ex. 62

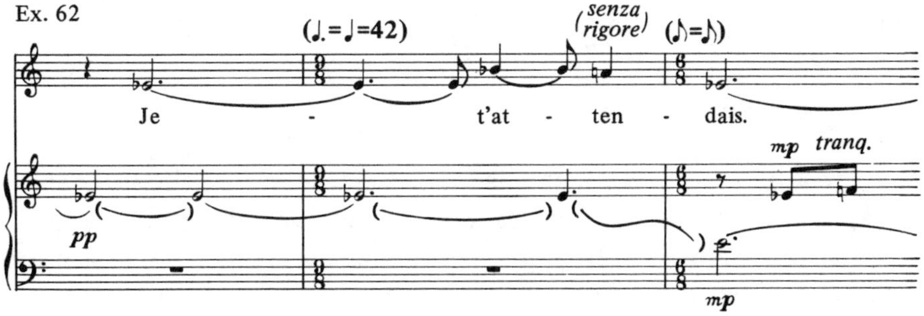

This enigmatic and terrifying leitmotiv symbolizes hatred and oppression. Played pianissimo by the double-basses against the background of muffled trumpets and trombones in its present version, it differs much from its prototype, its shape becoming ephemeral now, though the former regularity of motion still persists. So, vagueness on one hand and some measure of precision on the other contribute, each in its own way, to make the newly formed leitmotiv look both fantastic and at the same time real.

To achieve such metamorphosis, Enesco uses various methods of development, including the symphonic one. Its intensive application enables him to produce some very interesting results also where the transformation of secondary leitmotivs is concerned. Appearing at different moments, they change themselves in conformity with the situation, often acting as an important psychological factor.

Among many others, let us quote the flute motive, first appearing when shepherds bring gifts to celebrate the birth of the royal baby (ex. n 63). It is interesting to observe that this instrument plays a substantial role in the course of further events, its sound being used in special circumstances as a kind of leitmotiv.

Ex. 63

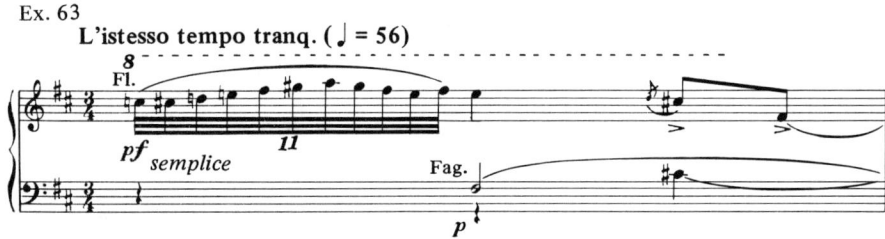

The flute motive has affinities not only with the shepherds' dance, but also with a number of passages marking the dramatic development of events further on (ex. n 64).

Ex. 64

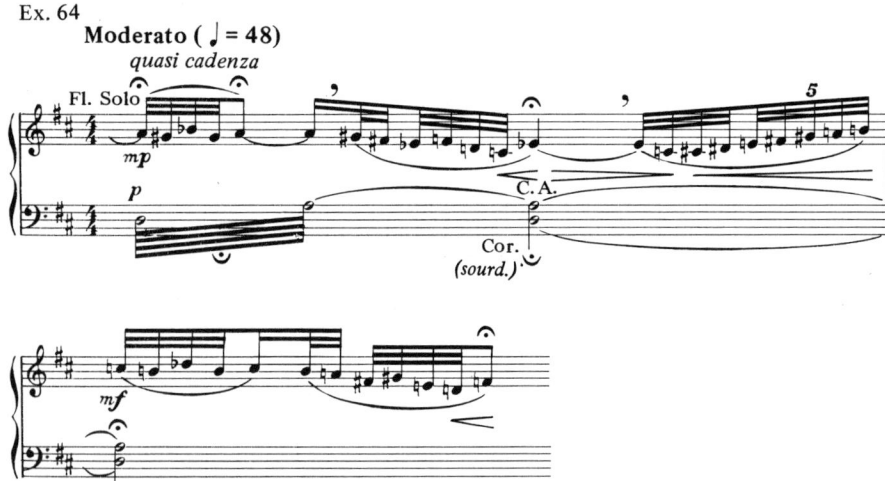

A striking modification of this motive takes place in the sinister atmosphere of the scene of parricide. Like a sorrowful improvisation the twisted melody of the flute sounds sharply, contrasting with the cruel leitmotiv of parricide (ex. n 65). The flute motive reappears at

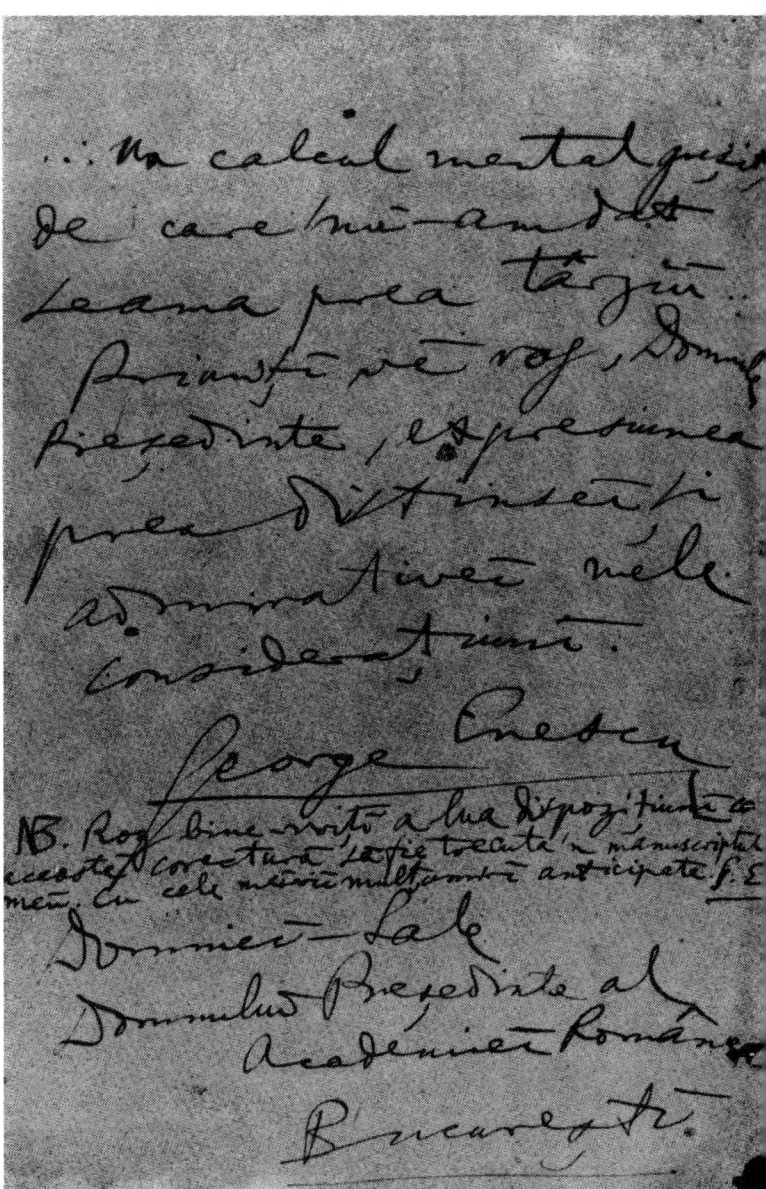

Enesco's letter from New York to the president of the Academia Romana.

the moment when Oedipus lifts his club against Fate; it is heard in a distorted form when Laios falls, struck down by his son (ex. n 66 "a" and ex. n 66 "b").

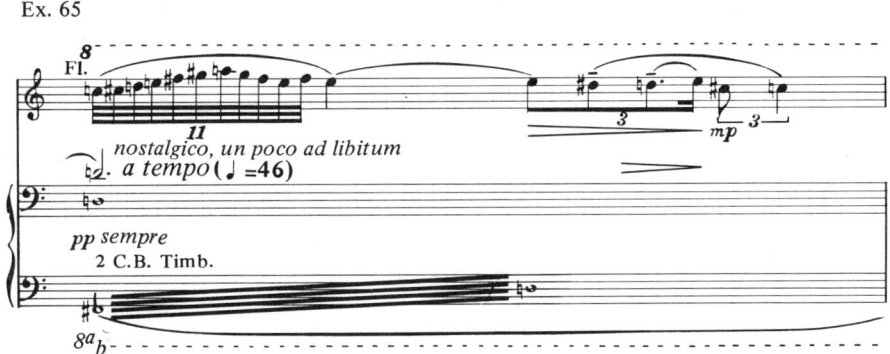

Ex. 65

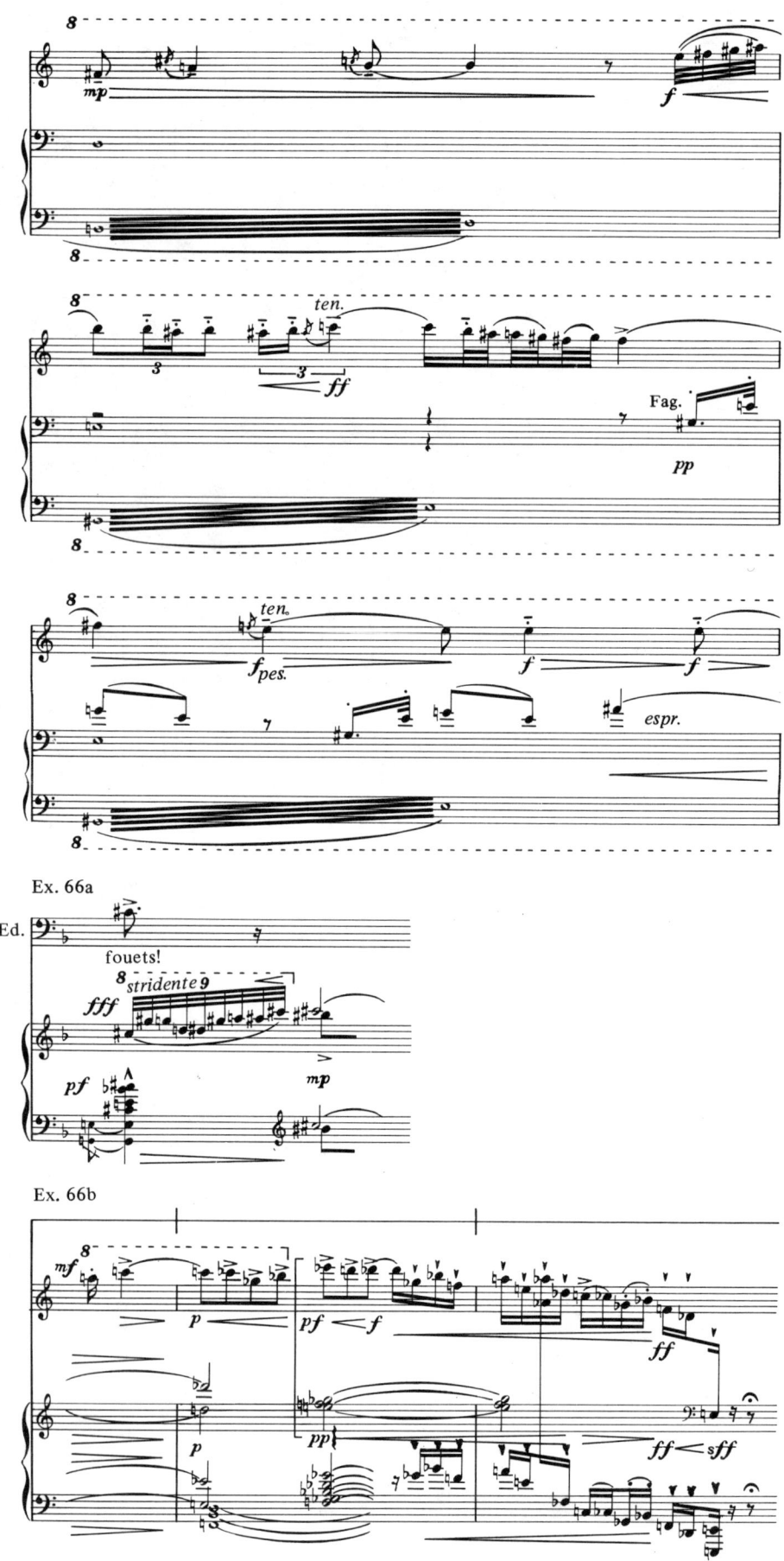

Ex. 66a

Ex. 66b

138

Quite a special role in the opera is reserved to the leitmotiv of Jocaste. Representing a symbol of moral purity and true love, it asserts Jocaste's innocence, for she, like Oedipus, is but a victim of the arbitrary will of despotic Fate. Having absorbed some elements belonging to a number of nuclei from the leitmotiv of Fate, her leitmotiv represents a very individualized expressive phrase which, at the same time, stands out as an embodiment of love and devotion in general (ex. n 67).

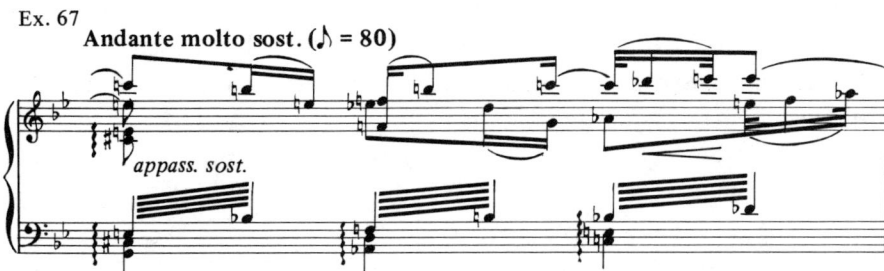

Ex. 67

This leitmotiv is very dear to Enesco who puts it in the foreground among other themes which carry the entire dramatic idea of the work generalized in the symphonic prelude to the opera.[95] Following immediately after the sinister motive of parricide, this lyrical leitmotiv leads to the culmination of the prelude, marking the superiority of humaneness over inhumanity. When fascism was cynically violating elementary human rights, to acclaim this superiority, as an expression of moral purity, spiritual strength and dignity of man, meant to western music of the early thirties as much as did Gorky's words to world literature of the beginning of this century "a man — this sounds proud!"

The significance attached to the leitmotiv of Jocaste determined the fact that it plays a substantial role at crucial points in the opera, although Jocaste, as a character, figures only in the prologue, at the end of the fourth scene and in the third act. Her leitmotiv is heard in the orchestra when, asked by the grand priest what name to give to the child, Jocaste tries to find out what the future has in store for her baby.

There is an allusion to her leitmotiv during the dialogue between Oedipus and Merope (scene II) where it sounds in a modified version changing under the influence of the dramatic story about the monstrous crimes Oedipus was doomed to perpetrate (ex. n 69 "a" and 69 "b"). The first time it gives birth to an expressive phrase, sung fortissimo by the flute, clarinet and the violins, which significantly enough emphasizes the words uttered so bitterly by Oedipus: "I shall be leaving!"; the second time Jocaste's motive appears in a distorted manner as a figuration whose nervous pace is underlined by the piercing sound of the small flute — this transformation expressing the young man's disarray after the terrible forecast.

Here then, the charming Jocaste is moving forward to meet the conqueror of the Sphinx enthusiastically acclaimed by the inhabitants of liberated Thebes (scene IV). And again her leitmotiv is heard in the orchestra, modified and darkened as an omen of misfortune awaiting the mother and the son who do not know each other and are doomed to become husband and wife (ex. n 70). In its present form, the leitmotiv of Jocaste constitutes a striking contrast compared with the general jubilation. Such a confrontation of two contrasting spheres — the inner and the outer one — brings this episode close to the best examples of psychological realism in the dramaturgical art of Mussorgsky, Bizet and Tchaikovsky. At the moment when Jocaste and Oedipus join hands, a synthesis of three leitmotivs is heard in the orchestra symbolizing the forthcoming misfortune; the composer foretells it by combining the leitmotiv of Fate with those of parricide and Jocaste (ex. n 71). Another subtle

A sketch of Georges Enesco.

example of forecasting a future tragedy by combining various musical characterizations is afforded by the synthesis of the leitmotivs of Jocaste, of the parricide and of the shepherds' dance which takes place in the orchestra just as Laios is handing the baby over to the shepherd.

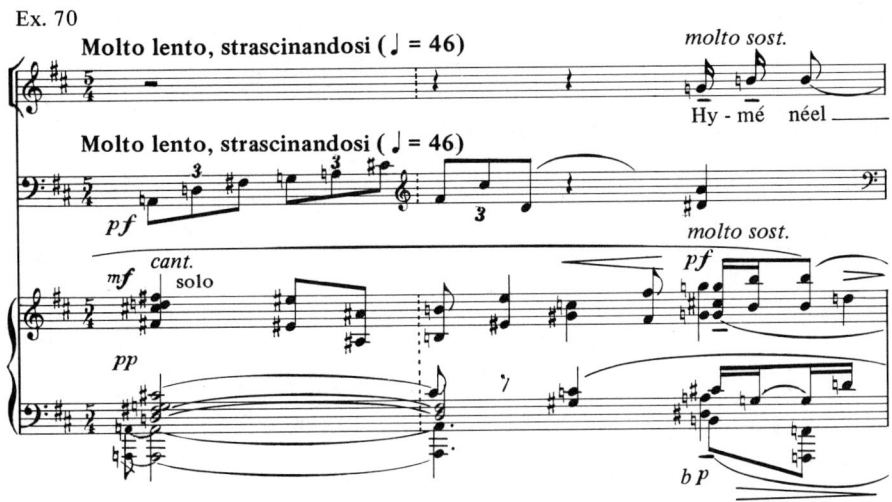

Ex. 70

Ex. 71

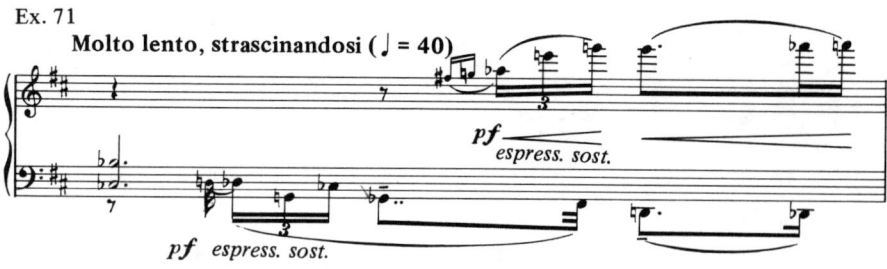

Ex. 72

A true psychological implication acquires the merger of the leitmotiv of Jocaste with the second nucleus of the leitmotiv of Fate when Jocaste appeals to Oedipus (act III) in the name of their chaste love at the critical moment on the eve of the dreadful outcome.

Ex. 73

Among numerous cases of transfiguration of her leitmotiv, perhaps, one of the most dramatic occurs when Oedipus, having blinded himself, addresses the inhabitants of the city he has once liberated.

Ex. 74

And finally, when Oedipus again asserts his innocence in the crimes he has committed against his will (last act), he is accompanied twice by a distorted version of the leitmotiv of Jocaste: the first time it sounds full of agonizing anguish when he mentions their tarnished nuptial bed, and the second time — dignified as he speaks out to defend her unmarred memory.

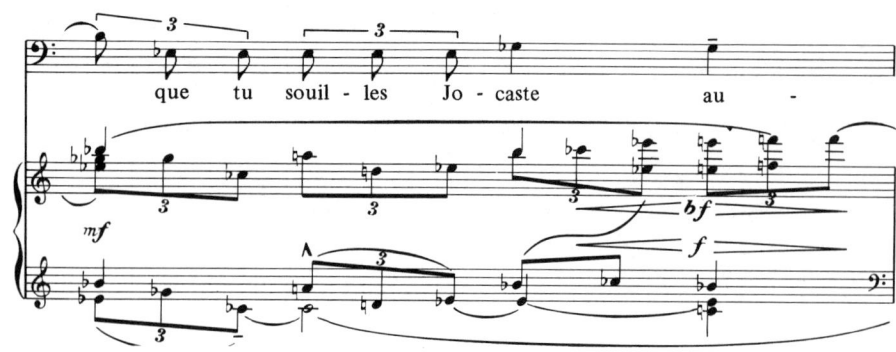

Jocaste's image, as a symbol of innocence, does not fade away with her death, for everything she stood for continues to live in Antigone. That gentle creature overtakes the role she played in Oedipus' struggle against the tyranny of Fate. Antigone's devoted support becomes, as we already know, a very important psychological factor at the crucial turning point of the drama. The true meaning of the part she has now assumed as a living embodiment of purity and faithfulness is brought to the surface by the use of an expressive strain of melody from the vocal part of Jocaste (viz. ex. n 73). It recurs just as the girl says to Oedipus from whom everybody turned away: "Father, I will follow you!" (ex. n 76). It is hardly possible to overestimate the moral implication of this touching gesture.

Enesco, like Stravinsky, saw in Oedipus a universal character. But the Rumanian composer did not choose the path which led to the obliteration of national characteristics or to the restoration of archaism. True to himself, he kept at his disposal the whole wealth of musical art, including that of his own people, from which he chose the means he deemed appropriate for his opera. Introducing a number of episodes of a distinct national character, the composer increases the international significance of his work. Among such episodes, besides the shepherds' dance and the sorrowful improvisation on the flute referred to earlier, one should mention the opening pages of the score (after the rise of the curtain). Here the idyllic atmosphere of the scene owes much to that placid way of writing which is typical of Enesco when, in his mature works, he sets about to poeticize the landscape of his native country. The Rumanian national flavor is even more obvious in the female chorus sounding

The last page of *Oedipe*.

from behind the stage (scene II). Its music, depicting the beauty of a blue sea on a moonlit summer night, is full of languor and voluptuousness associated with the love affairs of Adonis and Aphrodite. Apart from its own merits, the main purpose of that sensuous music is to create a contrasting background against which the bitter complaint of the unhappy Oedipus stands out with particular dramatic insistence. Thanks to intonational connections with the chorus, the vocal part of Merope too acquires a certain degree of national coloring. The latter becomes very pronounced in the orchestral interlude leading from the second scene to the third. Speaking about the national character of these episodes, it is worth pointing out that it comes, not as a result of a sophisticated stylization, but as a natural consequence of the composer's background and his imaginative thinking.

The same applies to the use of quarter-tones, for instance, in the parts of Oedipus and Sphinx (ex. n 77 "a" and 77 "b"). As in the case of the *Third Violin and Piano Sonata,* quartertone technique adds an extra touch of expression to those parts otherwise similar in many respects to ordinary declamatory speech. Enesco used this technique not as a modernistic trick, but as a means which, in his opinion, was perfectly suited to convey "certain special effects".[96] "I had," he said, "to depict the awakening of the Sphinx slumbering in a fading twilight, by sounds of far-off music."[97]

Emphatically stressing that the means of expression must keep in harmony with a given artistic task, Enesco thereby defined his attitude to the problem of modernism. If he deemed it necessary, he could use certain devices belonging even to the most extreme modernistic schools, but he never regarded them as a set system. Thus, being a tireless advocate of tonal music, he used atonal harmonies on several occasions, provided they fell in line with his intentions and were justified by artistic requirements. As to the quarter-tone technique, it interested Enesco not because he fell under the influence of some fashionable trend; using it, he had no desire to copy something or somebody. As a matter of fact he was one of the path-finders in this direction, for, as he remarks, his quarter-tone writing had anticipated the achievements of contemporary music.[98]

Ex. 77a

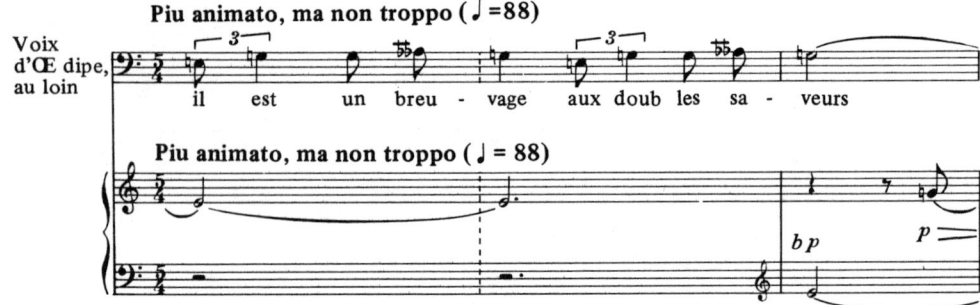

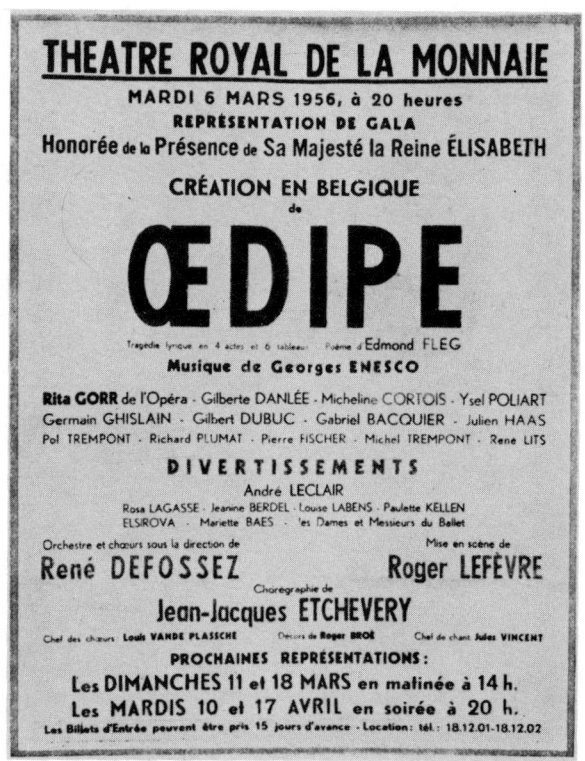

Bill for the 1956 Belgian revival of *Oedipe*, "honored by the presence of Her Majesty Queen Elisabeth."

For him quarter-tones were not a mathematical phenomenon, but a means capable of overcoming the limitations of temperament in order to enrich the art of intonation.

If it is wrong to attribute his quarter-tone technique to the fashion of the day, it would be equally erroneous to seek its origin in the ancient Greek enharmonic modes, as they were no more than antics for him. Being convinced ". . . that there is nothing more terrible than a parody of music"[99] he chose quite another way. His aforementioned technique sprang from the national background and popular traditions of his way of musical thinking which played so important a part in fostering the specific character of his art, both in the field of composition and concert performance.

In this respect the foregoing example from the vocal part of Oedipus before his duel with the Sphinx is sufficiently convincing. In fact, his twisted melodic line, drastically squeezed, as it were, in-

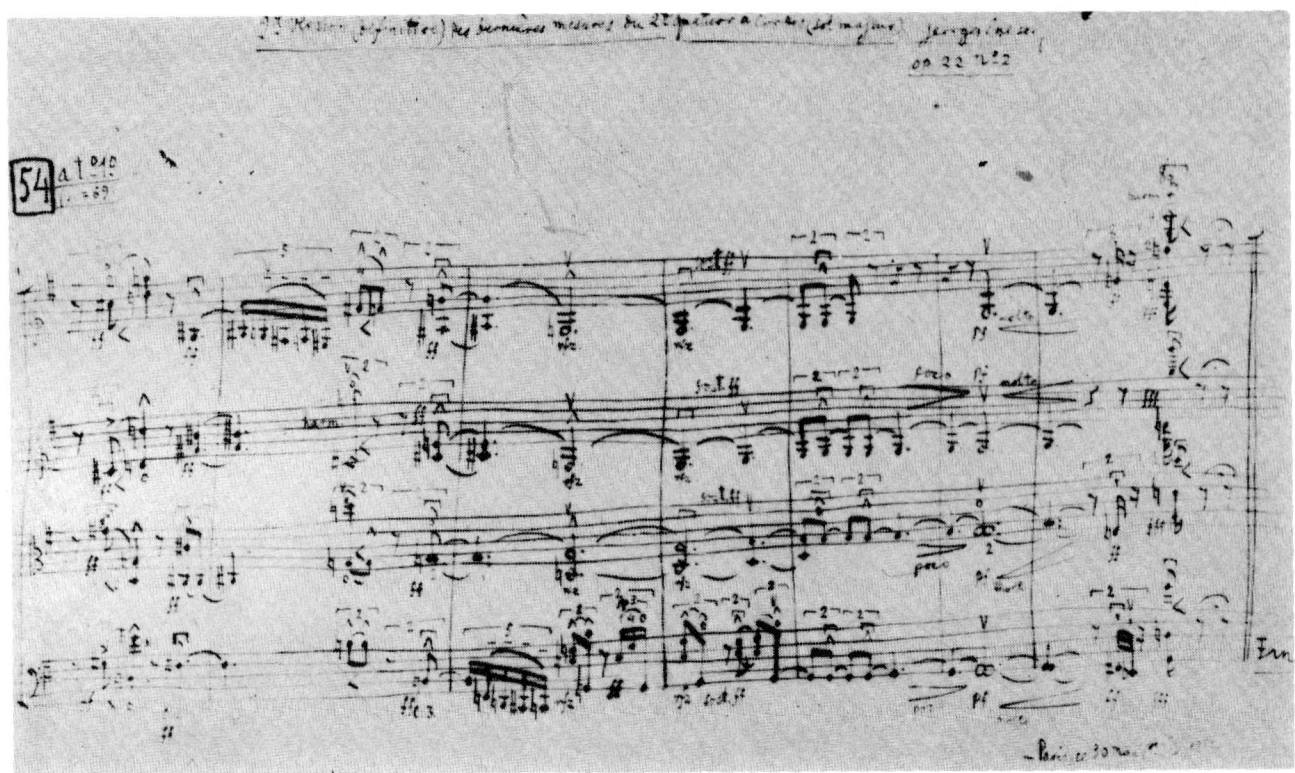

The last bars of the Second String Quartet.

to the narrow limits of a diminished fifth, points to the influence of diminished modes met with in mournful lamentations belonging to the oldest strata of the Rumanian musical folklore. As to the practice of making the intonation of certain notes more acute, a practice which leads here to the occurrence of quarter-tones, it belongs to the interpretative art of lautars.

With his opera *Oedipe*, which A. Honegger qualified as one of the greatest achievements in lyrical music of all times,[100] Enesco had created in the mid-thirties a highly artistic sample of the optimistic approach to a tragic theme of great philosophical and ethical significance.

The Grande Opera Theatre resumed the presentation of *Oedipe* in June 1937. In May 1955, to mark the death of the composer, his opera was broadcast by the French radio; in March of the next year, it was presented at the Bruxelles Opera Theatre de La Monnais. Nowadays *Oedipe* is regularly staged by the Bucharest Opera Theatre, and despite its complexity, continues to produce a great impression on contemporary audiences, its music remaining as fresh and moving as ever.

After *Oedipe*, apart from the already-mentioned compositions, Enesco wrote only chamber music works, the single exception being his symphonic poem *Vox maris* (The voice of the sea) finished not long before his death.[101] This poem belongs to those of his compositions whose programme is disclosed by the author himself. Here too Enesco takes up the idea of man's struggle against adverse forces, but unlike *Oedipe*, this idea, judging by the plot, was to have received in the poem a quite different interpretation. The daring sailor who dives courageously into the roaring sea is to become not a conqueror of the cruel elements, but a victim sacrificed to appease the god of the sea.[102] The fact that for a number of years the poem remained unfinished, although during this period Enesco wrote two more large-scale compositions (the *Second String Quartet* and *Chamber Symphony for Twelve Solo Instruments*), shows that such a passive mood was but transitory. This assumption seems all the more well-founded because his last works, dramatic as they are in substance, have no pessimistic implication.

Creating in suffering and joy, this great son of the Rumanian people was living the life of his time and could therefore echo its pulsation as a true artist always does.[103] A keen understanding of contemporary reality in all its multiplicity adds vitality to the best works of Enesco who not only traced the way of further development of the Rumanian musical school, but also made a valuable contribution to the commonwealth of world musical art.

Georges Enesco before a recital, in 1904.

Chapter 7

Enesco retains a very important place in the history of world performing art. Referring to this great violinist and conductor of his time, Casals said: "Georges Enesco is an interpreter of genius for whom my admiration is boundless."[104] How then did his talent for interpretation develop?

During the five years of studies at the Paris Conservatoire, his interpretative gift was gradually gaining in strength until it finally asserted itself. The credit for this must go to a great extent to his professor, M.P. Marsick—an excellent teacher who knew how to find the approach best suited for the development of the young violinist. He succeeded in preserving his personality while constantly endeavoring to enrich it. True to his principle of not interfering with the natural course of developing his pupils' individual qualities, he brilliantly solved the difficult task of successfully nurturing two violinists so distinct in character and artistic aspirations as Jacques Thibaud and Georges Enesco. Following the traditions of the best representatives of the French violin school, Marsick cultivated in Enesco the greatest care for maximum expression in interpretation while harmoniously developing his artistic taste and technical possibilities. At the same time, he made him retain everything he had learned from J. Hellmesberger. Thanks to his new teacher, Enesco's interpretative style luckily combined the best achievements of the Viennese and French violin schools: stern classical accuracy, logic and depth of conception, amplitude and breadth of sound, impeccable technical precision on one hand with warmth and flexibility of tone, meticulous sorting out of even the minutest details, elegant "bravura" and grace of playing on the other. Marsick's method, based on the most valuable experience accumulated by the French violin school, however, did not exclude the achievements of other schools. Like Gabriel Fauré, being a man and a musician of large vision, he always tended to enrich his experience by the achievements of world violin art. His resilient approach helped him to understand that new artistic demands required new means of expression determining a revaluation of technical devices. While highly appreciating the contributions that H. Wieniawski and L. Auer had made to the development of modern violin art, he was eager to take advantage of their innovations. He recognized that the high positioning of the right elbow and the deep-grip-manner of holding the bow, practiced by the Russian school, opened up new possibilities as far as coloring and intensity of sound were concerned. Eventually he recommended them to those for whom they were suitable from a temperamental and anatomical standpoint. Enesco was one of those who benefitted from them.

During the years spent at the Paris Conservatoire, Enesco was working hard perfecting his tone, phrasing and velocity at the same time introducing new pieces into his repertory. Among them were works by Vieuxtemps, Wieniawski, Lalo, Saint-Saëns, Grieg, Franck, Chausson and many others. His phenomenal musical memory made it easy for him to learn by heart everything he played. He could enlarge his artistic horizon without any risk of dissipating his attention for, even as a teen-ager, he combined an unabating curiosity with a strong sense of purpose and self-discipline.

He was first fully recognized as a violinist in 1900 following the performance at a Colonne concert of two works which were to remain among his favorite pieces for the whole of his life—the Concertos by Beethoven and Saint-Saëns (B minor). This performance at once established his reputation as one of the most outstanding violinists of his time. Soon one concert tour followed another, taking him to many countries throughout both hemispheres. Wherever he played—in London, Oslo or Brussels, in Moscow, Berlin or New York—his concerts ranked as remarkable events in musical life.

For Enesco, concert playing was an active means of promoting musical art. His intention was to bring this art to as large a number of listeners as possible, and therefore he would give concerts not only in capital cities, but also in small provincial towns, especially in his own country.

His way of playing fascinated people by its sincerity and freshness of emotion, by its temperamental drive combined with a clear and well-defined artistic conception. The more his artistic personality developed, the more obvious became his ability to penetrate deep into the core of music as well as his gift to convey a wide emotional spectrum with all its finest shades. His interpretation was never one sided; there was equal room in it for dramatic tension, moving lyrical intimacy, burning passions and recollections touched with a tinge of melancholy. He could therefore switch with amazing ease from one disposition to another, bringing side by side even the most contradictory feelings. In this he was strengthened by the unfailing youthful freshness of emotions so typical of him as a man and a musician. Despite the subtle interplay of contrasting feelings reflecting the riches of his inner world, Enesco's interpretation never failed to maintain its natural simplicity in the best sense of the word. Remaining always expressive, his style did not look far-fetched or intentionally complicated. He was freed of such danger by his con-

Camille Saint-Saëns.

Georges Enesco during the intermission of a concert (1937).

stant endeavor to obtain in music that kind of freshness, simplicity, and spontaneity which prevailed in genuine popular music-making.

In Enesco's interpretation, the emotional and intellectual factors were organically interwoven; his interpretative style never became scholastic or abstract. Rational approach coexisted on an equal footing with a rich creative imagination, highly developed sensibility and even with improvisation. These apparently contradictory features merged into a single harmonious and very original whole, welded together by his creative will. The unity of purpose in his conception, as in composition, affected both the main issue and its particular manifestations. Much as he paid attention to matters of craftsmanship, working them out to the highest possible level, he always made them serve a definite artistic purpose to which everything else was subordinated according to a general plan. This plan was uppermost in his mind as a guideline to which details had to be adjusted.

In the performing art of Enesco, just as in composition, realism played a leading role. His interpretative style was rooted in popular art which had made a deep impression on him since his early childhood.

This sound background made him immune to certain negative trends in performing art; he felt no inclination for insipid sentimentalism in fashion with the drawing-room public. Nor was he interested in concert pieces of little or no artistic value meant solely for light entertainment. In this respect, he was much more consistent than many other famous musicians who included in their programmes such light-hearted miniatures side by side with the greatest masterpieces they superbly performed.

Repeating Beethoven's words, Enesco wanted music to expand "from heart to heart." These words became his guideline in the art of interpretation no less than in composition. In his hands, the violin transformed itself into a singing instrument. He made the utmost use of its singing propensity not only in melodic phrases, but also in virtuoso passages. His technique was brilliant and expressive, but for him it was only a means of realization of artistic intentions. That is why, even in virtuoso pieces, his technical skill was never conspicuous.

Enesco possessed a tone of a great magnitude and emotional vigor notable for its flexibility and wide range of expressive power. His way of extracting the sound seemed to have nothing to do with the physical side of the instrument; listening to him, one had the impression that the bow was a natural extension of the arm and that the violin was a part of the player's body. A violinist, said Enesco, had to merge with his instrument to such a degree as to be able to impart to the sound any shade of color he liked. Indeed, his tone, remaining always crystal-clear, could be at his will now deeply dramatic and then warm, charming and graceful. In this display of different shades of expression, vibrato assumed a special part whose variety one could compare only with that inexhaustible diversity of colors which is met with in the world of nature.

A sound technical basis and a well-developed sense of style allowed Enesco to enlarge his concert repertory considerably. It would not be an overstatement to say that it included all the main violin works from the old Italian and French masters to Ravel and Khatchaturian. How wide-ranging his artistic interests and technical possibilities were can be illustrated by the following example: over a period of about three months, lasting from the end of November 1915 to the end of February 1916, he presented a cycle of sixteen

Two drawings of Chaliapin by his son.

concerts covering almost the three hundred years' history of violin compositions.

Enesco usually arranged the programmes of his concerts and recitals in such a way as to acquaint the public with a very large range of works. The following programmes of four concerts given by Enesco during March and May 1927 in various Rumanian towns, are typical:

1. Bach: *E-major Partita;* Tchaikovsky: *Violin concerto;* Ysaÿe: *Winter song* and *Rondo*; Beethoven: *Romance in F-major;* Bach: *Aria;* Couperin-Kreisler: *The Song of Louis XIII* and *Pavane;* Ravel: *Tzigane.*

2. Händel: *Sonata in A major*; Mozart: *Concerto in E-flat major;* Chausson: *Poem;* Leclair-Kreisler: *Tambourin;* Scarlatesco: *Bagatelle in the Rumanian Style*; Sarasate: *Habanera.*

3. Bach: *D-minor Partita;* Ravel: *Kaddisch;* Debussy: *Menestrel;* Wieniawski: *Les Souvenirs de Moscou;* Enesco: *Sonata no. 3 for violin and piano* "In Rumanian popular character."

4. Nardini: *Concerto in E-minor;* Lalo: *Symphonie Espagnole*; Beethoven: *Sonata n 9* (Kreutzer).

A musician capable of mounting four such programmes in as many consecutive days had to possess a highly developed understanding of stylistic matters. Enesco was not only perfectly familiar with the specific characteristics of various styles, but had at his command an amazing gift for transfiguration thanks to which he was able to identify himself with the music of various masters. Such a gift involved an ability to control one's own personality even to the point of splitting it into two if necessary. As has already been said, such a split did not mean for Enesco obliteration of his individuality or its subservience to the will of a composer, but presupposed an identification of the interpretation with an author in a single creative process. The main thing, said Enesco, "is to recreate in oneself what someone else wanted to create." Performing art must strive to produce "A genuine substitute for an already existing work." Developing this thought, Enesco concludes: "thus, while performing, I am creating in recreating." His ideal in this respect was Chaliapin.[105] "Chaliapin—this great singer—is recreating everything."

Re-echoing the well-known opinion held by Chaliapin, Enesco says: "Speaking in general, I want to point out that as an interpreter I am not entitled to have a personal attitude to a composer or to a work I am playing. My opinion is that it is necessary to merge with the composer's intentions and to follow with reverence the instructions indicated by the creator."[106] Living in the exercise of the recreating as he says, Enesco adds: "I am trying to get into the world of those whom I am interpreting. Of course, it is a very great joy for me. I am seeking the truth and, maybe I am near to it. Everything I achieved is due to the sympathy,[107] to a reverent esteem of these masters" (Enesco has in mind Brahms, R. Strauss, Debussy, Fauré and the school of Franck—B.K.) "as well as to my strenuous efforts."[108]

Advising Y. Menuhin on matters of violin mastery, Enesco throws a light on the possible way communion between a player and a composer can be achieved. He writes: "When dealing with a work we must consider the personality and the intentions of the composer. The composer's ideal has to speak for itself. Emphasizing without exaggeration what the composer intended to express, keeps intact the esthetic side of the work, the balance of its parts and nuances. In building up your interpretative conception, think of a work as if it were a monument having a base, a core and a dome crowning the whole difference. Do your best to make the work you are playing clear, bright, expressive and convincing. Be enthusiastic, but at the same time do not lose lucidity of thought. In spite of everything that has been said, remember—spontaneity must remain intact."[109]

Enesco believed that a player had to study attentively the history of music, the conditions in which composers lived, their background, epoch and style.

These principles are particularly interesting as they help to grasp the stylistic characteristics of Enesco the violinist, conductor and composer. They testify to a conscious endeavor to combine freedom of expression with strict emotional discipline. They again remind us of one of his maxims—"To create one must restrain one's self." And indeed, his interpretation, vibrant and original as it always was, never lost that sense of self-control which made it so convincing. His original treatment of any work he played was always conditioned by a careful approach to the author's text and strict observance of the composer's will. The words Enesco addressed to the young Rumanian composers may be applied also to his art as a concert player:

A program of a recital given in 1946 by a young Yehudi Menuhin, accompanied on the piano by Georges Enesco.

Enesco with his protege Menuhin.

J.S. Bach.

"Be true to yourselves. If you have something to say, say it in your own way, and it will be very well. If you have nothing to say, the best thing you can do is to keep silent. . . . Do not bother about the problems of renewal in art: progress in art can be achieved only given a very long time. Do not seek a special new language; look for your own language, that is to say, for your own means of expressing the feelings you have. Originality comes to those who do not seek it."[110]

Enesco was an excellent interpreter of the great masterpieces of Mozart, Beethoven, Brahms, Franck, Debussy and Ravel. But it was in Bach's immortal works that he reached the heights of his mastery.

To convey to the public the music of Bach in all its artistic magnitude was for Enesco a matter of honor and exceptional responsibility. He had at his disposal everything such a difficult task required, namely: great artistic and technical skill, deep understanding of Bach's style and a full command of all the resources of the violin.[111]

Playing Bach, he succeeded in revealing the profound humane essence of his music which, in his interpretation, appealed to large audiences. His conception totally denounced the scholastic view of Bach as being a dull dogmatic composer of a clerical type. In Bach's music, he revealed its progressive character reflecting the genuine humaneness and passionate attachment to life of this great master.

Enesco played all the works of Bach involving the violin: solo sonatas and partitas, sonatas for the violin and keyboard instrument, *Aria*, solo concertos and the double concerto which he used to perform together with the greatest violinists of his time.

Enesco's interpretation of the solo sonatas and partitas was very profound in character and clear in design regarding the form as a whole and the various melodic lines making up the contrapuntal structure, each individual part being brought out with exquisite skill. As if unfolding a magic ball of yarn, he was weaving with a firm and gentle hand melodic patterns whose main threads could be easily picked up amidst the intricate tangle of hidden polyphony.[112] Nothing was allowed to disrupt the even flow of a melodic phrase, including bow skip from one string to another, complicated chords or position shifts.

Enesco knew how much the expressive character of a phrase depended on the right allocation of nuances and handled them with perfect taste and extraordinary skill. They were so well balanced that it is hard to say in which of them he was at his best. However, special mention should be made of his masterly sustained, lasting piano and long gradually rising crescendo which left an unforgettable impression.

In slow movements of sonatas and partitas as well as in fugues, he attained an organ-like volume of sound. This was particularly so, for instance, in the Andante from the *A-minor Sonata* or the Adagio from the *C-major Sonata*. In his interpretation, this Andante sounded like a real duo for a self-accompanied single violin. The Adagio with its two notes ostinato figure gave him ample opportunity for displaying his ability to build up tremendous emotional concentration creating an obsessive feeling similar to an "idée fixe."

The *C-major Fugue* can be cited as an outstanding example of constructive thinking in performing art. Played by Enesco, it resembled a giant column towering high up in the sky just like the "monument" about which he was speaking in his advice to Y. Menuhin. At its base, it had the theme which Enesco filled with a sentiment of elevated ecstasy that gave an impulse to the whole movement. Majestic in its proportions and exquisite in detail, this fugue was undoubtedly one of the best achievements of the violinist.

It is also impossible to forget the impression left by the Adagio from the *G-minor Sonata* in his interpretation. In his artistic vision, it transformed itself into a pathetic monologue full of inner expressive power and warmth coming from the bottom of his heart.

But only when hearing him play the *Chaconne* could one appreciate in full the talent of this great artist, for it was in this monumental poem of human emotions that he reached the very heights of his mastery. Serene lyrical dispositions, dramatic outbursts and epic tranquility were succeeding one another only to lead eventually to a storm of frantic passions betraying the pathos of struggle, the joy of existence and the triumph of the victory to come.

Georges Enesco, Jacques Thibaud, and Georges Georgesco at a concert in Bucharest, in May 1924.

His conception of the *Chaconne* stressed the profound philosophical meaning of this work. The main theme in this conception was the idea of struggle and ultimate victory of good over evil which we already know from his compositions.

Bach's solo violin concertos gave Enesco yet another opportunity for displaying all the resources of his art of phrasing which, being original and imaginative, was always logical and placid. He interpreted them with so high a degree of perfection that it would hardly be possible to draw attention to any particular detail. Nonetheless, summing up the effect he produced in these works, three main qualities should be mentioned: great care for melodic expression, an active role of the rhythmic factor and an impeccable sense of tempi. The transparent atmosphere of the *A-minor Concerto* was conveyed by him with a moving simplicity, preserving both the happy Vivaldian air and the depth of thought so typical of Bach. Enesco was very fond of the *E-major Concerto* from which the Adagio produced in his interpretation an especially great impression. He maintained it throughout the movement, starting with a magic crescendo on the opening G-sharp which gradually asserted itself against the background of expressive phrases in the orchestra. In this Adagio, as well as in the Aria, the stern sincerity of his phrasing had in its perfect beauty something of an antique masterpiece.

Enesco played Mozart with much warmth mingled with cheerfulness, taking particular delight in bringing out the human qualities of his divine music. Enesco seemed to prove that there was hardly another master who required greater precision in interpretation than Mozart, and he served him faithfully to the best of his ability. It was really surprising with what skill he combined perfect precision with flexibility, and this applied especially to rhythm and bow strokes which were precise to the highest point, but not at all rigid. His interpretation of Mozart's concertos, sonatas and the *G-major Rondo* could be regarded as a model of artistic taste, sound stylistic judgment and an overall sense of proportion.

How well Enesco felt Mozart's style can be seen from the following extract from his cadenza to the *Concerto No. 7* discovered at the beginning of our century, which he was one of the first to play.[113]

Ex. 78

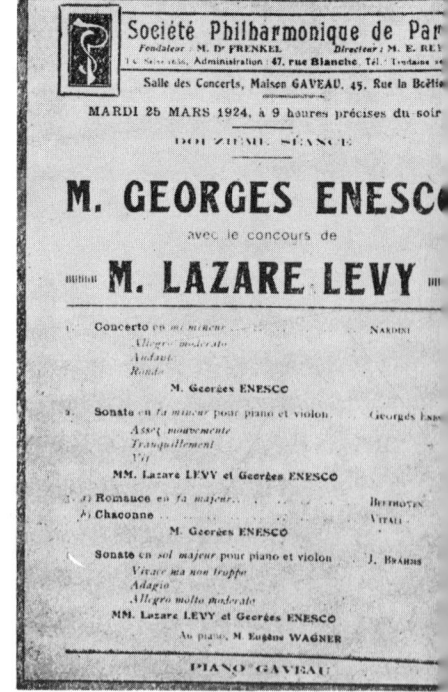

Program of a recital by Georges Enesco and Lazare Lévy in Paris, 1924.

At the same time, this example shows that while preserving the purity of Mozart's style, Enesco could enrich eighteenth century violin writing with modern technique, provided, of course, it was in keeping with the specific character of the work.

Enesco attached particular importance to the interpretation of music by Beethoven and Brahms whose works he played in the best realistic tradition.

His manner of performing Beethoven's *Concerto* was fully subordinated to the task of conveying the whole depth of this immortal composition. Hearing him play this work, it seemed that his art in combining the emotional and the rational factors into one unified conception reached its highest point. It enabled him to recreate the whole wealth of Beethoven's emotional world, including his lyrics, in all its integrity without the slightest hint of rigidity or sentimentalism so hated by the master himself. In this connection, his manner of performing the lyrical episode from the development section of the first movement of the violin concerto or the *Romance in*

F-major can be referred to as an example of sublime lyricism which, despite its intimate character, was totally free of any sentimentalism.

In his interpretation of the concerto, Enesco was strict and yet very imaginative. Among many interesting instances of his expressive power, one should mention the unforgettable way of switching from the cadenza to the second subject of the first movement. This was a moment of great psychological suspense that kept the hearer guessing as to what would follow. Here the violinist gave the impression of stopping to ponder for a short while, and although this lasted for only a moment, it seemed an eternity. And suddenly, as if something inevitable predetermined from the start, but yet somehow quite unexpected, there came the sublime lyrical theme. After this intriguing transition, its entry signaled a long awaited relief.

No less impressive in its way was his phrasing in the episode from the second movement marked "Sempre perdendosi." He made the melody on E string sound in a very dignified and charming poetic manner, achieving a considerable emotional concentration by using a sustained but sufficiently saturated singing piano and the full spell of his unique vibrato.

The third movement in his interpretation gave a striking example of an acute sense of rhythm which played a decisive role in creating the specific character of the Rondo. An interesting indication as to how Enesco understood this character comes from one of his pupils, at present professor at the Krakow Conservatoire, Eugenia Uminska. Speaking in a letter to the author of these lines about her studies with Enesco in Paris, she recalls the following episode which gives an insight not only of his conception of the Finale, but also of his approach to the rhythmic factor in general. "Maestro," she writes, ". . . who was not satisfied with my articulation in the main theme of the Rondo, once asked me: "Have you seen Rembrandt's pictures portraying rural scenes with a lot of people about enjoying themselves, full of exultation and vitality? There's a rhythm which emanates from their bodies!" This vivid association instantly gave me the clue to my problem."[114]

Enesco was very particular about the true character of this main theme, stressing that its measurement is one of $\frac{6}{8}$ and should never produce the impression of $\frac{2}{4}$ time. To avoid this, he would recommend to his pupils to see that the quaver be exactly twice as long as the following crochet and to emphasize the proper accentuation. In exchanges between the soloist and the orchestra, he advised them to stretch to the utmost the solo violin responses rhythmically, giving them an extra weight, for otherwise they would seem quite negligible and lose all their significance. As to the central episode in Rondo, which Enesco played with exquisite charm, he warned not to make a trivial little sentimental waltz out of it.

In Brahms, Enesco fascinated the listener by his ability to combine a very warm personal feeling with a deep penetration into the complex conception of the master's music. He managed to reveal its dramatic force in a striking way, the poetic spell of romantic dispositions and the colorful character of popular images, especially in the *Hungarian Dances* and the *Violin Concerto*. From its very beginning, he struck the imagination by a passionate drive which nonetheless never became disorderly. On the other hand, what a subtle poetic feeling and tenderness he displayed in the following Calando and dolce! Here he used all his skill in ingenuously modifying his vibrato and the coloring of sound as if enhanced by the mysterious beauty of Brahms' superb harmonization. In the development section of the first movement, he showed an amazing ability to switch almost at will from one disposition to another, reaching an extremely high degree of dramatic intensity in the culmination.

Enesco wrote a cadenza to the Brahms' concerto which was published for the first time by D. Oistrakh in the magazine "Sovietskaia muzika" No. 8, 1961. This cadenza, like the one to the Mozart concerto, is very original and at the same time shows a great understanding of Brahms's style. Being treated very freely in improvisational manner so typical of Enesco in general, it fits quite well with the main character of the work.

The themes of the Finale acquired, in his interpretation, a special flavor: he made them sound significant but not ponderous, alert but not hasty, clear-cut but not pedantic. He stressed every detail of the solo part while keeping it strictly in line with the orchestral score which he knew perfectly well. His treatment of works by Brahms, as

Georges Enesco and the cellist Dimitrie Dinicu.

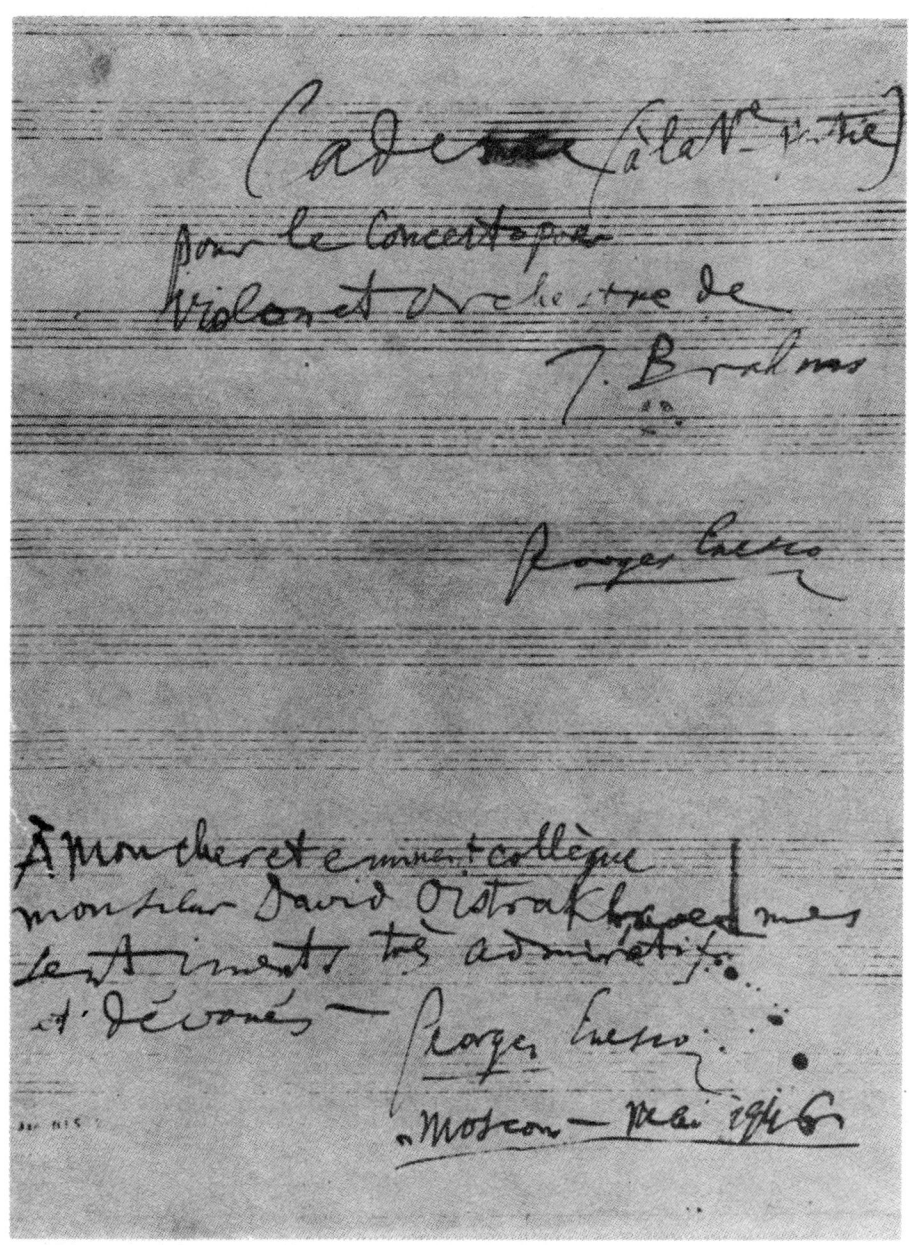

Title page of the manuscript of Enesco's cadenza for the Brahms violin concerto, with the dedication "to my dear and eminent colleague Mr. David Oistrakh, with my most admiring and devoted sentiments. Georges Enesco, Moscow, May 1946."

well as those by Beethoven, displayed his practice of a symphonist and orchestra conductor.[115]

Enesco possessed a many-sided interpretative gift which enabled him to perform on the highest artistic level not only classical violin music, but also the works of contemporary French composers such as Saint-Saëns, Lalo, Franck, Chausson, Debussy and Ravel. Playing the music of the latter composers and, especially, *The Poem* by Chausson, he attained subtle effects by interchanging light and shadow in the best traditions of the impressionist painters. But this did not exclude sweeping glittering strokes, all the more impressive in comparison with the deliberately faint "water-color" sounds he could extract, thanks to his expert bowing. It is hardly possible to describe in words the large spectrum of sound-effects he displayed in Chausson's *Poem* or Debussy's *Sonata*. As to the works by Ravel,

Enesco found for them quite a different coloring. This was especially the case with the *Tzigane* which he rendered with an overwhelming passion, creating a very intense emotional atmosphere right from the start of the solo violin melody on G-string. The improvisational and declamatory character of this piece seemed to be quite familiar to him, probably because it had so much in common with the art of his own people. This, and particularly his firsthand knowledge of the specific lautar style, which gave so much flavor to his violin compositions, made his interpretation of the *Tzigane* very convincing.

In an original way, Enesco interpreted the works of modern composers and particularly the *Violin Concerto* of the Soviet composer, Aram Khatchaturian. The inclusion of this remarkable work in his repertoire showed that in his sixties he was as keenly interested as ever in everything new.

Enesco played the concerto by Khatchaturian for the first time during his visit to Moscow in the spring of 1946. His interpretation of it was highly appreciated by the Soviet musicians. The composer, deeply impressed by his performance, wrote the Rumanian violinist the following letter:

> Yesterday the language difficulty prevented me from expressing to you my admiration of your art in proper terms and from thanking you for the pleasure you had given me by your interpretation of Bach and Chausson. I am also very grateful to you for your interpretation of my concerto which I very much admire. To learn a new large concerto at your advanced age is a heroic feat indeed.[116]
>
> Your conception is very original and convincing and I am sure that many young violinists will try to reproduce it. There is much poetic feeling and romantic drive in your interpretation. I was following it yesterday with deep emotion and I would like to write now a new work for violin and orchestra."[117]

Speaking about Enesco's interpretative style, it is impossible not to mention here the way he played his own violin compositions. He performed them in a unique personal manner that made them acquire an additional unforgettable flavor. In his inspired interpretation, the *Second* and *Third Sonatas,* as well as *The Impressions of Childhood* could be regarded as models of fine taste, imagination and technical skill. He played them with so much ease that they seemed to contain no difficulty whatsoever, leaving the specialists to wonder how on earth he managed to combine so freely into an organic whole the most sophisticated concert virtuosity with the specific lautar technique. Using in a very subtle individual way a great variety of sound-colors, as well of vibrato and intonation, including quartertones, Enesco attained striking coloristic effects. Elaborated as they

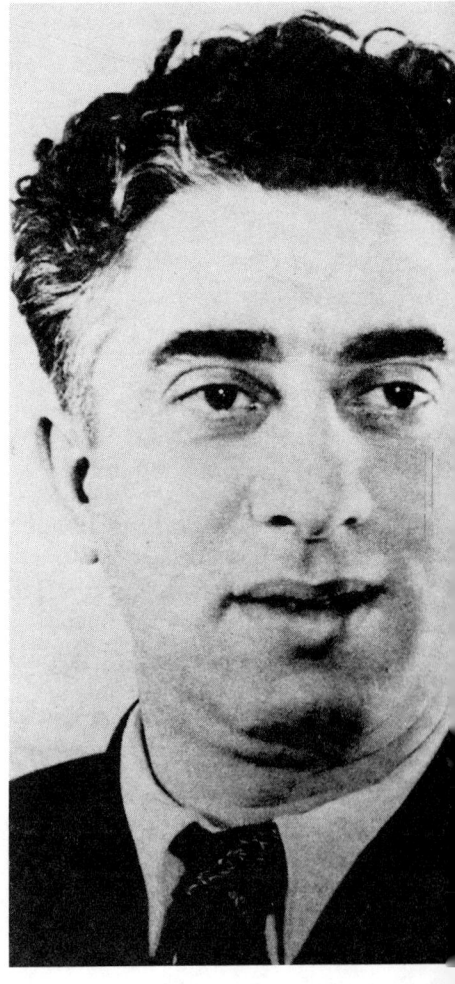

Aram Khachaturian.

Enesco and Alfred Cortot rehearsing.

were these effects served him as a means of vitalizing the musical idea in the best tradition of popular art. Spontaneous and improvisational in character, his interpretation preserved that inner logic which he displayed in Bach or Beethoven, constituting the highest achievement of its kind. Besides its purely artistic value, this achievement presents considerable interest from an analytical point of view as it completes our knowledge of his interpretative style which will be dealt with in the concluding chapter.

Enesco devoted much attention to chamber music. He had come to love it as a boy, thanks to Hellmesberger who led one of the best quartets of the Austrian capital. In Paris, his interest in chamber music grew even stronger. This was largely due to Marsick who, together with the Russian cellist, A. Brandukov, in 1886 had formed the first string quartet permanently functioning in France.[118] This interest was stimulated further by Enesco's musical environment in Paris. He would regularly meet with Kreisler, Ysaÿe, Casals and Cortot to play together chamber music in their spare time.

As the years passed, Enesco became an expert chamber music player and that probably accounts for the fact that chamber music works are so prominent in his heritage.

Already in 1902 Enesco, together with A. Casella and L. Fournier, organized a trio in Paris and in 1904, a string quartet with F. Schneider, H. Casadesus and L. Fournier. Being an excellent pianist, he often played the piano part in various ensembles.[119] In the course of his long interpretative career, he played together with many world famous musicians including Casals,[120] Cortot, R. Strauss, M. Ravel, B. Bartok, E. Risler, Y. Menuhin, D. Oistrakh, D. Shafran and others.

Enesco's chamber music repertoire was extensive. It included the bulk of existing works belonging to various epochs and styles. In performing them, he showed perfect command of ensemble playing characterized by his ability to view a chamber music work as a single whole in which the part of every instrument was subordinated to an overriding artistic goal. This applied not only to the general character of music, but also to all the details alike and, especially, to the coordinated rendering of polyphonic design in which all the contrapuntal lines were properly balanced. He tended to transform an ensemble into a communion of equal partners complementing one another. In this connection, among many striking examples, one could mention Enesco's performance together with D. Lipatti of his *Third Violin and Piano Sonata,* which stands out as an achievement of the highest class.[121]

Enesco played sonatas not only in his solo recitals, but liked to give concert cyles illustrating the history of this genre. Such cycles could contain up to eighty works, all of which he always played by heart.

The Rumanian violinist attributed the greatest importance to the knowledge of quartet literature which he considered an essential part of musical education. He was convinced that the development of a virtuoso player would be incomplete without quartet music which should be studied with the utmost attention. Realizing how great the educational value of quartet music was, he often would carry out (particularly in Rumania) the general rehearsal of his chamber music concerts in public, especially for the students. Thus, in the Rumanian city of Iasi during the First World War, Enesco played specially for students and then for the general public all the string quartets of Beethoven.[122]

These quartets Enesco valued very much and interpreted them in an inspired and masterly way. Extremely demanding of himself, he was never completely satisfied with his performance. Once, after playing the *C-sharp minor quartet* (op. 131) at one of such rehearsals, he said to the students who surrounded him and who were scarcely able to contain their emotion: "Beethoven's quartets produce such a big impression on me that my interpretation does not seem to me good enough."[123]

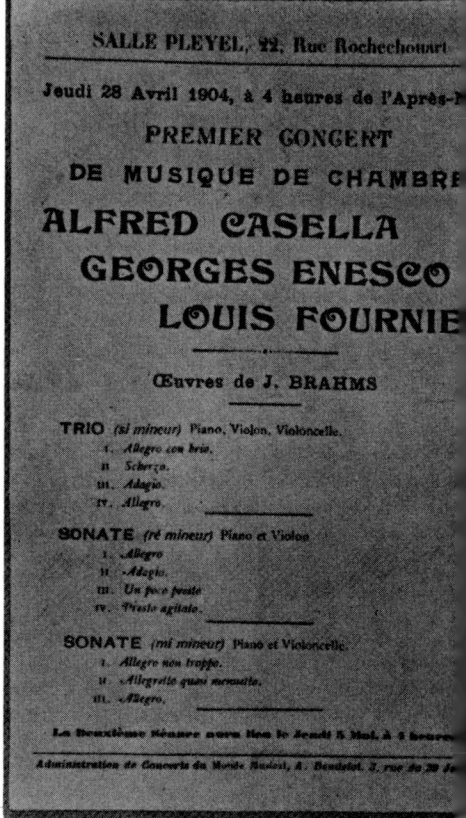

Bill for the first concert of the Casella-Enesco-Fournier trio.

Top: A 1904 photo of the Casella-Enesco-Fournier trio; **Bottom:** Enesco and Yehudi Menuhin.

In addition to quartets, Enesco also often participated in trio playing at different times, together with Cortot and Casals. With the latter, he performed the *Double Concerto for Violin and Cello* by Brahms several times. He had in his repertoire Mozart's *Concert Symphony for Violin and Viola,* as well as the *Concerto for Two Violins* by Bach, playing it with a number of celebrated violinists such as, for instance, Ysaÿe, Kreisler, Thibaud, Menuhin and D. Oistrakh.[124]

Enesco attached much importance to piano playing. He had a complete command of the keyboard which is best exemplified by his own piano compositions.[125] He could easily have become a concert pianist had he wanted to. No piano piece, however difficult, seemed to be beyond his reach. His pianistic qualities enabled him to improvise and to accompany in a perfect way.

Among the well-known soloists whom Enesco accompanied on the piano, was the Russian tenor I. Altchevsky. He performed for the first time Enesco's vocal cycle of seven melodies on verses by C. Marot, with the composer at the piano. This performance, which took place at the Georges Enesco Festival in Paris in 1908, gave the singer an opportunity to express his admiration for the Rumanian artist's music and piano playing. The outstanding Soviet cellist D. Shafran, who played D. Shostakovitch's sonata with him in Bucharest, which had just been liberated from the fascist occupation, enthusiastically spoke about Enesco as a pianist. In 1899 as a youth, Enesco at the piano and on the violin accompanied the Russian opera singer F. Litvin whose Paris salon he, Fauré, R. Hahn and other outstanding musicians had very often frequented.[126]

Any study written on Enesco would be incomplete without a review of his pedagogic activity. This was very wide-ranging and important in its consequences although Enesco could not be called a teacher in the ordinary sense of this word.

His role as a pedagogue was not confined solely to the master classes he conducted for a number of years in Paris and other cities. It was not restricted to those violinists who actually studied with him, but was felt by many musicians who came in contact with this remarkable artist. His every recital, chamber music or symphonic concert, every rehearsal, in fact, amounted to a most valuable lesson. That is why so many violinists benefitted from his experience which he so generously shared.

The pedagogical character of Enesco's activity was determined mainly by its very nature. With violin in hand, at the conductor's stand or at the piano, he was always ready to answer any question, to explain what he had been doing, to hear what others had to say. Talking in his usual frank and outspoken manner, he would soon put the newcomer at ease by his benevolent attitude. Enesco was open to criticism; being very much a man of principle, he criticized others objectively without any bias, showing the greatest respect for the opinion and individuality of his opponent. As the author of this

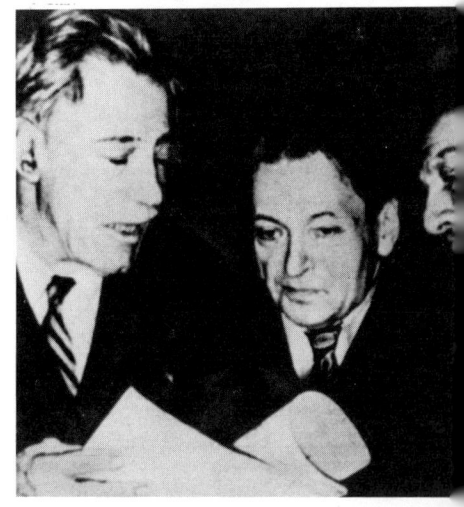

Fritz Kreisler, Georges Enesco, and Jacques Thibaud (left to right).

Top left:
Enesco accompanying David Oistrakh in a 1946 Moscow concert.
Top right:
Eugène Ysaÿe, one of the many celebrated violin virtuosi with whom Enesco played the Bach *Concerto for Two Violins*.
Bottom:
Amazingly versatile, Enesco was also a keyboard virtuoso.

book himself had been privileged to experience, Enesco, an extremely busy man, would always find time for a young violinist seeking his advice; he showed great understanding of one's problems and knew how to encourage people with a kind word.

It would be of great interest if one could have recorded at least some of the remarks Enesco had made on numerous occasions concerning various professional questions, particularly those referring to playing and teaching the violin. Unfortunately it is impossible to fix them all since, in the majority of cases these were never written down. The following represents a modest attempt to gather here those thoughts and recommendations this author has heard, either directly from Enesco or from other violinists, who had also known the maestro, particularly from the late professor of the Liège Conservatoire, Henri Koch.

Enesco maintained that the main task of any violinist in training his right hand must be the extraction of a pure, full, flexible and expressive tone. A continued tone of a large respiration—that was his ideal. To achieve it, one should be able to change the direction of the bow very smoothly at any given point, handling it with complete freedom of action all along its length, down-bow and up-bow being equally even and firm. Enesco said that the bow must "stick" to the string ("L'archet doit coller à la corde"), but the violinist should not force his right arm, taking advantage instead of its natural weight. Echoing Tartini's famous maxim—"Force without rigidity and strain, softness without laxity and sluggishness"—Enesco based his work on the assumption that force came through flexibility of movements. A fine tone, he used to say, requires much strenuous

An aging Darius Milhaud with the Polish violinist Roman Totenberg, who studied with Enesco in Paris.

work with special emphasis on its expressive qualities and freedom of movement, particularly in legato and détaché. He recommended practicing them in various parts of the bow, tempi, rhythms and registers changing nuances and paying attention to the purity and expressiveness of tone.

Enesco attached much significance to work on scales. Like Ysaÿe, he recommended practicing them in all tonalities, using the whole length of the bow détaché and martellé in all nuances from pianissimo to fortissimo. He considered this type of exercise very useful, and those who heard him play the Prelude from Bach's *E-major Partita* or the *Prelude and Allegro* by Pugniani-Kreisler, could see for themselves how effective they were. He would also stress that the right way to cross the strings without any undue accentuation constitutes an essential element of a sound bow technique.

So far as the left hand is concerned, Enesco was very particular with regard to the accurate intonation, especially of semi-tones, considering it a very important factor not only from a technical, but perhaps even more, an expressive point of view. Here too his main preoccupation was to develop freedom and elasticity of movement and not sheer force. He left no doubt that it was not speed that mattered, but ease and velocity so essential for the right finger technique, shifts of positions and a flexible vibrato which he could fashion at will.

Enesco was convinced that trill had to play an important role in finger exercises. And again the key to the problem lay here not in speed, but in regularity of well balanced motion. Speed comes later, he remarked, as if by itself when any unwarranted tension disappeared, thanks to persistent work. Even the most rapid trill should always remain accurate and organized, never becoming nervous and convulsive. A trill must be regarded not as an outside enbellishment, but as an integral part of musical fabric which ought to be subordinated to the general poetic idea. In this way, a trill in all its variety could be used as a true expressive means. How masterly Enesco handled his trills could be seen in his interpretation of the sonata, *Trille du Diable* by Tartini, the *Poem* of Chausson or the first movement of Beethoven's *Violin Concerto*. In every one of these works Enesco made the trill sound in a different manner: demonically malicious, calm and transparent like a murmuring stream or relaxed and soothing as a quiet summer dusk.

According to Enesco, a violinist had to practice regularly not only special exercises but also études. A number of études, not omitting, of course, the *Caprices* by Paganini, had to become a lifetime companion of every concert player. Like Wieniawski, Enesco highly appreciated Kreutzer's studies, considering them extremely useful for the development and maintenance of a number of essential elements without which both the left and right hand technique would be incomplete. He attached particular importance to the studies numbers 15, 18, 19 and 20 for the work on trill, and to those Nos. 2, 7, 10 and

13 on various bowings.[127] He recommended practicing the latter, as well as the study No. 5 by Dont (Op. 35), using various rhythmic figures and nuances legato and other bowings. In his opinion, those two studies represented excellent material for perfecting the string-crossing and the right-hand technique. It is interesting to note that, according to Professor Koch, Enesco, even at the height of his worldwide concert career, would periodically take up some études, particularly the number 13 by Kreutzer which he practiced to perfect the handling of the bow at the heel, staccato runs up-and-down-bow, as well as other bowings.

Enesco also appreciated very much the études by P. Rode. These studies, some of which consist of a slow melodic introduction and a more rapid technical section, are destined to acquire both an expressive tone and a brilliant virtuoso technique. From the point of view of phrasing, he considered study number 14 (Adagio con espressione) to be one of the most useful. He believed that its main difficulty consisted of very even distribution of the bow in accordance with the requirements of musical phrases.

Tending to subordinate his interpretation to the requirements of

Gruia Panescu's friendly caricature of Enesco.

A sketch by Otilia Michail of Enesco as a conductor.

the music he performed, Enesco did not treat various elements of phrasing separately one from another, regarding them as an organic whole. Slurs, nuances, fingering and the like, being part of an overall complex pattern, should be dealt with as a single aggregate, taking into account the specific nature of all its elements.

It is known that Enesco, who had always set for himself the highest possible standards, actually never stopped working to maintain his technique at an appropriate level. To achieve this, he endeavored to use the utmost every minute he had to spare. His manifold activities and frequent engagements left him little time to practice the violin regularly; to make up for this he carried with him a pocket violin board which he used for "mute" exercises. In this connection, it is interesting to recall that in general Enesco was very skeptical about the so-called theories of "innate mastery" or "natural technique". Ironically laughing at those who were naive enough to support such theories, he liked to say: "A true mastery means 70 percent of labor and 30 percent of talent."

Unfortunately, it is impossible to sum up Enesco's views on playing and teaching the violin. As has been already said, he usually made his remarks orally to various people if and when necessary. Many of his recommendations were sketched in brief on pages of musical works which are no longer available; others are scattered in private diaries and may be lost forever. Therefore, the author does not pretend to have surveyed them here exhaustively, but scanty as they are, they are quite sufficient to show that Enesco's main purpose was the formation of true artists fully in command of their instruments and with the knowledge of how to make them serve their creative imagination.

Enesco was the type of musician who simply could not do without conducting. As he became more mature, he grew increasingly fond of it, realizing all the possibilities of that highest form of interpretive art, and eventually his desire to take it up became an imperative necessity.

"A conductor", he wrote, "experiences a far greater moral satisfaction than a violinist, and that kind of satisfaction is much more in keeping with my aspirations. My baton is for me a 'liberated' bow.[128] I don't care very much for applause. But when the orchestra understands the idea I want to convey, when it is following me, when it identifies with me, when all the instruments are translating my intentions into sounds, then I feel happy indeed; it's a wonderful experience which can't be described. One has to pass through it to understand this feeling."[129]

His imagination was captured by the expressive potential of the symphonic orchestra and chorus; he saw in them one of the most valuable achievements of human civilization, the most perfect "instrument" men possessed to express the entire wealth of their emotional world.

The way Enesco conducted the orchestra had, of course, very much in common with his interpretive style in general, but in some respects it was even more characteristic of his universal talent. It enabled him to master an orchestral score in all its infinite variety as a single musical edifice that stood out in his interpretation as if designed by himself. His conception was broad and profound, and, although carefully worked out, never lost its emotional appeal. Paying attention to the main idea of the work, he would thoroughly sort out all the details reflecting a wide spectrum of nuances with no detriment to the majestic structure as a whole. As a conductor, Enesco was especially good at combining various timbres and obtaining a proper sound balance of all orchestral groups. Emphasizing or shading some instrument or group of instruments, he obtained from the orchestra sounds of different kinds just as a painter mixes several dyes together to get the color he wants. And an orchestra

Poster for a 1914 benefit concert (under the baton of Enesco) featuring Beethoven's Symphony no. 9.

under Enesco was as colorful as the palette of a painter. It seemed that his coloristic and dynamic possibilities were inexhaustible.

The acute sense of coloring, so typical of Enesco as a composer, violinist and conductor, developed very much thanks to the French school. He admired French composers for their ability to preserve the specific character and "even the individuality of every instrument" – a quality the Rumanian musician regarded as a matter of capital importance in the building up of a symphonic work.[130]

He saw in Berlioz and Saint-Saëns ideal examples of perfect scoring and rated them, along with Rimsky-Korsakov, Dvořák and Mahler, as the world's greatest masters of orchestration.[131] A high tribute to Enesco's skill in handling orchestral coloring comes from his most famous violin pupil, Y. Menuhin: "When Enesco stood at the rostrum he succeeded in extracting from the orchestra such wonderful sounds that other, sometimes more authoritative, conductors would not even dare to have dreamt of.[132] This was made possible probably because the orchestra, as Enesco said, had been a means capable '... to express everything that constituted the beauty and full intensity of life. The orchestra is some entity which I can modulate to achieve the most perfect interpretation.[133] The art of a conductor is a very difficult thing.' Enumerating the qualities a conductor must possess, Enesco stressed that he must never lose his spirit, be in full command of the score and know how to play the principal orchestral instruments."[134]

Before starting his first rehearsal, Enesco would usually play the full work on the piano to acquaint the orchestra with his conception of it. He knew by heart all the scores he was going to conduct and could render any of them freely on the piano.

A full knowledge of the score was, in his opinion, one of the essentials of a conductor's know-how. His ideal in this respect was exemplified by A. Toscanini who had a phenomenal ability to know by heart the slightest detail of any score. According to Enesco, "the work of a conductor begins in earnest only after he has freed himself completely from a printed score. Only when a work has already taken shape in imagination," he said, "can the conductor achieve a personal approach that is completely of his own; only then all details and nuances will be in line with the basic idea of the work." Aiming at the maximum expressiveness, but never losing self-control, he rejected affectation in conducting as firmly as in any other facet of his concert activity. Expression and over-reaction were for him two absolutely distinct things. He would criticize second rate conductors for substituting bad taste sentimentalism for a truly sincere emotion recommending them "to take an example from A. Nikisch in the past and Toscanini at present."[135]

Enesco's debut as a conductor took place in 1898 when in Bucharest his *Rumanian Poem* for symphony orchestra was performed under his direction. After that he would appear more and more often as the conductor of his own symphonic compositions. Among them the two *Rumanian Rhapsodies* were, as has already been mentioned, most frequently performed. These colorful works, which in his spirited interpretation gained widespread popularity, gave him the opportunity of acquainting the concert public for the first time with the achievements of Rumanian music.

Enesco's career as a conductor took a new turn in 1909 when he began to perform symphonic works written by other composers. The first concert he gave abroad, at which he conducted more than his own compositions, took place in Russia.

From then on, he more and more frequently took his place at the conductor's stand, constantly enlarging the number of works he performed.

Enesco's symphonic repertoire was perhaps even larger than the

Glière's student, the Russian composer Miaskovsky.

A group photo at the historic Russian concerts in Paris, May 1907. Among the people may be found: 2. Georges Enesco; 3. S. Koussevitsky; 5. F. Shalyapin; 7. A. Casadesus; 8. S. Rakhmaninov; 11. C. Saint-Saëns; 15. N. Rimsky-Korsakov; 17. Wanda Landowska.

one he presented as a violinist. It comprised a very large number of works written by classical, romantic and contemporary composers. Music by Bach, Beethoven and Brahms, whom he used to call "my three gods", was especially prominent in it. He also often conducted works of Russian composers with whom he had long-standing ties. The high level of Russian musical culture attracted him, and he felt deep respect for those who represented it. The first occasion Enesco had to meet some personally, occurred in 1907 at the reception given by Saint-Saëns at the Pleyel Hall in Paris in honor of Rimsky-Korsakov, Rachmaninov, Chaliapin and Litvin. On several occasions later, Enesco met with such composers as S. Prokofiev, N. Miaskovsky and R. Glière, as well as with violinists L. Auer, K. Sibor and others. His Russian ties deepened considerably, thanks to his concert tours.

Enesco first visited Russia in 1909 at the invitation of the Russian Musical Society. His concerts were awaited with great interest as the Russian public had already heard about the successes of the young Rumanian musician abroad who combined a triple talent of violinist, composer and conductor.

Enesco's Russian debut took place in St. Petersburg on October 10, 1909 in a concert series organized by the well-known pianist and conductor, A. Ziloti. The programme of this concert consisted of the *Violin Concerto No. 7* by Mozart with Enesco as the soloist, the two *Rumanian Rhapsodies* conducted by the composer and J.S. Bach's *Piano Concerto No. 1* played by Ziloti with Enesco conducting.

Enesco was warmly received by the Russian musical press. Referring to his first concert, the "Russian Musical Gazette" critic wrote:

"The young Rumanian violinist... showed himself to be a gifted, serious and accomplished artist not content with superficial virtuoso effects, but seeking the soul of art and finding it!" The critic was enthusiastic about the way Enesco played Mozart: "... one could witness a fairy maid's song reverberating in the second movement ... the smile and ... intermittent tears of an angel which appear now and then throughout the work and the sparkling joy of rhythm ..." The critic also liked Bach's *Aria* played by the violinist as an encore. Pointing out that the first half of the concert was fully and truly delightful, the critic exclaims: "What an abundant beauty, what a luxurious beauty, what a dignity of youth mighty in its creative power!" And as if having guessed Enesco's intention, the critic continues: "... the feeling with which one hears it (the music—B.K.) has nothing to do with amusement or curiosity, being itself a symbol of harmony it evokes in the listener such a harmonious state of mind that the phenomenon involving the mysterious identity of good and beauty seems to become for a while a tangible reality."[136]

This concert also got favorable comments in the magazine "Novoe Vremia". Paying tribute to the beauty and originality of Enesco's scoring, its critic wrote: "The composer himself very well conducted his own compositions."[137]

A week later the Rumanian musician appeared in Moscow at the first symphonic concert of the season conducted by M. Ippolitov-Ivanov. There, as in St. Petersburg, he played the *Seventh Violin Concerto* by Mozart and conducted his two rhapsodies.

The impression Enesco produced at these concerts found an echo not only in newspapers. An interesting reference to this event is to be found, for instance, in the memoirs written by the niece of A. Ziloti, Z. Pribytkova. Recollecting the first acquaintance of the Rus-

The greatest of contemporary Russian composers, S. Prokofiev.

Fritz Kreisler, Enesco, and Zino Francescatti (left to right).

sian public with the young Rumanian musician and praising his excellent interpretation of Mozart's concerto, she writes: "Ziloti . . . had a good eye for discovering talented people . . . Now Enesco is an artist Rumania and the entire musical world is proud of. Today Ziloti could have said with satisfaction that he had been the first to show Russia this wonderful Rumanian musician."[138]

Enesco's ties with Russia acquired a new meaning in 1917 when his visit assumed the character of a friendly gesture towards an allied country whose armed forces had been fighting at the Rumanian front during the First World War. His concert in Petrograd on March 10th that year went off in unusual circumstances caused by the troubled events of the time. Referring to this concert, the French ambassador to Russia, M. Paleologue recalls the impression produced on him by Enesco's inspired playing against the background of the tense atmosphere prevailing in the capital constantly patrolled by armed revolutionary guards. "Never before," he says, "has this remarkable artist, this acknowledged rival of such geniuses as Ysaye and Kreisler, produced on me a more striking impression by his straightforward and spirited interpretation capable of expressing the most subtle, as well as the most powerful emotions."[139]

Another point of interest concerning this concert and demonstrating the friendly attitude of Enesco towards Russia is that on his return home, he made a donation of a thousand lei to the Russian Red Cross — quite a substantial sum at the time. Reporting this fact to his government, the Russian ambassador in Bucharest emphasizes Enesco's benevolence due, as he puts it, ". . . to his sincere and profound sympathy for us . . ."[140]

Enesco had in his repertoire works of Russian composers not confined to those of the last century. He often performed the music of Stravinsky whom he considered a composer of genius. "Best of all", wrote Enesco, "I like *Petrushka* and *The Firebird* though it is cast more in the French than Russian fashion. As regards *The Rite of*

Spring, it seems to me that it is prejudiced from the point of view of emotional graduation by a too much pronounced parallelism between the first and the second part. Nevertheless this is music of great value."[141]

Reacting swiftly to everything new, Enesco was keenly interested in Soviet music. He was the first to popularize it in Rumania, backing it with his full authority. He did much in this respect not only by performing the works of Soviet composers, but also by writing articles about them. "The Soviet music," he wrote in one of his articles, "is very original, and I am sure that the effort to make it known to the Rumanian public will be successful as it merits to be."[142] It is worth noticing that this declaration was published not in a special musical journal, but in a popular feminine newspaper. This choice of media indicates a clear desire to address a mass reader. This article, coinciding with the liberation of Rumania, acquired not only an artistic, but also a political meaning. It showed Enesco's attitude to a new cultural factor and expressed his friendly feelings towards the country whose sacrifices in the war contributed also to the liberation of the Rumanian people. "I know the music of the composer S. Prokofiev", wrote Enesco in the same newspaper, "and appreciate it very much." The Rumanian musician was deeply moved by Shostakovitch's *Seventh Symphony*. "I regard Shostakovitch," he wrote, "as one of the greatest musicians of today. The *Seventh*, ("Leningrad") *Symphony* is a work of a high class, written by a highly talented musician possessing a perfect technique. I like very much the first movement and the Finale. Of course, there are many other extremely beautiful pages in the symphony, but its beginning and the Finale, as well as the transition from the third to the fourth movement are marvelous and deeply moving. There are absolutely new themes in this work . . .: the themes of war horrors and sufferings endured by Leningrad during the siege when Shostakovitch was composing the *Seventh Symphony*."[143]

When, as a result of the heroic deeds of the Soviet people, the hour of liberation from fascism had struck for Rumania, Enesco heralded his country's new era by the sounds of Russian and Soviet music.[144] He was one of the first to sign the act which inaugurated the foundation of the Rumano-Soviet Friendship Society and became chairman of its musical section. He was delighted to receive in his country a group of Soviet musicians including Oistrakh, L. Oborin, Shafran, M. Kozolupova, I. Briushkov and the members of the Vuillaume Quartet with all of whom he participated in solo, chamber music and symphonic concerts. Referring to these experiences, Shafran wrote in April 1946: "Leaving Rumania I want to say that Georges Enesco made on me the greatest possible impression. Our meetings, conversations with him and playing together were for me a true revelation. He will come to the Soviet Union as a messenger of Rumanian music, and I am happy that our people will hear this great musician."[145]

David Oistrakh, Enesco, and Lev Oborin (left to right).

The program of a concert conducted by Georges Enesco.

Top:
Dmitry Shostakovich and Georges Enesco.
Bottom:
Enesco and Mihail Andricu (first on the left) with members of the Vuillaume Quartet from Kiev, with whom Enesco gave several concerts in Bucharest (1945).

And indeed, Moscow soon again welcomed Enesco on the occasion of his return visit. Appearing once more in his triple capacity, he gave three symphonic concerts: the programmes of two of them included the *Fifth Symphony* by Beethoven, the *Fourth* by Tchaikovsky, two Rumanian rhapsodies and his *Second Orchestral Suite*, as well as works of the Rumanian composer M. Jora; one night he was the soloist in a violin concerto by Bach, the *Poem* by Chausson and the already mentioned Khatchaturian *Violin Concerto*. Other soloists in these concerts were: E. Gilels, who played the *C-major Concerto* by Beethoven and the *E-flat-minor Concerto* of Tchaikovsky, and Oistrakh who, together with Enesco, performed the *Double Concerto* by Bach. Besides, at a chamber music evening the Rumanian guest together with the pianist L. Oborin played Mozart's and Franck's violin sonatas, then switching to the piano, he performed with Oistrakh the *C-minor Sonata* by Grieg. Enesco was warmly received at the Union of Soviet Composers where he played his compositions on the piano, including fragments from the opera *Oedipe*. "Concerts given by Enesco in Moscow," wrote G. Shneerson, "caused the public to experience many strikingly vivid impressions. The programmes of his concerts were varied and interesting. Pointing to his exceptional gift as a violinist, conductor, composer and pianist, they were beneficial also to the players from the State Symphony Orchestra of the Soviet Union who found working with this outstanding master an excellent new stimulus in their creative activity.

Enesco, before departing for the Soviet Union, takes leave of his fans.

Those who were lucky enough to meet him personally and to contact Enesco would keep in their memory the noble image of this great musician and great man forever.[146]

The warm reception which was extended to him in the USSR deeply moved the old maestro. Speaking on his return home at the reception given by the Rumanian Society of Cultural Relations with the Soviet Union on the 17th of May 1946, he said with emotion: "I was received in such a manner which I think I do not deserve. I especially appreciate the support given to me by the Soviet orchestra, its efficiency and discipline, its endeavor to carry out all the indications and its deep comprehension of the essence of music. I want to mention the cult of beauty which is being practiced on a large scale in the Soviet Union as a serious matter based on merit and work."

That is how the elderly master, who had devoted his entire life to foster in people the sense of beauty, expressed his attitude to the musical art in the USSR.

The role Enesco played as a conductor had a special importance for his own country. At the beginning of the century, Rumanian musical life was lagging behind, compared with more developed European countries. Thanks to Enesco, this situation was completely changed. Now when Rumania enjoys the reputation of a country musically advanced, his part in bringing this about must not be

Emil Gilels.

David Oistrakh.

underestimated.

Spending several months every year in his native country, Enesco regularly gave symphonic concerts. True to his principles, he conducted them not only in Bucharest and other major cities, but in small towns, as well as promoting music among people of all walks of life.

Thanks to him, his fellow countrymen had an opportunity to hear such capital works as Beethoven's *Ninth Symphony, Romeo and Juliet* and *Damnation de Faust* by Berlioz, the third act of Wagner's opera *Parsifal,* the *Leningrad Symphony* of Shostakovitch and others, some of which were performed in Rumania for the first time. A number of his concerts, given during the First World War, acquired a meaning that went beyond a purely musical event. Thus, in the days when the Rumanian authorities instigated nationalistic passions he continued to make up his concert programmes irrespective of the composer's nationality. Enesco, who regarded all true artists as his brothers, firmly rejected all attempts from any quarter to exclude from the programmes German or other composers only because they were subjects of an enemy state. In this respect, his performance of Berlioz's *Damnation de Faust*, which took place in Bucharest on the 24th of April 1916, is very symptomatic. By that time Rumania, under the pressure of the Entente, entered the war against Germany and Austro-Hungary. The reactionary Rumanian bourgeoisie, which had been whipping up a chauvinistic hysteria in the country, came out against the performance of the Rakocze March, considering the introduction of anything connected with Hungary to be antipatriotic. Despite a frenzied campaign against him, Enesco flatly refused to omit this march from the programme which made the concert assume the character of an antimilitarist manifestation. The same can be said about the three concerts given by Enesco in Kishinev in March 1918, the programmes of which included works of German, French, Austrian and Russian composers.

Besides its cultural value, this wide-ranging concert activity contributed to the setting up of a number of symphony orchestras and a national opera theatre in Rumania. He was fully aware of the importance of such a theatre and had been striving for a long time to bring it into being. As early as 1915 he wrote: "Rumanian opera theatre is my long-standing dream. I want to see a theatre where our singers could perform in our language the great masterpieces by Gluck, Mozart, Beethoven, Weber, by the superhuman Wagner and also such outstanding contemporary operas as Debussy's *Pelléas and Mélisande*, "Ariane and Bluebeard" by Paul Dukas, Mussorgsky's *Boris Godunov, Salome* by Richard Strauss, and later Rumanian lyrical works. Our current repertoire shall have to consist of true masterpieces, of works that are pure, noble and elevated.[147]

These words became guidelines for the Bucharest National Theatre of Opera and Ballet which, since its inauguration, had staged the best works of the world's operatic repertoire. Performing at home and abroad, visiting Paris, Moscow and other cities, the theatre established its reputation as a highly efficient company capable of tackling successfully the most complex artistic problems.

Enesco also did much to popularize Rumanian music. Conducting his concerts, as an artist-patriot he was doing his best to make it known abroad, to assert it in the international arena. Rumanian music began its advance through the concert halls of the world with his *Rumanian Poem*, as well as the two Rumanian rhapsodies. Enesco deemed it his duty to popularize the music written by the young Rumanian composers whose development he had been nurturing with so much love and care. He conducted works by M. Jora, S. Dragoi, D. Cuclin, A. Alessandresco, I.N. Otesco, A. Mendelsohn, T. Rogalski, S. Golestan and many others. He included them in his concert programmes wherever he went, and it was thanks to him that they became known to the public at large. He achieved this in different ways, either by including a Rumanian work in a concert mainly devoted to famous composers, or making up the whole programme of pieces composed by his fellow countrymen. The latter course was eventually put to the final test in 1937 at the first Rumanian symphonic concert ever mounted in Paris, proving even to the most exacting critics that the Rumanian

Enesco and Mihail Jora in Enesco's house in Dorohoi (1932).

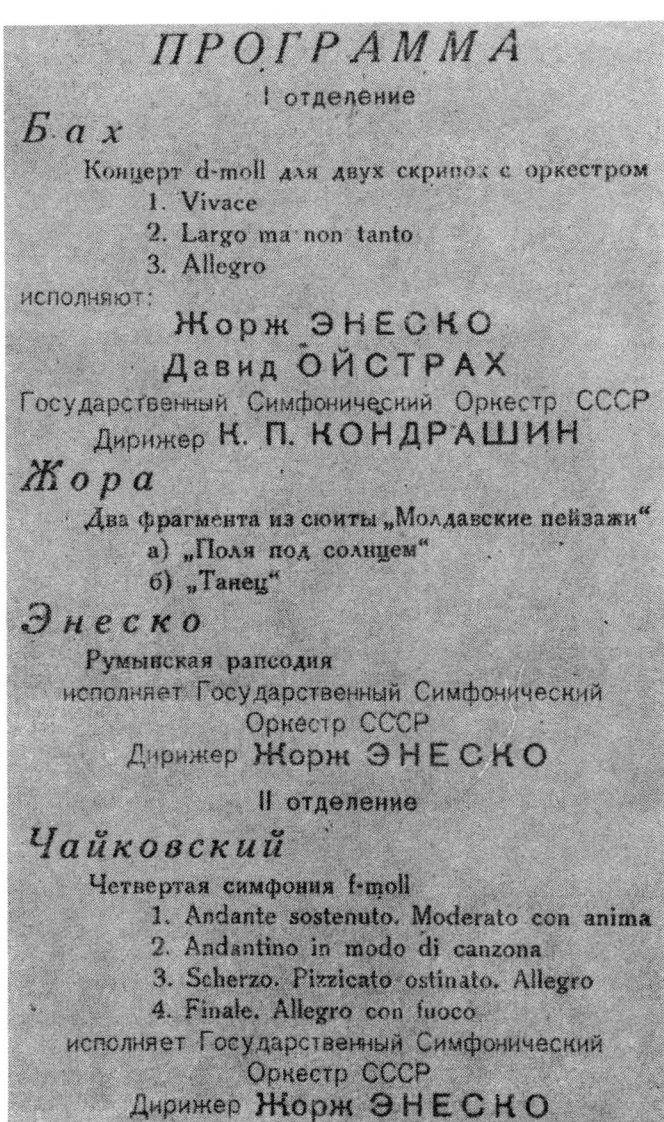

Left:
Enesco and the composer Alfred Alexandrescu at the Rumanian Atheneum (1936).
Right:
Program of a Moscow concert featuring Enesco both as conductor and violin soloist.

school of composition had been making rapid progress.

Enesco also contributed directly or indirectly to the development of many Rumanian conductors whose names are well-known in a number of countries. A mere enumeration of musicians such as A. Ciolan, G. Georgesco, C. Silvestri, I. Perlea, M. Basarab and M. Cristesco will suffice to illustrate how much the Rumanian school of conductors owed to his activity. Developing their individual style, Rumanian conductors are continuing Enesco's traditions, and this is the best reward for the great master.

His art as a conductor is still alive. It is preserved for posterity by numerous gramophone records which provide valuable data for those students of performing art who did not have the chance to hear him live. Interesting information on the subject is supplied by Shneerson who gives an eyewitness account of Enesco's qualities as a conductor: "The skill of Enesco in dealing with the orchestra is very high. The interpretation of Beethoven's *Fifth Symphony* had been overwhelming by the magnitude and integrity of conception, by its daring power and temperament. Enesco knows how to emphasize a phrase in an amazingly simple and yet expressive way. His rhythm is always lively and full of sweeping emotion. His symphonic works, as well as the interesting symphonic poem by the Rumanian composer M. Jora, have been rendered in a splendid expressive way and with complete freedom... Enesco conducts in a seemingly very simple manner without any superficial pause. His gestures are simple and clear, as are his intentions. Knowing the score perfectly and the possibilities of the orchestra, he can freely obtain any effect he wants, including striking tone contrasts, formidable crescendos, transparent pianissimos, and all of them are being achieved by means that seem to be very modest and unsophisticated. He is extremely good at handling the strings which he makes to sound like one instrument fully obeying the conductor's will.[148]

But neither the recollections of his contemporaries, nor even gramophone records can convey in full that charm and vital power which Enesco's magic baton seemed to generate. The real impact of his performing art can be traced best in the achievements of those musicians who in one way or another were in contact with him and those who were helped to find their own way in art by the example of this great master.

All the various forms of Enesco's artistic activity are characterized by his views on education. As has already been said, his aim was to promote music among the masses, to develop in ordinary people good taste and love for the fine arts. Sharing the view that music can enlighten and unite people, he considered it his moral and civic duty to popularize it. In pursuit of his aim, he gave concerts in Rumania during the war years, visiting the remotest places of the country despite difficult conditions. The receipts from these concerts would usually go to various cultural and charitable institutions. For instance, he helped financially to organize a number of churches and schools; in 1912 he made a grant to set up a yearly composition contest bearing his name, contributed in 1915 to the cost of an organ for the concert hall Ateneum in Bucharest and so forth. Devoting much attention to the plight of wounded soldiers, he was trying to alleviate their sufferings. Thanks to his efforts, a sum of six hundred thousand lei in gold was collected for the wounded of the First World War.

But Enesco did not think that his patriotic duty involved material assistance only. Whatever he did was always according to the utmost importance of the moral factor, and remaining true to himself, he often played in military hospitals. No matter where, amidst the wounded, students or children, at the bedside of his dying friend the painter Luchian, whom he had come to console by the sounds of his violin, his humane art was producing a lasting impression, evoking a profound and warm feeling of sincere gratitude.[149] The emotional impact of his art was so great that it evoked a touching, sometimes

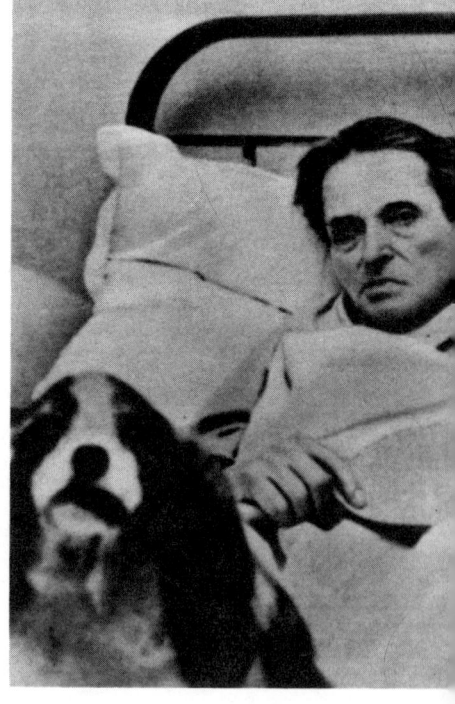

Enesco and furry friend.

Top: Enesco on the deck of a ship, during his last trip from the U.S. to Europe (1949); **Bottom:** Georges Enesco with writer and academician Mihail Sadoreanu.

Bill for a recital of Beethoven violin-and-piano sonatas in the Salle Pleyel.

A letter from Enesco to the president of Rumania.

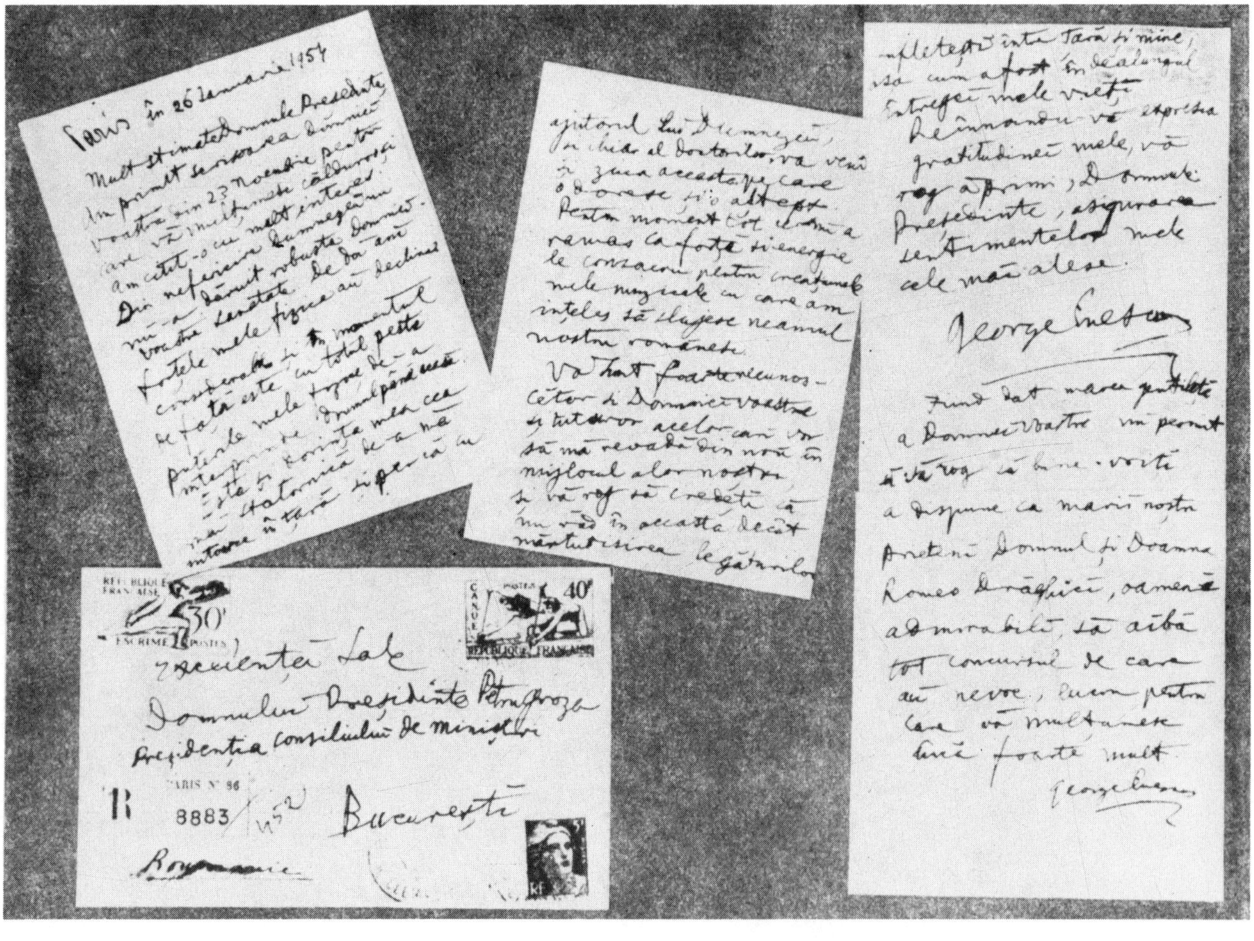

Georges Enesco's last resting place.

rather naïve, reaction especially on behalf of simple folk. Thus, after a concert, given by Enesco in a small provincial town, a porter once told him that he would carry his luggage free of charge if only he came to play again there. Such simple reactions coming from the bottom of the heart were for the Rumanian musician the highest possible reward.

Enesco's activity was so manifold and intense in all its manifestations that one can only marvel at his inexhaustible energy and endurance. He always found in creative labor a source of happiness and moral satisfaction. It seemed that work only helped him to gain strength and new momentum, enabling him to undertake an ever-increasing number of tasks. So, his various engagements did not prevent him from taking a most active part in the setting up of the Union of Rumanian Composers. As the Union's chairman, he laid the foundation of a folkloric department which grew with time into one of the largest folkloric institutes in the world.

He realized the need to gather and study popular music not as a result of pure scientific curiosity, but in direct consequence of the essence of his activity. He was convinced that a thorough knowledge of the artistic wealth accumulated by the people was essential for the development of a progressive professional art. He saw in folklore, and particularly in its rural specimens, a force which could counteract the growing commercialization of the Rumanian bourgeois art in the thirties. With this problem very much in mind, Enesco wrote in 1934: "While the middle class public has fallen under the influence of dubious taste, the village is unequivocally remaining an unlimited source of pure and original popular art. A peasant is a poet, an artist, a creator by his very nature. It is necessary to save the village from the mechanized forms of art."[150]

When Enesco found himself in foreign parts towards the end of his life, he kept intact the ties that had united him with his native country. In his letter of January 25 1954, addressed to the President of the Grand National Assembly of the Rumanian Popular Republic, he wrote about his most cherished desire to return home, but circumstances made it impossible. After a prolonged severe illness, Enesco died in Paris on May 4, 1955.

A sketch of Enesco in his old age.

Chapter 8

Enesco, one of the most cultured artists of our time, strove all his life for an art that really belonged to the people. Knowing how difficult it was for ordinary folk during his lifetime to have easy access to art, he insisted that people occupied with physical work, ". . . who were deprived of any spiritual joy, should be able to take advantage of all that is beautiful and noble."[151] He had no illusions as to what jeopardized such a contention in the world and sharply criticized those social factors which transform art into "a chained Prometheus", Enesco wrote: "Sad as it is, one has to recognize that art is being considerably prejudiced by economic and social factors. It is impossible to speak, nay even to raise the question of improving artistic taste until people have something to eat. So long as they are made to hear music on an empty stomach, they can not be blamed for remaining indifferent to a concert or a poem. Governments must think first of all to provide everybody with means of subsistence. Only when the basic requirements of the body have been met can the struggle for preserving and multiplying cultural values be resumed. Bread, heating, public baths and education—these are things we must make available to all people."[152]

Advocating the need to create proper conditions enabling art to fulfill its noble function, Enesco came to realize the necessity of social reforms. He saw to what extent progress was impaired by reactionary forces and consequently he could not remain indifferent in the struggle for democracy which he supported as a man and an artist. To act otherwise would have countervailed his humane principles. His declaration welcoming the setting up of the united antifascist front in France, which we have already quoted above, showed that he had no hesitation on this issue. Moreover, in 1934 Enesco wrote: "We are living at the time of extraordinary changes. We have to be ready for the emergence of a new social basis."[152] A hint as to how he viewed such "a new basis" can be found in the following statement: "I know that art cannot flourish where hatred and oppression exist."[154]

Enesco's profound humanism, his democratic views brought him into the ranks of those who had been struggling against the threat of war. He raised his voice passionately in the defense of peace especially when Hitler's war hysteria was in full swing. "I am a convinced pacifist", he exclaimed.[155] "Artists of all countries have to be apostles of peace."[156] Urging the artists to collaborate, he put before them a concrete aim: "In this cruel time we have to promote art and purity of thought as much as we can raise mankind once again to the level that makes men superior to other beings."[157] In 1942, when there seemed to be no way out of the impasse Rumania had been pushed into by Hitler's Germany, Enesco wrote: "My only desire is that our country, our wonderful people find their way to a bright future. That is how I feel, that is how everyone ought to feel."[158] His voice was heard again when, during the post-war years, the intrigues of international reaction created once more an alarmed situation: "An artist shows mankind the path to harmony which is to be found in happiness and peace."[159] He was making these statements in the firm belief that ". . . a man's soul unfolds itself only in peace."[160]

Friendship between peoples, based on full mutual understanding, respect and equality, was for Enesco one of the main pre-conditions of peace. Deeply loving his country and his people, he made no distinction between nations and condemned any manifestation of nationalistic feelings which, in his opinion, ran contrary to the sense of justice and human dignity. He would never judge people on racial or religious grounds. Attempts to instigate national hatred provoked in him disgust and indignation. "Art," he insisted, "does not know race restrictions. I cannot understand how an artist can hate a man only because he belonged by birth to another group of men."[161] "Those who believe in art are my brothers irrespective of race, nationality or religion."[162] When fascist vandalism was at its peak, he kept intact his belief in the moral strength of men and its final triumph over evil and obscurantism. With unabated optimism he proclaimed that ". . . the rulers, who now, (*i.e.,* 1934 B.K.) — are recurring to nationalistic theories, find themselves at the edge of an abyss. Dictators shall tumble down as their predecessors did in the past.

"Culture shall survive! Too much labor and belief in all that we have cherished and assimilated throughout so many centuries have been accumulated for it all to be erased from the surface of the earth at a single stroke. History has already experienced crises that seemed to be unsurmountable but they all have been overcome, thanks to the heroic power of survival men possess. This time too we will have enough courage; let us then keep our faith and we shall triumph."[163]

It is this belief in the final victory which emphasized the optimistic character of Enesco's outlook so typical of his art in general. This optimism is rooted in his contention that the very nature of man is inseparable from the creative impulse which eventually triumphs over darkness and oppression.

This belief made him react all the more bitterly to the reality that surrounded him. In this connection his attitude to the musical art of

Enesco composing.

Top: Bust of Enesco by Lavrillier-Cossaceanu; **Bottom:** Plaster cast of Enesco's right hand.

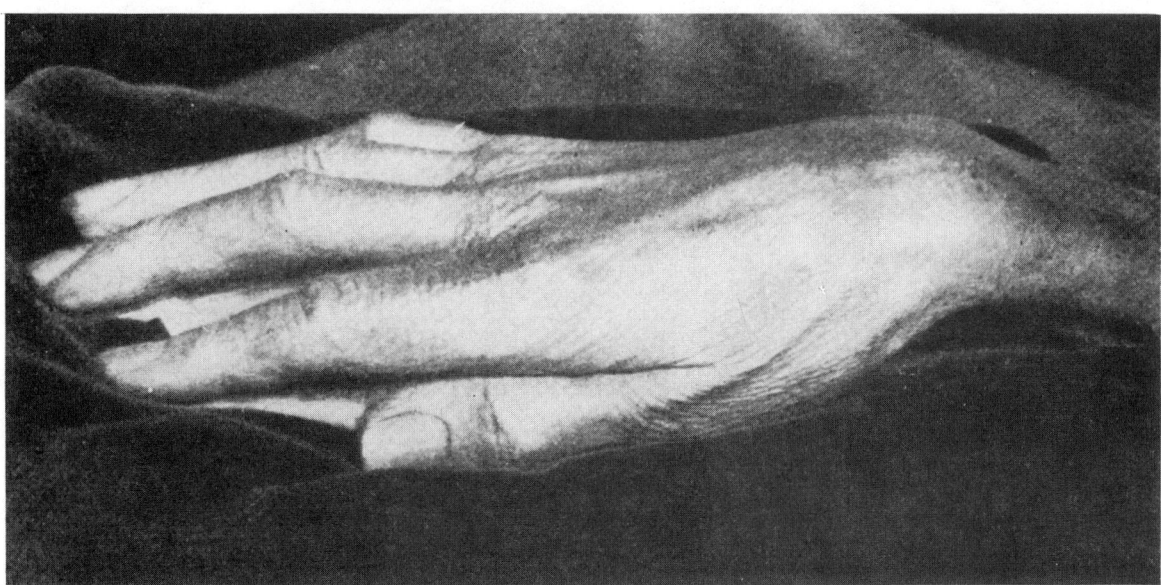

his time is fully representative of his overall conception. This attitude, which took its final shape during the period between the two world wars, can be characterized by the following words of the well-known French musical figure, René Dumesnil: "Hindemith's music—more intellectual than emotional—has not remained without influence on the young French composers who have been attracted more by construction than by emotion and are often inclined to regard as a mistake everything that seemed in their art to touch on emotionality."[164] Referring to the same topic, Enesco gives it a similar characterization: "In art, as in music, there is no more harmony which, as the ancients assumed, could appease even ferocious beasts. The legend of Orpheus is forgotten. The world nowadays is aggressive. Military marches, factory and traffic noise, the roar of engines are heard everywhere. Genuine music has many times been subjected to a mechanical invasion. Present day music—mainly mechanical, brutal and desperate—smacks of violence and automation. Generally speaking, the world today is inundated by excesses of cruelty. I think that in literature the situation is much the same."[165]

But this outspoken assessment did not lead Enesco to pessimistic conclusions. Unhappy but never discouraged, he went on viewing the future with unabating hope in a firm belief that, to quote Shelley, "If winter comes, can spring be far behind?" "I hope," wrote Enesco, "that after this war there shall come, as I would put it, 'un retour à la sensibilité.' It is to be hoped that we will return to sincerity and tend to integrate the intellect of an artist with his emotionality in accordance with human nature."[166] This was a realism not of "lost illusions", but of soaring hopes, a realism of a positive kind asserting the triumphant impetus of life. Its humane essence manifested itself in a deeply compassionate attitude to people for whose fate Enesco showed so much concern. In the "world of cruelty" this artist was referring to, the following words acquire a special meaning: "I believe that art must radiate virtue carrying relief and consolation."[167]

It is characteristic of Enesco's esthetic conception that, while viewing life realistically, he would not put up with the implacable course of daily events in the midst of which a new dawn was about to break, just as the bright opening of the Finale of his *Third Symphony* evolved from the terrible nightmare of the preceding movement. This coming dawn was his life's dream, a dream that was part of his very being. In his inner vision, this dream was not tantamount to Maeterlinck's evasive "blue bird" tempting people to a vain pursuit of unattainable happiness, nor was it a vague sterile symbol brought about by a moral vacuum, but a very tangible manifestation of a humanitarian ideal. He was convinced that this ideal can be attained and this turned his dream into a reliable driving force. He saw in it a burning torch highlighting the aspirations of an artist who, as he said in his "Souvenirs" ". . . is to find nothing if his im-

The Master in his studio.

agination is not constantly guided by a noble aim."

While remaining aware of various artistic trends, Enesco formed his own mature and original conception. It represents an organic whole which synthesizes such characteristic features of classical music as the magnitude of the poetic idea coupled with a profound and wide-ranging philosophical generalization of dialectical contradictions inherent in the existing reality, as well as the freedom of spontaneous self-expression so typical of the romantic art. Enesco, who called himself "a romantic and a classic by instinct", wrote: "it is necessary . . . to learn how to combine the classical unity of form with the utmost freedom and dynamism of expression hindering in no way the spontaneity of emotion."[168]

Speaking of his esthetic conception, it is interesting to note that Enesco was not satisfied with any of the new artistic trends of his time. He paid much less tribute to neo-classicism than many of his contemporaries and parted from it in the main as early as 1907. He felt he was a stranger in the sphere of abstract constructions and showed no interest for stylistic display which, no matter how masterly, cannot rekindle a dying flame by resuscitating the spirit of a living creation. Nor did he share the desire of some of his colleagues to modernize old forms and means of expression.

He believed that sheer reproduction of art forms could not have lasting results. "In music, as in literature and painting," he maintained, "every work must have an inner origin of its own, free of any formalized conception which we deem successful or which actually was successful in another case."[169] That is why he did not think it right to transplant the achievements of one epoch mechanically into another one without taking into account the change of situation. The perfection of form or style, which should be, in his opinion, the constant care of every artist, was regarded by him only as an indispensable attribute of a true art work; moreover, such perfection was, in his view, not an abstract and self-imposing notion, but a direct result of that creative impulse which, to use his own expression, ". . . brings forth a link between the artist and universality."[170]

Arguing with those who taught that music could not express anything but itself, he insisted that "The sacred goal of music is to

Georges Enesco in the Garden of his villa "Luminis" in Sinaia (1945).

put out hatred, to soothe passions and to unite the hearts of men in a sincere fraternal communion as it was understood during the epoch of the great antiquity which had created the myth about Orpheus."[171]

In view of the importance Enesco attached to the emotional factor in music, it is natural that he had not been tempted by constructivism. Having mastered the logical side of musical thinking, he rejected sterile models; he saw no purpose in building structures purely for the sake of construction. He felt that the intellectual factor reveals itself in art through sensual images; he wanted above all to see them as lively as possible. In dealing with this problem, he was fully aware that art and logic each have laws of their own. With this in mind, he wrote: "It is true that music is related to mathematics, but the great composers were not mathematicians, or, if we want, they were mathematicians only in an instinctive way. Bach's genius detected correlations of the highest order between various component parts of a musical work. Of course, his compositions can also express mathematic elements and proportions, but Bach did not establish them by means of logical deduction. He had no time to indulge in logical exercises. The influx of emotions and daring ideas organized themselves into symmetrical esthetic forms, not under the tyrannical control of learned mathematical principles. A composer can be said to be a mathematician in the sense that he becomes possessed by the spirit of mathematics, or more correctly, that this spirit penetrates into his mind. I think the same thing occurs in other art too. Poetry also contains formalized relationships which can be expressed in mathematical terms, but a poet does not calculate the metrical structure of a verse, for his inspiration is rushing much more quickly than even the most dynamic versifications. Rhythmic cadences find their right positions themselves, seemingly without any outside interference."[172] The above statement makes it clear why the constructivist standpoint was unacceptable to Enesco either in practice or in theory.

The optimistic quality of Enesco's humanism made him immune to the influence of some other artistic currents prevailing in western music during the period between the two world wars—called in French "les folles anées" ("the crazy years"). While sharing its tragedy with mankind, as an artist he was saved, thanks to this quality, from the tragic split of personality desperately trying to assert itself under the onslaught of rushing events. In his search for maximum expressiveness, he did not succumb to expressionist exaggerations. He was not satisfied with the exquisite refinement of impressionistic art, nor with the vague post-romantic mysticism; nevertheless, he remained outside the influence of the deliberate primitivism or urbanistic excesses indulged in by some representatives of "The group of six." Enlarging the tonal and modal sphere during his period of maturity, he did not become an advocate of atonalism or dodecaphony. He was not attracted by fashion or extravagance merely for the sake of innovation. Both as a composer and an interpreter he rebuked those "inventors" who devote all their attention to technical details at the expense of artistic unity in a desire to demonstrate their self-styled originality simply by repeating these details.[173] Technical skill had for him but a single purpose—to serve a given artistic task. It had to disclose the content of an art work, and to achieve this, Enesco used any means of expression provided it pursued the assigned aim. By using such means at his discretion, he would never formalize them into a strict system, for "In music," as he said, "there were no laws prescribed in advance to express a feeling."[174]

These words, characterizing the artist as a champion of truth in art, may offer a clue to the understanding of his style.

Its formation was very much influenced by the Rumanian popular art with which the great master had been so closely linked. For him this art represented an inexhaustible creative source and not an exotic ethnographic rarity or museum relic. He saw in it a reflection of the national and psychological character of the people, of the best manifestations of its soul. Enesco summed up his attitude to it in the following words: "The Rumanian peasant is carrying music in himself. Music has been his faithful companion in lonely mountains and fields; it is alleviating his anxieties, helping him to air his sacred aspirations, the yearning and nostalgia that are overwhelming his heart. Born through the sufferings of the Rumanian people subjugated by greedy rulers, this music is full of pain and dignity even in dance rhythms. In itself this music represents a wealth Rumania can be proud of."[175]

In his native folklore Enesco valued most its emotional riches in which various contrasting dispositions are organically combined. Turning again to this subject, he says: "Our folklore is not only dignified and beautiful, but it makes people capable of understanding everything. It is more savant than the entire savant music, as it is called, and, for that matter, everything in it is due to instinct. It is more melodious than any melody, and in the most natural way it is tender, ironic, sad, gay and wistful."[176]

No less characteristic of Enesco is his admiration for what he termed ". . . the sense of proportion enshrined intuitively in popular art, its ability to exert a maximum emotional influence by a minimum of means . . ." an ability which in his opinion constitutes ". . . the secret of beauty and universality of popular music."[177]

To grasp the nature of Enesco's style, it is important to bear in mind that his concept of "universality" presumed an integration of the individual factor with that common to all mankind. It must be added that as time went on, popular music became for him a symbol of his native land. The fact that the world-famous artist had to spend much of his time abroad also contributed to this effect, making him homesick and strengthening even more his ties with the music of his country.

The great Hungarian composer and collector of folk music, Béla Bartók.

Bust of Enesco by Gheorghe Anghel.

Enesco was attracted by many folkloric genres showing a special interest for the idiomatic emotional and intonational structure of the doina, nostalgic lyrical songs, mournful lamentation melodies, heroic ballads, Christmas and New Year's carols and instrumental tunes. On several occasions, he would focus his attention on some archaic melodies as, for instance, in his *Dixtuor* where the principal subject of the first movement is based on an ancient carol. In such cases, the composer always singled out the most vital and active elements of the old specimen. He was never tempted by the archaic aspect of folkloric melodies so dear to Bartók or Szymanowsky in his later years. Unlike his great Hungarian colleague, Enesco sought in folklore neither archaisms nor barbarisms. Bartók, deeply distressed by the agony of our century, turned to the idealization of the patriarchal way of life of the peasant, as the Soviet musicologist I. Nestev rightly points out, and, seeing no other way out, he advocated "a return to nature", giving prominence to poetic images evoked by the "resuscitated primary momentum of barbarity."[178] The great Rumanian musician envisaged the salvation of mankind in the triumph of enlightened humanistic ideals which reflect the best aspirations of our epoch.

Many of the musical themes created by Enesco usually preserve folkloric links so far as their intonational and generic origin is concerned, but the use of direct folkloric quotations was not at all typical of his style except such early works as *The Rumanian Poem* and the two *Rumanian Rhapsodies*. As has already been seen, all his best compositions constitute an excellent example of creative evaluation of the idiomatic sphere of popular music. In this respect it is interesting to note that Enesco often warned young musicians of the danger resulting from an incorrect approach to popular or folkloric material. Insisting on the correct understanding of the problem, he wrote: "It has to be borne in mind that the notion 'popular' must not be trivialized." He often stressed that the culture to be promoted among the broad masses should be of the highest class which would require prolonged educational work. Summing up, he concludes: "The art for the people must precede popular art."[179] Enesco's attitude to folklore in general and his way to use it are well characterized by his words addressed to the young composers: "I will repeat what I have so frequently said to my Rumanian colleagues: folklore itself is perfect and should not be dressed in unsuitable garments. To combine folkloric material with an unsuitable scoring is vandalism! Folklore as a motive for inspiration—yes, but its treatment must be original, free of school dogmas and far-fetched complications. The simpler a popular melody is presented, the more strikingly it shines in all its beauty. An original artistic process must

Postage stamp issued in Enesco's honor.

tend to create music in popular spirit."[180] "Turning to our young composers — the hope of our national art — I am glad to welcome the growing tendency to come nearer to the Rumanian soil, the tendency to absorb the subtle fragrance coming from its music which seems to be a sound-picture of our wonderful and enduring motherland."[181]

Enesco more than once drew to the attention of the young composers the fact that folkloric material must neither be copied mechanically, nor treated extravagantly with regard to harmony, counterpoint and means of development which are not in full keeping with its nature.

Folkloric links are especially prominent in Enesco's melodic thinking which determines, to a large extent, the expressive qualities of his style. Arguing against the tendency to renounce melodic expression as advocated by some modern composers, the Rumanian master, who called himself "an incorrigible lyric", maintained that the melodic line — "the leading motive", as he said, "constituted the principal channel through which the musical idea revealed itself.[182] Melodic themes created by Enesco represent an amalgamation of popular intonations generalized in his own individual manner. He drew the material for such a generalization mainly from the rural folklore so widely represented in the art of the lautars. This can be exemplified, for instance, by the main theme from the second movement of his *Violin and Piano Sonata Number Two* or by "The Cradle Song" from his *Impressions of Childhood*. Singling out a characteristic strain of melody from a popular tune, the composer would frequently introduce it in a melodic design of his own as, for example, in the following extract from the third movement of his *Dixtuor* (ex. n 79). Here, in the oboe part we find a tiny musical figure deduced from the cadential clause of the initial theme in the first *Rumanian Rhapsody* (compare with musical example number 1).

Ex. 79

Enesco's melodic patterns are characterized by the fact that they combine placidity with great intonational tension. They portray an affinity with the even-flowing phrases typical of a popular song, as well as with the active intervallic motion characteristic of the folkloric instrumental tunes. Their intonational tension is largely due to an active shift of basic modal sounds coupled with their frequent alteration which gives the composer an opportunity to produce, on a diatonic basis, chromatic scales much similar to those which exist in Rumanian popular music. As a result of chromatization of the II, IV, VI, VII and even III degree, Enesco obtains various scales consisting of anything from seven up to twelve notes. In a number of cases a scale, including the twelve-note one, is enriched by the introduction of quarter-tones (viz. examples quoted above from the *Third Violin and Piano Sonata* or the opera *Oedipe*. Enesco uses quarter-tones within the limits of the basic intervallic zones (*i.e.,* bands consisting of frequencies of closely related rate) of a given sound.[183] Such quarter-tones emerge due to maximum use of modal gravitations which make the intonation more acute, owing to the heightening or lowering of a given note. As a result, such a note, far from losing its individuality, acquires new expressive qualities. Quarter-tones are usually employed by Enesco while approaching a basic modal sound which in his works, just as in Rumanian popular music, may be represented by the II degree of the prevailing mode (viz., for instance, the principal subject of the first movement from his *Third Violin and Piano Sonata*). A point deserving special mention is that quarter-tones in Enesco's music are of functional origin conditioned by the very nature of zonal pitch and therefore have nothing to do with the dodecaphonic system. Leading to an enrichment of the intonational sphere, just as they do in popular music, they enlarge a mode, as it were, from within, taking advantage of its potentialities, but they do not destroy the modal or tonal entity.

Another characteristic of his melodic patterns is that they are based on a wide range of scales which can be used in a complete or incomplete form, irrespective of whether their ambitus is wide or

Books and magazines about Georges Enesco, which were published after his death.

The title page of Enesco's acceptance speech at the Academia Romana.

narrow. In the latter case, nuclei as narrow as a third, fourth and fifth are more frequently met with. In themes of a large melodic range, the scale, as a rule, is extended, but even such themes are often also made up of small separate nuclei as, for instance, in the opening theme from the middle movement of the *Third Violin and Piano Sonata.*

Enesco's melodic designs are in most cases neither symmetrical, nor complete from a structural point of view. They usually represent a free-type structure consisting of separate asymmetrical nuclei which, however, preserve common intonational and intervallic characteristics and constitute various links of a single chain formed in the course of uninterrupted development. This particularity is well demonstrated by the principal subjects of the first movements of the *Third Symphony,* F-sharp-minor *Piano Sonata* or the *Third*

Sonata for Violin and Piano. Melodic formations of this kind are connected with the monothematic nature of the composer's thinking, resulting in a wide-ranging application of variational technique. Thanks to it, a given characteristic nucleus (usually taken from the opening section of the theme) undergoes a series of modifications altering its original profile. In this connection, it is interesting to point out that Enesco uses this technique not only to develop, but also to build up these themes. Another point of interest is that such a technique comes as a consequence of the improvisational nature of his melodic thinking.

There are many things in common between improvisation in the art of Enesco and that of lautars. In either case it is characterized by an unimpeded change of contrasting images which, despite their spontaneous nature, are governed by the inner logic of a continued creative impulse. In this type of improvisation, the freedom of expression and its orderly character represent a dialectical entity in which opposing tendencies mutually complement one another.

The improvisational nature of Enesco's art, which is largely responsible for its romantic flavor, has much to do with the improvisational sphere so typical of the slow part of an instrumental doina. In it, as in his music, we find plenty of spontaneous contrasts brought about by a rapid switch from an even-flowing song-like melody to a declamatory type of recitation as well as by other factors, such as changes of melodic motion, ornamental and rhythmic design. On the other hand, the improvisational technique of Enesco also speaks of romantic influences especially when we think of his *Third Violin and Piano Sonata* or *Impressions of Childhood.* These works, in some respects, are reminiscent of Ysaÿe's art.[184]

Improvisational tendencies are also clearly visible in the texture of Enesco's music. It fluctuates sometimes to the point of becoming unstable; it may be dense or light and transparent, but always it reflects the slightest change of mood. Unexpected shifts from one register to another, together with contrasting dynamic and bowing markings, make it assume a very emphatic expressive character. When required, the texture becomes very picturesque largely because of abundant melismatic formations, which animate the musical tissue, as well as various onomatopoeic effects reproducing the sound of sundry popular instruments or voices of the pastoral world (viz. the analysis of musical works and especially that of the *Third Violin and Piano Sonata*).

If we turn to the rhythmic side of Enesco's music, we find that it has the same improvisational background. Of course, he also uses clear-cut rhythmic patterns of a dance or march origin, full of defiant elegant grace or steady self-confidence, such as, for instance, in the second subject from the first movement of the *Third Violin and Piano Sonata* or in the basic motive of the second movement of the *C-major Symphony,* but they are not the most characteristic of his style. Its specific character owes much to the use of freely cast

Honegger's review of Enesco's memoirs.

rubato type rhythms which the composer evolved from the declamatory-recitative elements of the doina and which in popular musical practice do not always agree with the generally accepted metro-rhythmic scheme. A frequent succession of long and short value notes, abundant irregular rhythmic groupings made up of even and uneven numbers of sounds, richly ornamented cadencial-type passages consisting of extended melodic figurations or tiny fiorituras, prolonged fermatos, unexpected accelerando and relantando, emphatic accents—here are but some of the main devices that constitute an inexhaustible source of expressiveness. This source has for ages been used by lautars, particularly in doinas and brilliant concert virtuoso pieces, but Enesco's merit is that these devices were for the first time made to express such a variety of poetic images in works of great artistic value and became an organic part of his individual style. It is the use of this particular source that determines the specific style of the Rumanian musician who, unlike Stravinsky, Bartok or Szymanowsky, did not limit himself to the use of popular rhythms mainly of the so-called justo type. Speaking of the innovational role of Enesco, it is interesting to mention the hypothesis put forward by the Rumanian composer and musicologist C. Taranu who suggests that he anticipated some of the principles of Messiaen's rhythmic theory.[185]

The variety of Enesco's rhythmic patterns is also due to the use of rapidly changing double and triple measurements as well as simple and compound times frequently met with in his compositions (viz.

the *Second Violin and Piano Sonata* or the suite *Impressions of Childhood*).

In this connection, one should also mention the frequent employment of complex polymetric and polyrhythmic combinations occurring at moments of intense development or as a means of stressing the independent character of various melodic lines which in its turn determines some of the characteristic features of his polyphonic technique.

Finally, another individual feature of his music is the non-coincidence in timing of similar melodic motives based actually on the same rhythmic figure subjected, however, to constant modification. Such rhythmic "discrepancies" are usually used by him as an additional means to heighten tension leading to a climax as, for example, in the coda from the Finale of the *Third Violin and Piano Sonata*.

A special role in increasing the expressive power of Enesco's musical language is played by ostinato already met with in his works analyzed above. The intensive development and widespread use of this device is apparently due to one of the tendencies of contemporary music, a tendency which, though known already in the past, assumed at present a new meaning. This tendency leads to an emphatic intensification of expressiveness particularly in conveying haunting psycho-complexes of obsession brought about by the feeling of the instability, moral disarray and general nervousness of modern times. However, ostinato in Enesco's music, as well as its improvisational nature, is of a different origin. On one hand, it is rooted in the traditions of his national art and especially in those of taraf playing, and on the other, in romantic traditions. As to the first, he took advantage of the long-standing taraf habit of playing a melodic phrase against the background of a sustained note (or a repeated group of notes) thanks to which a dynamic and a static factor could be concurrently combined. So far as the second is concerned, Enesco knew how often the mid-nineteenth century romantic composers associated ostinato with emotional stagnation as did, for instance, Schubert in the song "The Favorite Color" from his vocal cycle *Schöne Müllerin*. Unlike his friend A. Honegger and certain tendencies in contemporary opera, Enesco used ostinato not as a harmonic means destined to pull together a complex orchestral tissue,[186] but mainly as a device capable of expressing in an emphatic manner man's reaction provoked by an adverse force threatening him from outside as, for example, the expression of a bitter complaint (the opening of the second movement from the *Third Violin and Piano Sonata*), or of an angry protest (the Finale of the *First Piano Sonata*), or of a fatal menace (the introduction to the opera *Oedipe*).

In all these cases, ostinato is conceived as a dialectical complex consisting of two opposing factors: an insistent obsessive repetition of a sustained note in one voice and a tense melodic line in another.

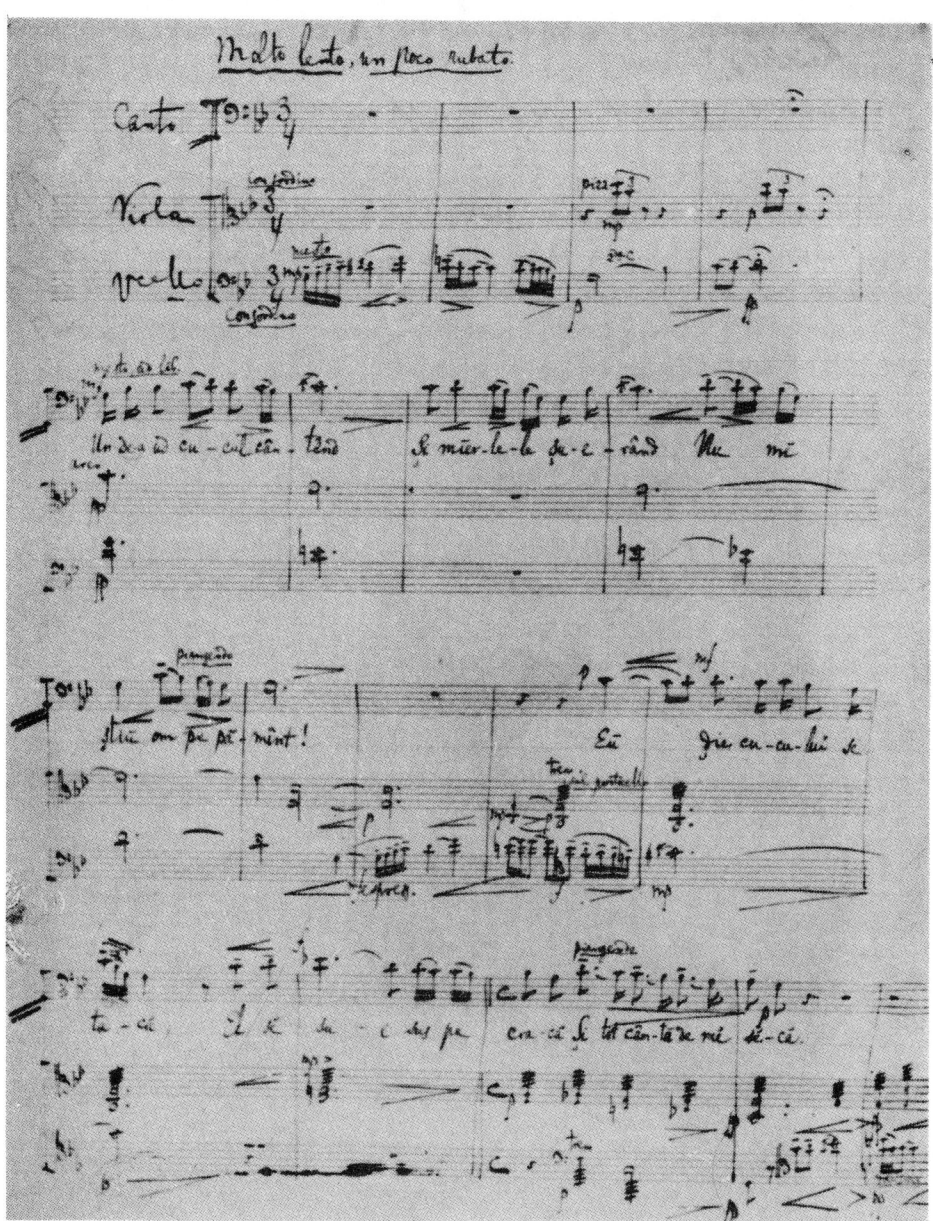

A page of the manuscript of "Doina."

This confrontation between a potentially explosive melodic phrase and an ostinato device, meant, as it were, to immobilize it, reproduces one of the characteristic features of a doina. The latter usually begins with a richly ornamented and intonationally very tense melodic figuration sounded against the background of a long drawn-out tonic harmony that seems to impair its free deployment. Comparing this popular practice with that of Enesco, one gets the impression that in either case a freely flowing melodic stream, twining 'round like a vine, clashes head on with the prolonged restraining sound trying to liberate itself from its firm grip.

Enesco's harmonic language has a pronounced modal basis which has already been pointed out while dealing with his melodic style. This basis has much in common with the modal structure of Rumanian popular music, including the widespread use of chromatically

207

extended diatonic scales already mentioned. This affinity contributed to the widening of the very notion of tonality leading to the use of specific harmonies inside the tonal complex as well as to the employment of chords belonging to different keys treated either as a brief tonal deviation or as a modulation in the proper sense of this term. Correlated as they were, these features of the composer's harmonic thinking could manifest themselves both concurrently and separately.

As to the first case, Enesco's harmonic writing is characterized by the use of keys which, owing to an intense alteration of a number of degrees, represent complex scales of a different intervallic structure but based on a single common tonic. If we take, for instance, the principal subject from the opening movement of the *Third Violin and Piano Sonata* we will see there a "fluctuating" minor mode marked by an oscillation on the same tonic between the Dorian, Aeolian and harmonic minor modes, all of which have their IV degree heightened. In a number of cases, the composer returns to bitonal formations in which the dominant (sometimes the subdominant, one of the mediants or another degree) assumes the function of the tonic. The presence of several tonics may come as a result of polymelodism when various independent melodic lines are superim-

Enesco at 50.

A hall of the Georges Enesco Permanent Display in Bucharest.

posed one above the other. In such cases Enesco, unlike D. Milhaud who favors polymelodic patterns made up of complete themes, usually superimposes a number of melodic segments deduced from a single thematic nucleus. One of the results of this technique is the extension of horizontal scales in the course of which a basic tone of one of them may acquire, within a newly derived formation, the function of a tonic. In so doing, Enesco does not destroy the tonal entity, but merely widens the limits of a tonal complex (viz. the development sections of the first and last movements from the *Third Violin and Piano Sonata*, the *First Piano Sonata* as well as the opening movement of the *C-major Symphony*). The use of complex harmonies, such as the chords of tonic 7th or 9th, can also contribute to this effect.

As has already been pointed out, the Rumanian master was not an advocate of atonalism which, however, did not prevent him from using harmonies that lay beyond the tonal conception, provided they were in full keeping with his artistic requirements (viz. the last chord of the *Third Violin and Piano Sonata*). In light of this, it is all the more significant that in the coda of the same sonata he takes great care to reiterate emphatically the basic tonal note—the tonic "A".

Regarding the choice of particular harmonies within a given tonality, the following examples are probably the most characteristic of Enesco's style: the appearance of the subdominant major chord within the framework of a minor key treated as the Dorian mode (viz., for instance, the principal subject or the development section from the first movement of the aforementioned sonata) and the use of the dominant minor chord which acquires a peculiar expressive quality against the background of the Mixolydian mode (viz. the principal subject from the opening movement of the *Third Symphony*).

As for modulations, Enesco was very fond of modal and tonal shifts in the course of which a sound is made to behave as a new fundamental tone for which he frequently chooses the II or the IV degree. On several occasions, he gives preference to a sequence of keys, each of which is situated at an interval of a third or second respectively, the former being met with in various kinds and not restricted to the notion of relative tonalities. Thus Enesco combined in his technique a sequence of major and minor relative keys, so typical of his native music, with the widespread romantic practice of confronting far distant tonalities separated one from another by an interval of a minor or major third. Of course, his modulation technique did not rely solely on the enumerated above devices.

Enesco could freely make use of some device characteristic of any harmonic school if only his artistic tasks demanded it. His style assimilated certain achievements of impressionist music, particularly sequences of parallel fourths and fifths (viz. among others the closing bars of the middle movement from the *Second Violin and Piano Sonata*, the development section in the opening movement of the *First Piano Sonata* or the beginning of scene IV from the opera

Oedipe) as well as some of the most discursive sound-effects used by expressionist composers (viz. the duel between Oedipus and the Sphinx in the same scene of the opera). The Rumanian artist differentiated his harmonic means according to its intentions. It was the type of music, its character and dramaturgic lay-out that conditioned the use of the classical or modern harmony as, for instance, in the *Concert Piece for Viola and Piano* where the former is met with in the exposition and recapitulation while the latter in development sections. This early work, written in 1906, shows a tendency to depart from the functional principle of harmonic thinking when intense development is concerned.

During his mature period, Enesco developed a harmonic style of writing characterized by a qualified use of intensely dissonant harmonies involving various combinations of seconds, fourths and fifths. Such harmonies come as a result of a special technique involving appoggiaturas being added to one or several notes of a given chord. This technique, often used by lautars, actually leads to a superposition of two chords whose fundamentals form an interval of a fifth. Similar complex chords occur at moments of exceptionally high emotional tension as, for example, towards the end of the development section from the first movement of the *Third Violin and Piano Sonata*. But the composer employs harsh discursive chords not only for dramatic purposes; in a number of cases they are used to emphasize the generic character of the music (viz. examples from the last movement of the said sonata imitating taraf style or the sound of popular plucked instruments). On other occasions such chords occur as a means of creating special tone-color effects as, for instance, in the episode from the recapitulation of the opening movement of the same sonata or the middle section from its finale. Here we find a chord in the piano part consisting of three notes (A, D-sharp and E) which represents a vertical version of a melodic figure frequently used by lautars (ex. n 80). Such tone-color "splashes" add a specific flavor to the music at the same time highlighting the expressive qualities of the violin melody.

Ex. 80

Like many contemporary composers, Enesco preserves a close link between his harmonic language and polyphonic thinking. In a large number of cases, his harmonic progressions originated as a result of horizontal motion of various melodic voices. Having been brought up on the basis of Bach's polyphony, he attached the utmost importance to the emotional logic and coherence of voice progressions. He always showed the greatest care for the precision of each melodic part in his polyphonic designs. Inherent in his character as it was, this tendency developed greatly under the influence of Gédalge and Massenet who had played a significant role in his for-

Enesco conducting in the Rumanian Atheneum in Bucharest.

mative years. There was yet another factor that also contributed to this effect namely the violin, whose singing propensity had done so much to cultivate Enesco's melodic thinking. A symphonist by nature, he did not conceive a musical fabric outside polyphonic treatment. The polyphonic character of his musical way of thinking was so pronounced that the multi-storied structure of the sound matter often came into the foreground from the beginning of a theme as, for example, in the principal subject from the first movement of the *C-major Symphony* where its third nucleus takes shape as a contrapuntal voice.

One of the most specific hallmarks of Enesco's style comes from his ability to combine imitational polyphony with variational technique. It manifests itself in various ways, the most typical involving the building up of complex structures characterized by the presence in different voices of two or more melodic figures which are akin, from an intonational point of view. This original polyphonic technique is connected with the composer's monothematic and variational methods as well as with the popular roots of his art in general. To see it at work, it will suffice to refer the reader to the development section from the first movement of the *Third Violin and Piano Sonata* which abounds in splendid examples of this technique. The same popular roots account for the presence in Enesco's music of heterophonic elements in his polyphonic patterns making their texture very florid. In highlighting this feature, one should remember that heterophony still lives in the taraf way of playing; it can also be traced in the older strata of the composer's native vocal folklore. He must be credited with developing and modernizing this ancient popular device, transforming it into one of the most specific features of his original style.

Like his other means of expression, Enesco's polyphonic technique is very dynamic, which makes it even more suitable as an effective means of intense development. This role of his polyphonic thinking becomes especially significant when he wants to disclose either the internal contradictions of an image or a conflict between the opposing inner and outer factors (for instance Oedipus's psychological reaction to the haunting curse of destiny). In general, the more the conflicting forces are popularized, the more active the polyphonisation of the musical material becomes. The composer makes extensive use of polyphonic devices in building up dramatic tension, sharp climaxes or monumental sound frescos as, for example in the coronation scene following the defeat of the Sphinx and the liberation of Thebes by Oedipus (scene IV of the opera). In cases of a very intense dramatic buildup, the application of polyphonic devices is often coupled with a marked intensification of the rhythmic factor which results in the occurrence of complex manifestations of rhythmopolyphony. Enesco's contrapuntal writing in special circumstances can acquire certain features of

The first page of the program notes for an Enesco festival.

linear polyphony. This usually happens when he sets about to portray some scene of horrors, to convey an onslaught of destructive forces as, for instance, the middle movements of the *C-major Symphony* or the *First Piano Sonata* marked by the use of strongly dissonant harmonies. In fact, the uglier the image he wants to convey, the harsher his musical language becomes. This is well exemplified by the emphatic use of a succession of parallel seconds in the middle movement of the said sonata where the furious forces of destruction seem for a moment to be gaining the upper hand.

As a composer and performer, Enesco paid much attention to the problem of form and cycle in music, the treatment of which is very characteristic of his style as a whole. Most of his major compositions, except the two *Rumanian Rhapsodies*, are based on the sonata-cyclic principle which, however, is not applied in a formal way. As we already know, he regarded the sonata-form as the highest type of musical organization, totally free of any schematic approach. In his large-scale works, cast as a cycle consisting of several movements, he makes extensive use of his monothematic method, thanks to which one phase of the composition is prepared by the preceding one, both from the thematic and emotional points of view. He envisaged such cyclic principle as an essential means of building up the entire composition as a consistent whole or its various movements. This refers to nearly all of his large-scale instrumental works whether or not they are formally entitled a suite or a poem. As a matter of fact, his first publicly performed orchestral composition, *The Rumanian Poem*, contains, as has already been said, certain features of the sonata-form while his three orchestral suites and the suite *Impressions of Childhood* are actually conceived not as suites in the proper sense of the term, but rather as symphonic cycles. As an exception to this general trend we may mention his two early works—the *Piano Suite,* "In old style" Op. 3 and *Piano Suite* Op. 10 which are cast on the pattern of the pre-classical suite. In his large symphonic and chamber-music compositions, Enesco favors a three-part form based on a pronounced contrast of poetical ideas and tempi following the model of an instrumental solo concerto with its characteristic formula—fast, slow, fast. The framework of the opera *Oedipe* taken as a whole and also in a number of separate sections contains certain attributes of the sonata structure.

Enesco's conception of the sonata-form is marked by a tendency towards the utmost intensification of thinking which has become one of the characteristic features of contemporary musical art in general. In dealing with this form, he rejected all abstract formal schemes while preserving, in his way, certain features characteristic of his epoch. The first movements of his works are, as a rule, molded in sonata-allegro form, which treatment implies a combination of the expositional phase with that of development probably to a far greater degree than in music of his predecessors. Following this practice, he creates contrasting complexes in which such a combination is so organic that sometimes it is hardly possible to draw a formal line between the end of the initial phase and the beginning of development (viz., for instance, the exposition from the first movements of the *Third Violin and Piano Sonata*, the *C-major Symphony* or the *First Piano Sonata*). These exposition sections, reminiscent of the well-known traditions of Mahler, are fully self-contained from the point of view of their emotional function, but at the same time represent structurally incomplete patterns. This makes it possible to build them up, as well as the next sections of the movement, consistently maintaining an uninterrupted line of intense development. At the same time, development technique becomes a regular feature in the course of the exposition of various themes. Both principal and second subjects in Enesco's works usually represent large, freely-conceived designs, incomplete from the structural point of view. Contrasting as they often are, they do not necessarily require a transition section as is the case in the first movement of the *Third Violin and Piano Sonata*. In other instances, the transition section can acquire very large proportions continuing the line of development set off in the principal subject (viz. the exposition from the first movement of the *C-major Symphony*). This work can be considered an extremely original example of a new approach to the sonata-allegro form. As indicated above, the first movement begins with quite a long stretch of music in a slow tempo which, at first glance, seems to be an introduction, but in reality constitutes the principal subject.

The closing section of exposition is also conceived by the composer as a new stage of development and not as a generalization of the previous material. Hence a new image, thematic material and tonality of the closing section which nonetheless represents, together with the other sections of the exposition, a new successive phase in the modification of the main musical idea.

The development section follows the exposition as its logical outcome and leads just as naturally into the recapitulation. It takes up at a new and higher level the drive triggered in the exposition, especially as it manifested itself in the course of the transition section. To make the development as varied and intense as possible, the composer applies a wide range of devices.

No less original is his approach to the recapitulation, which is characterized by the fact that the principal and second subjects merge into a single theme as, for example, in the recapitulations from the opening movements of the sonata and symphony. This completely alters the usual profile of the recapitulation, but here again the composer avoids standardization, achieving this merger in different ways. One of them consists of combining the rhythmic design of the second subject with the thematic material of the principal subject as is the case in the recapitulation from the initial movement of the *Third Violin and Piano Sonata*. The other makes the second subject to engulf as it were, modified intonations typical

The Master in old age.

of the principal subject as exemplified in the recapitulation from the first movement of the *C-major Symphony*. In choosing one way or the other, Enesco is guided solely by a consideration determined by the dramaturgic layout of the work in question, that is to say, which of the two themes—the principal or the second subject—plays a decisive role in influencing the course of the development section. To redress the balance tipped by the lack of the second theme, the composer introduces an episode into the recapitulation as seen in the *Third Violin and Piano Sonata*. But here the term "episode" should not be applied literally, for the thematic material of such an additional formation is not a new one but represents a new manifestation of the monothematic modification of the chief musical idea.

As to the coda, it marks the completion of the whole previous development and at the same time synthesizes it. This twofold function of the coda makes it possible to assert the main idea of the work in a very convincing manner. In the course of this process, there may appear seemingly new material which, however, takes its roots in some previous nucleus, one hitherto of secondary importance from the thematic standpoint. Surprisingly enough, it is just this kind of material that the composer chooses to carry the brunt of his principal idea, as in the coda from the first movement of the *C-major Symphony*.

The analysis of Enesco's art would be incomplete without a study of his instrumental style, of his way of handling solo voices in chamber and orchestral music. This style is inseparable from the vast experience he gained as a concert violinist, conductor, quartet player and pianist.

As we have already seen, as a violinist, he had at his disposal a wide variety of means aimed at achieving striking expressive results. Besides the phrasing and other qualities mentioned previously, these were largely due to his ability to modulate his tone for which

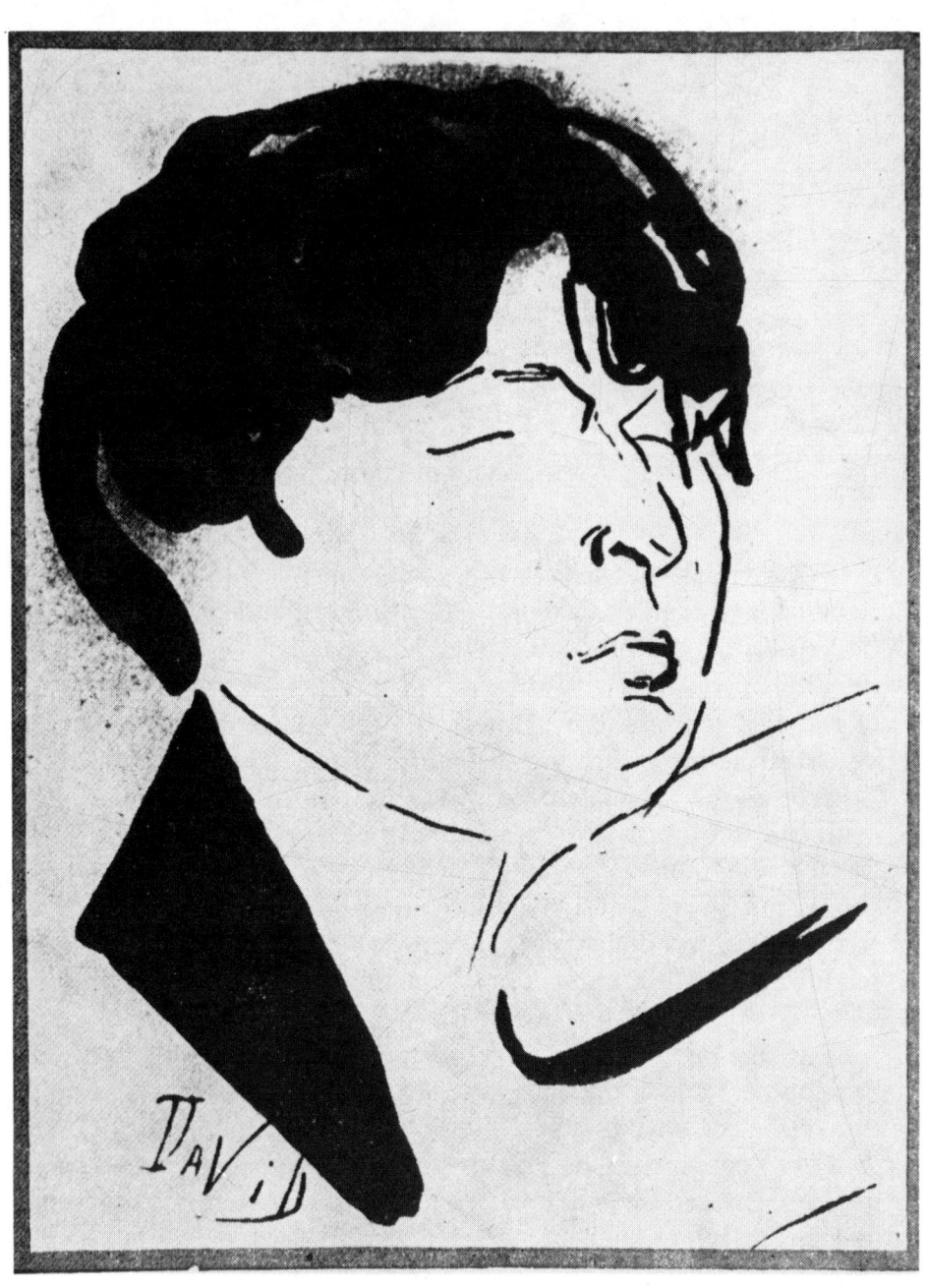

A caricature of Enesco by David.

he had been so justly renowned. He could, in fact, make it assume any character he wanted by using a technique seldom excelled by other famous violinists. It involved a subtle combination of frequency and amplitude changes of vibrato with a special positioning of the bow. Changing its place between the bridge and the board of the violin as well as altering the angle formed by the bow and the string, he modified the rate of upper-and-under-tones, thereby giving the sound new coloring. This technique is especially manifest in his own compositions, such as the *Third Violin and Piano Sonata* and the suite *Impressions of Childhood*. They also provide many other examples illustrating the specific character of Enesco's instrumental style. Probably the most edifying are those which concern the employment of trills and melismata. Following the popular tradition, Enesco uses them abundantly as a means of vitalizing the musical tissue. They appear not only on the main notes, but also on passing notes; they literally electrify the musical fabric with rapid sparkling trills, mordents and all sorts of appoggiaturas.

With regard to the works just mentioned, it must be said that they constitute a document unique in violin literature inasmuch as they show how popular traditions can be combined with the highest manifestations of the virtuoso concert technique. With the greatest reverence for Vivaldi and Ravel, it must be recognized that neither the former's *Seasons*, nor the latter's *Tzigane*, splendid as they are, go as far in this respect as does Enesco in his *Third Violin and Piano Sonata* or in "The lautar" and "The bird in a cage" from the *Impressions of Childhood*. Besides their artistic value, the significance of these two works lies in the fact that they expand horizons in this direction, showing an example which, it is hoped, will be followed by other composers.

Reviewing Enesco's style, the role of the piano should not be underestimated. He treated it as a universal instrument capable of expressing the most subtle gradations of human emotions, an instrument whose registers could be used as different voices or groups of voices of the orchestra. This attitude had already manifested itself in his early piano suite "In the Old Style" where there is a definite relationship between contrasting emotional dispositions and various kinds of touche and piano texture. This is felt especially in the third movement of the suite—Adagio—in which the organ-like large flowing sonority evokes associations with a profound restrained emotion. In the course of years, his writing becomes more varied, as can be seen in his piano sonatas, whose complex texture looks like an orchestral score abundantly displaying various tone-color effects. The affinity between his orchestral and piano writing is exemplified in many ways, particularly in the fact that he often indicates, in one bar, different phrasing markings to be followed simultaneously in the right and left hand parts.

In the *Concert Piece for Viola and Piano*, the former is treated as a solo instrument, but the piano is assigned a role that goes far beyond the requirements of sheer accompaniment. The viola part is very developed and varied and deserves all the more attention considering that at the time (1906), the viola had been rather neglected as a solo instrument. A point of interest in this respect is that Enesco makes use of the full range of the instrument from the lower C to F third octave—a range clearly connected with solo violin writing. Besides, the viola part contains many tone-color effects reproducing the sound of woodwind and popular plucked instruments. With his *Concert Piece,* Enesco fostered the renewal of interest in the viola on behalf of other composers who, like Hindemith, devote a great deal of attention to this instrument.

Enesco's instrumental style acquires new features in his chamber music works, becoming more and more elaborate. In his violin or cello sonatas, it attains such a high degree of virtuosity that those works could in fact be rightly called "concertos for two instruments without orchestra." Instrumental parts, especially in his mature ensembles, assume a very individualized character, forming a consistent whole. They are combined in such a way as to form an active dialogue in the course of which the participants exchange statements, often passing from one register to another. This lively "conversation" is rendered more vivid still, thanks to an extensive use of the various polyphonic devices spoken of above. All this contribute to creating a very dynamic fabric whose contrasting nature is further emphasized by varied applications of the rich technical resources of string and keyboard instruments. Particularly effective is the use of the "singing" propensity of the violin and cello which seems to be all the more impressive against the specific background of the piano part.

In his string quartets, the individualization of each instrumental part becomes especially evident. This refers particularly to the polyphonic framework where every melodic line is brought out with the greatest care.

Seeking new tone-color effects, Enesco turned to a combination of ten wind instruments unfamiliar in early twentieth century music. In so doing, he again anticipated what seems to be a general tendency of the time—the desire to bring to the forefront the group of wind instruments which later culminated in so many interesting works for wood and brass instruments by Hindemith, Schönberg, Milhaud, Stravinsky and other composers. In his *Dixtuor* Enesco shows even more clearly than in his previous compositions a desire for a solo treatment of various instruments forming an ensemble. This feature of his style, reflecting a tendency towards the "personification" of instrumental parts, manifested itself in full in his last work—*Chamber Symphony for Twelve Solo Instruments.* Here the solo instruments are used not to depict the pastoral world as in the *Dixtuor,* but to convey a human tragedy—the tragedy of the artist himself.

Throughout his life, the Rumanian composer had been fascinated

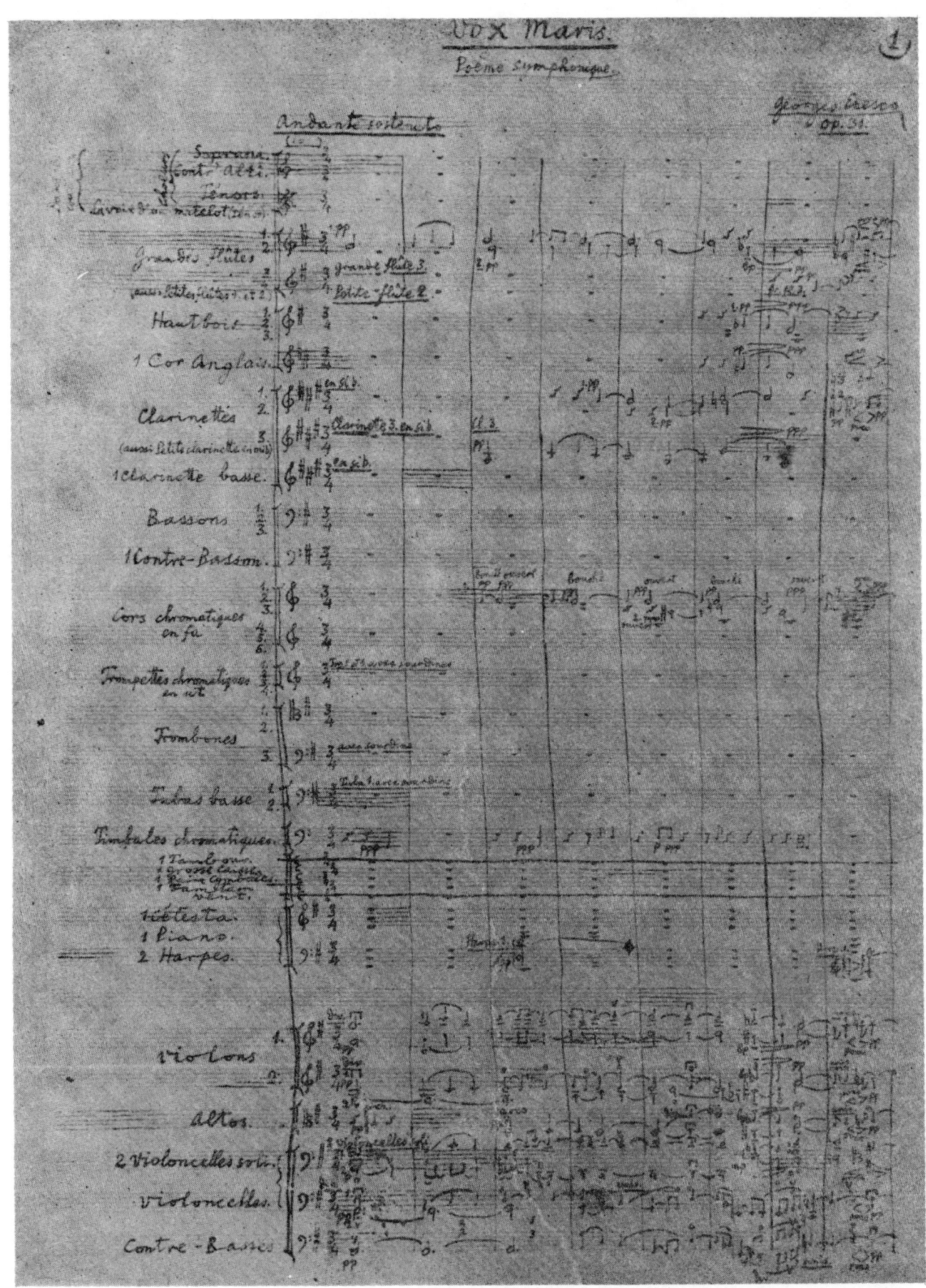

The first page of the score of the symphonic poem *Vox Maris*.

by the orchestra which he used to express his most cherished ideas. No matter how important in character and scope they were, he was never tempted by a grandiose orchestra. Unlike many of his colleagues, he felt no sympathy for extravagant instrumental combinations of the jazz-type orchestra. Nor did he write for electronic instruments so much favored by a number of his French friends. While he was a great admirer of popular instruments, he did not follow the example of Z. Kodaly or others who introduced them in their orchestras. He had no desire to replace the existing instruments by whistles, typewriters, hammers, iron plates or other noise-producing objects, the only exception being the wind and thunder machines he used in *Oedipe* and the poem *Vox maris*.

In his compositions, he kept to the traditional symphony orchestra with the addition, when necessary, of a small flute, corne anglaise, double-bass clarinet and bassoon, as well as one or two harps. When required, he would enlarge the orchestra's resources either by augmenting the number of already existing instruments or by introducing additional ones.[187] He often made use of the piano to enrich the orchestral coloring, taking advantage of its lowest register

One of the last pictures of Georges Enesco.

to darken the orchestral tissue or of its upper ones to give the strings a touch of harshness. On several occasions, Enesco uses muted instruments in his scores, applying this effect not only to the strings, but also to the brass, including the trumpet and the trombone. In fact, a series of parallel fourths and fifths played by muted trumpets and trombones accounts much for the peculiar atmosphere which surrounds the appearance of the Sphinx in the opera *Oedipe*. For coloristic purposes, kettledrums too can be muffled not only in the usual way, but also by using sticks wrapped in sponge.

For Enesco, it is rather unusual to employ a huge battery of percussion instruments so often found in contemporary music. In most cases he limits himself to a triangle, a large and a small drum, a pair of cymbals and castanets keeping tam-tam, various rattles and a bell for special effects, for example, in the *Third Symphony, Oedipe* and *Vox maris*.

In his orchestra, the composer very frequently uses solo instruments whose contrasting timbres provide him with an additional source of subtle expressive combinations. A characteristic feature of his style is that at a given moment he can single out any instrument from the orchestra for solo purposes. In so doing, he would pay special attention not only to the violin or viola, but to the cello and double bass as well, as for instance, in the opera *Oedipe* whose scoring was so highly praised by Vuillermoz in his aforementioned article from the magazine "Excelsior". Being precise as usual, Enesco indicates the exact number of instruments to be used solo in an orchestral group. This can be seen in the *C-major Symphony* where he specifies that of the twelve double-basses, two should be soli. Grouping the solo instruments into pairs, the composer apparently wants to preserve a proper sound balance between them and the rest of the orchestra. It is interesting to note that in so doing he differentiates between the two singled-out instruments in an evident desire to activate the role of each of them, as is the case in the opening bars of the *Third Symphony*. Developing this technique aimed at the utmost individualization of every instrumental part, the Rumanian master turns the contrast between his soli and tutti into a substantial source of additional expressive effects. The greater the difference between contrasting timbres, the more significant do these effects become. Developing this principle of orchestration still further, Enesco makes the timbre contrast serve a definite dramaturgic aim. His scores contain many examples showing how effective this technique may be. Among others, let us recall the tragic effect caused by the striking contrast he produced in opposing the animated improvisation of a "lonely" flute in its upper register against the ostinato background of the leitmotiv of parricide carried by the bassoon in the third scene of the opera *Oedipe*. It must be added that the composer applied this principle not only to solo instruments. Combining various instruments, he built up entire orchestral layers contrasting in coloring and intensity of sound whose skillful interconnection becomes a part of his timbre dramaturgy.

Its specific character and dynamic power depend very much on his approach to the violin part which he works out with special care. While other bow instruments are used—as a rule, only in separate solo passages of relatively brief duration—the solo violin can be assigned a far more conspicuous role. In this connection, let us mention the second subject from the first movement of the *C-major Symphony* whose emotional character and national coloring are, to a large extent due to the use of a solo violin. Confronting its improvisational figurations and freely ornamented texture with the rest of the orchestra, Enesco makes his instrumental writing acquire a very specific character (viz. the said movement of the symphony).

Another typical feature of Enesco's style constitutes a practice which leads to a split of the orchestral score. Thus, he can form a small ensemble inside an orchestra. This is exemplified in his *Second Rumanian Rhapsody* where he introduces a dance episode played by a string quartet. This makes one think of a group of gypsy players suddenly emerging to the proscenium from the orchestra to execute their clue number and afterwards regaining their former places, as individual performers used to do in the days of popular rondos. A similar way of singling out an instrumental ensemble within an orchestra as well as the use of a substantial solo violin improvisation emphasizes once again the popular and national background of Enesco's orchestral style.

Expertly using coloristic effects as a means to conjure up external circumstances and particularly a generic atmosphere, Enesco, as a composer and conductor, never envisaged these effects merely as a descriptive attribute. The fact that the sound coloring of his music fitted with a given poetic idea or emotional disposition eventually became one of the distinctive features of his art of orchestration. This is especially true of his mature scores in which leitcoloring or leittimbre plays a very prominent role. So, the leitmotiv of destiny identified itself with the morbid sound of the double-bassoon, tainted by the ostinato figure in the first violin part, while that of parricide from the same opera was associated with the gloomy coloring of the bassoon. But the fusion of coloring and image into a single whole is met not only in his opera score. Let us quote as an example the recapitulation from the first movement of the *C-major Symphony* which sounds particularly pure, due to the lucid timbre of the violins coupled with harp accompaniment.

The identification of coloring with an artistic image helps Enesco to strengthen the unity of an artwork. Among many cases of such a dramaturgic approach to the tone-color problem, it will suffice to mention the use of similar orchestration at the beginning of acts one and three of the opera.

Finally, speaking of the expressive qualities of Enesco's orchestral writing it must be said that he made extensive use of both pure and mixed timbres. The latter he would obtain in different ways: he

Enesco's letter of April 17, 1933 to the Academia Romana.

either combined instruments of various types from the outset, or, following the traditions of such masters as Wagner and Mahler, gradually put one instrumental coloring over the other. His usual way to build up such a color-pyramid was as follows: the first to enter were, for instance, one bassoon with one hautboy; then he coupled them with a clarinet combined with one flute, later adding some bow instrument and so on. Such examples of overlapping timbres are very numerous, especially in the opera *Oedipe* where they occur both in unison or octave doubling and in a single chord. Such consecutive timbre superpositions in his music acquire so prominent a role that to speak about the "timbre-polyphonic" character of his orchestral style is justified.

In a number of cases, Enesco enriches his symphonic scores by the use of chorus. This practice is adopted in his larger compositions, such as the *C-major Symphony*, the opera *Oedipe* and the symphonic poem *Vox maris*. In each of them the treatment of the chorus and choral writing are not the same, being determined respectively by the conception of the work in question. The Rumanian musicologist O.L. Cosma suggests that Enesco's choral writing combined certain features of the monumental oratorio style of Bach and Händel, the expressive laconism of Gluck's choruses with the plasticity and inner dynamism of Mussorgsky's music.[188] This characterization should be completed by special reference to the influence of Beethoven's *Fidelio* and the choral finale of his *Ninth Symphony* on the formation of Enesco's approach to the chorus as well as his links with Wagner's choral technique. *Oedipe* and *Boris Godunov* are also connected by the fact that the Rumanian composer, like Mussorgsky, treats the chorus in an active manner, regarding it as an embodiment of the people representing an effective force. This has been pointed out in the course of the above analysis of the lyrical tragedy written by Enesco. Beethoven's influence helped him to shape his attitude to the chorus as an important factor aimed at generalizing the content of the work, at the same time ascertaining its central idea. As for Wagner, his influence can account for the fact that for Enesco, the chorus, despite all its importance, is made only to continue the line of symphonic development whose driving impulse is centered on the orchestra.

On a number of occasions Enesco handles the chorus in a coloristic way as one of the voices of the symphonic score. This is especially the case in the *C-major Symphony* ending with a choral finale where the choir sings without words. In *Vox maris* the composer uses a reduced choir, made up of soprano, alto and tenor voices—and a tenor soloist, the text of whose part determines the programmatic content of the poem. The chorus here has a partly coloristic and a partly semantic function since it contains only one single exclamation—"ah!"—insistently recurring throughout the work. There appear episodically some words in the soprano solo part which underline the dramatic character of the music. But even

Modest Mussorgsky.

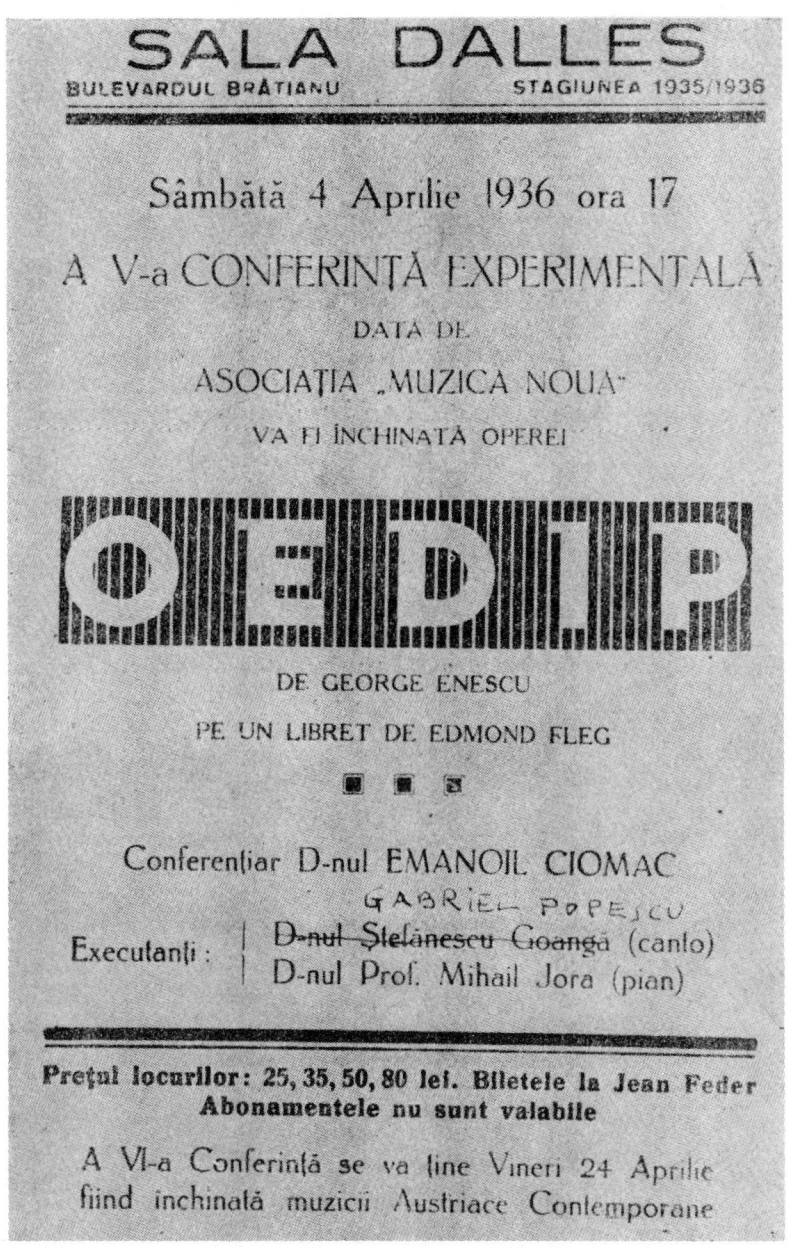

Poster for the *Muzica Noua's* fifth "experimental conference," at which excerpts from *Oedipe* were performed.

in the absence of a text, the chorus can fulfill the role of the most important dramatizing factor as is the case in some sections of the choral finale to the *C-major Symphony*.

Enesco uses a great variety of technical means in his choral writing. The whole choral body is usually called upon to strengthen focal points and dramatic climaxes. His favorite technique involves the confrontation of a female and a male singer or full or incomplete choirs as, for instance, in *Oedipe* or the finale of the *C-major Symphony*. Using a succession of contrasting choral groups, he obtains many expressive effects which enhance the emotional impact of his art. In the search for additional expressive means, he often singles out a solo voice from some choral group in much the same way as in dealing with his orchestra. In the main, his choral writing and or-

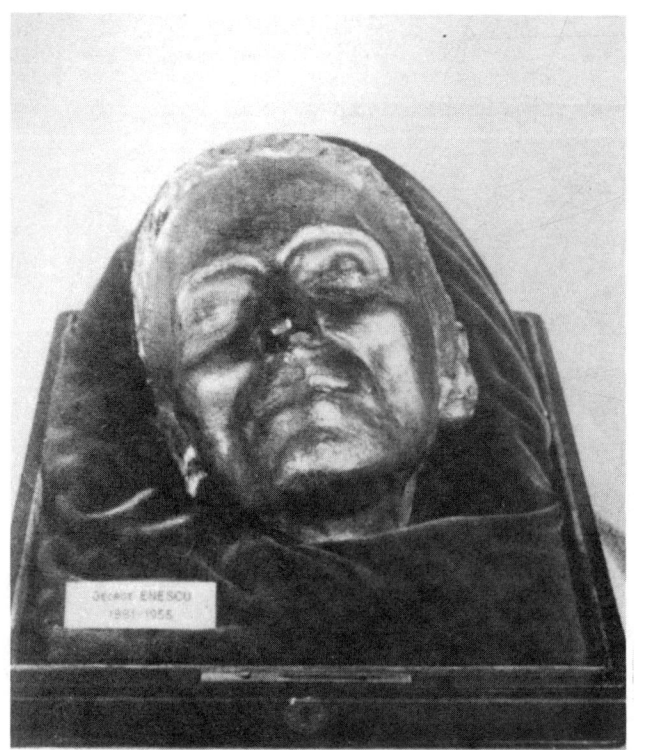

Top left: Enesco's death-mask; **top right:** A hall of the Georges Enesco Permanent Display.

Bottom: Rumanian composers and musicians at Enesco's grave in Paris (1956).

Poster for symphony concerts in memory of Georges Enesco (1955).

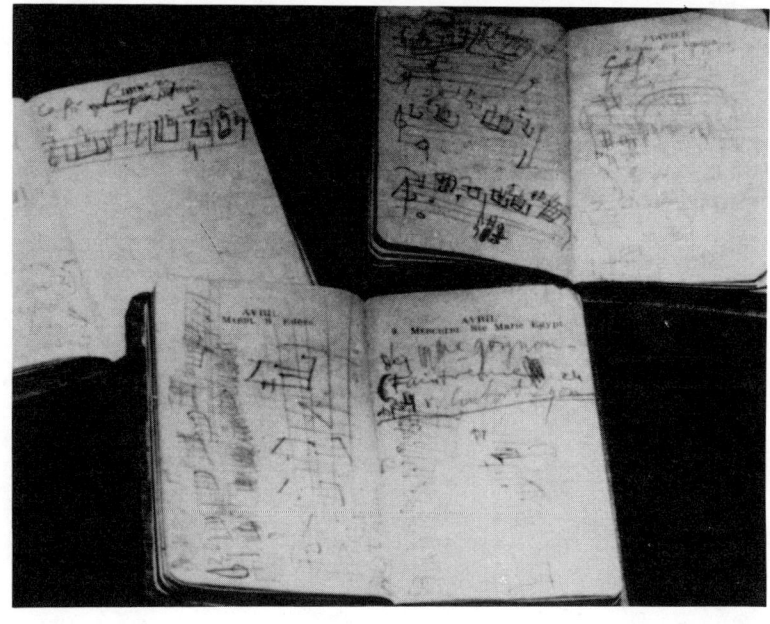

Enesco's composition notebooks.

chestral writing are in many respects identical, taking into consideration the specific nature of vocal and instrumental art. In the relationship between them, the latter plays a leading role and this makes his choral technique clearly assume the character of vocal "instrumentation."

To complete the survey of Enesco's choral style, it is necessary to mention one more characteristic feature, namely the use of collective speech recitation capable of producing effects of tremendous dramatic power as, for example, in the third act of the opera *Oedipe*. This type of recitation, expressing the people's reaction to the horrors that had befallen the city of Thebes, is all the more appropriate here since, according to the traditions of the Greek tragedy, the chorus represented the collective personality of the people.

★ ★ ★

The Rumanian government and the Rumanian people have been highly appreciative of the merits of Georges Enesco, who, as a celebrated musician, one of the founders of the National Academy

The headstone of Enesco's grave.

Gheorghe Anghel's sculpture of Enesco for the Rumanian Atheneum.

of Sciences and a member of the Grand People's Assembly, had contributed so much to the development of Rumanian as well as international musical art. To perpetuate his memory, an international competition and a festival bearing his name are held every three years in Bucharest. His name has been given to the Bucharest Philharmonic; a number of "Georges Enesco" scholarships have been regularly granted to the best students of the Bucharest Conservatoire; his native village Liveni is now called the village "Georges Enesco" where his native home has been transformed into a memorial museum; a Georges Enesco museum has been established in the capital and also in the town of Dorohoi. Recently, to mark the centenary of his birth, there has been issued a full edition of his recordings and a cinema version of the opera *Oedipe*. The centenary celebrations also included an international festival held in Bucharest at which many of the world's leading musical personalities gathered to pay their tribute to the memory of the great master.

Although Enesco died far from his beloved native homeland, his thoughts may have been of his young compatriots urging them to continue the cause he had served so devotedly to the last days of his life. And this bequest echoes again his words: "how lucky you, the young, must be who can fulfill what we have been unable to do!"[189] This appeal to the future reinforces the thoughts and feelings of a great artist and humanist who had unselfishly devoted his long eventful life to the service of the art whose aim was ". . . to lead people forward on the way to the better."[190]

Notes

[1] "Cuvintul liber", 1934, 17 martie, n 19. In a number of cases Enesco's quotations are reproduced in this book from the following set of articles: "Georges Enesco". Editura muzicala a uniunii compozitorilor din RPR, Bucuresti, 1964.

[2] B. Gavoty, Les souvenirs de G. Enesco, édition "Flammarion", Paris, 1955. This book represents a literary version of Enesco's Mémoires by the French musicologist Bernard Gavoty (Russian shortened edition—Georges Enesco—Reminiscences and Biographic Materials, 1966).

[3] This fact was communicated to me by the director of the "G. Enesco" Museum in Bucharest, R. Draghici (viz. the author's personal file at the Central State Archives of the MSSR, f. R-2960).

[4] B. Gavoty, ibid., p. 112.

[5] Cobza—a plucked folk instrument well-known in Rumania and Moldavia, used solo and in popular orchestra (taraf). Formerly its strings were plucked with a goose feather.

[6] In this connection it is interesting to note that the violin was already well-known in Moldavia as early as the beginning of the XV century (viz. B. Kotliarov, "About Violin Culture in Moldavia," Kishinjov, 1955.

[7] B. Gavoty, ibid., p. 84.

[8] B. Gavoty, ibid., p. 105.

[9] B. Gavoty, ibid.

[10] B. Gavoty, ibid., p. 180.

Chapter 1

[11] B. Gavoty, ibid., p. 180.

[12] B. Gavoty, ibid., p. 51.

[13] "Rampa noua ilustrata", 1916, n. 279, 19 Iunie.

[14] B. Gavoty, ibid., p. 117.

[15] B. Gavoty, ibid., p. 56.

[16] Idem, p. 60.

[17] "Muzica", 1921, n 5-6, p. 95, 96.

Chapter 2

[18] Romain Rolland—"Jean Christophe" Works, Vol. 4, Moscow, M., p. 324.

[19] B. Gavoty, ibid., p. 65, 66.

[20] B. Gavoty, ibid., p. 65.

[21] Idem, p. 68.

[22] French Music of the Second Half of the 19th Century. "Iskusstvo", M., 1938, p. 241.
[23] H.M. Corredor, "Conversations with Pablo Casals" "Muzgiz", 1960, p. 233.
[24] B. Gavoty, ibid., p. 75.
[25] Doina—a folk melody played or sung without accompaniment. Its emotional sphere is very wide, ranging from a lyrical lamentation to dramatic and epic images.

Instrumental doinas consist of a slow part and a rapid part, the first being improvisational and tuneful, the second rhythmically very well organized and sounding like a cheerful dance.

[26] That is how Enesco himself describes the program of the Rumanian Poem (B. Gavoty, ibid., p. 80).
[27] R. Rolland, ibid., p. 328.
[28] B. Gavoty, ibid., p. 73.
[29] B. Gavoty, ibid., p. 168.
[30] H.M. Corredor, ibid., p. 234.

Chapter 3

[31] Idem, p. 153.
[32] A. Tudor, "Enesco", Bucharest, 1957, p. 41-42.
[33] B. Gavoty, ibid., p. 158.
[34] Lautar—a professional folk-musician, a fiddler.
[35] The second sonata is available on record n 61-2 produced by the Rumanian firm "Electrecord".
[36] B. Gavoty, ibid., p. 159.
[37] B. Gavoty, ibid., p. 156.
[38] B. Gavoty, ibid., p. 156, 157.
[39] B. Gavoty, ibid., p. 85.
[40] B. Gavoty, ibid., p. 86.
[41] B. Gavoty, ibid., p. 83.
[42] B. Gavoty, ibid., p. 89-90.
[43] "Ciocarlia" is a brilliant concert piece based on improvisation in which lautars employing a virtuoso technique imitate the singing of birds.
[44] A. Tudor, ibid., p. 41.
[45] "Cuvintul liber", 17 martie, 1937.
[46] M. Gorky, "About Literature", M., 1935, p. 195.
[47] B. Gavoty, ibid., p. 89.
[48] H.M. Corredor, ibid., p. 233.

Chapter 4

[49] The author is unable to analyze the *Second Symphony,* for its score is not available.
[50] Several times Enesco was offered asylum in a number of countries, but did not want to change his citizenship.

Chapter 5

[51] Enesco held the view that melody itself, and especially a popular melody, contained the backbone of its most suitable harmonization.
[52] It is impossible to say whether Enesco knew the *Suite for Thirteen Wind In-*

struments Op. 4 by R. Strauss written in 1884 and first published in 1911. But it may be assumed that his Dixtuor prompted other composers, such as Milhaud and Stravinsky, to use a large number of wind instruments in their chamber-music works.

[53] Enesco as a violinist and a composer frequently made use of this device when he wanted to stress the national background of his art.

[54] Fluer — a type of shepherd's flute.

[55] Enesco deeply admired the sonata by Franck. To understand his attitude toward this great master, it is interesting to recall that, while playing the serene and profoundly humanitarian theme from the third movement of Franck's sonata, he whispered in reverence the following words from the Latin mass: "Agnus Dei, qui tollis peccata mundi" (B. Gavoty, ibid., p. 120).

[56] Gorky was inspired in this poem by the rising revolutionary tide on the eve of the revolution of 1905. He symbolized his enthusiasm in the romantic figure of the stormy petrel — a sea bird which enjoyed the storm.

[57] Whether travelling throughout the world, or living in France, Enesco would regularly return to Rumania and visit his native village. In his spare time he would enjoy strolling about the countryside, mingling with peasants at village dances, listening to their music and writing it down.

[58] In a number of cases Enesco employs intervals which cannot be fixed on paper within the limits of present musical notation. Although he introduced special signs, indicating one quarter or three quarters of a tone, these by no means account for all the variety of his intonational deviations.

[59] "The Way They Play", Book 2 by Samuel and Sada Appelbaum, Paganiniana Publications, Inc., Neptune City, N.J., 1973, p. 74.

[60] The first performance of this work took place on February 2, 1939 in Carnegie Hall under the direction of the composer. It was played by the New York Philharmonic Orchestra, to which Enesco dedicated his *Third Suite*.

[61] In this connection it is interesting to recall a real story told to the author of this work by an old lautar. Once he was asked by a peasant to play something for him. When the musician inquired what piece he wanted to hear, the peasant said: "Do play on your violin about how a wheel of my cart broke down."

[62] B. Gavoty, ibid., p. 36.

[63] B. Gavoty, idem, p. 36.

[64] Here Enesco has in mind the tiny stream in the garden of his native house in the village of Liveni.

[65] B. Gavoty, idem.

[66] The same technique was used by Schumann in "Paganini" from his *Carnaval*.

[67] In his desire always to be precise Enesco went so far as to indicate in certain cases how long the rest should be between two movements of a work. In his *Third Piano Sonata*, for instance, he stipulates that the finale should be preceded by a pause lasting no less than ten seconds.

[68] B. Gavoty, ibid., p. 35.

[69] B. Gavoty, ibid., p. 37.

[70] B. Gavoty, idem.

[71] A. Pushkin. Selected works in II volumes. V. I (poetry). "Progress" publishers, Moscow, 1979, p. 34.

[72] As is known, Pushkin in his "Ruslan and Liudmila," used legends he had heard from his nanny (A. Pushkin. Compl. works in X volumes. Second edition. V. IV. Published by the Academy of Sciences. Moscow, 1957. p. 547 (note).

[73] B. Gavoty, idem.

[74] "Georges Enesco". Editura musicala a Uniunii compozitorilor din RPR, Bucuresti, 1964, p. 255.

Chapter 6

[75] "Scanteia", 1955, n 3286, May 18, p. 2.

[76] "Universul", 1937, n 307, November 7.

[77] There is a controversy about the date when Enesco resumed the work on *Oedipe*. In his souvenirs he says it was in 1924 in Lausanne while some Rumanian authors, for instance, L. Voiculeco mention other dates and places. " G. Enesco and his opera *Oedipe*, Editura de stat pentru literatura si arta, Bucuresti, 1956, p. 192.

[78] In his letter of November 21, 1968 an old Akkerman journalist, F.I. Konstantiner, says that he used to accompany Enesco on his trips to the fortress. He recalls that the composer would spend much time examining the moss-covered towers and, often stopping amidst the ruins, "kept on pondering" (the author's personal file in the Central State Archives of the MMMS, R-2960).

[79] The opera was presented by the best French singers with André Pernet in the title role. It was conducted by Phillippe Gaubert, stage direction by Pierre Chéreau, decorations by André Boll. Enesco wanted Chaliapin to portray the part of Oedipus, but the great singer declined his offer because of failing health.

[80] Edmond Fleg (1875-1963) is a well-known author of a number of historical novels and plays. He understood well the requirements of a musical drama, having written before *Oedipe*, a libretto of the opera *Macbeth* for E. Bloch. Among many authors who wrote about Oedipus, he was the first to create a comprehensive account of the story of this hero covering the whole of his life from birth to death. Besides the main events dealt with by Sophocles in his tragedies "Oedipus Rex" and "Oedipus in Colon", Fleg introduced in his play a number of episodes reconstituted on the basis of various legends related to his hero. His versified play, written in French, is published by Calmann Lévy (Paris, 1936).

[81] "Amateur Scientists", A.L. Herzents, Vol. 9, Bk. 2, 1955, p. 36-37.

[82] Sofokl, "Tragedies," M. 1958, p. 7.

[83] Sophocles, ibid., p. 96.

[84] "Gazeta romaneasca", 1936, n 3, January 20.

[85] "Gazeta", 1936, n 542, January 1.

[86] "Scanteia", 1955, n 3286, May 18, p. 2.

[87] In the third and fourth acts Fleg concentrated the main episodes of Sophocles' "Oedipus Rex" and "Oedipus in Colon" respectively. As to the first two acts, he wrote them on the basis of a number of antique legends.

[88] B. Gavoty, ibid., p. 133.

[89] For example, at the Paris performance there were about 350 people on stage during the mass scene of celebrations of Oedipus's victory over the Sphinx and his entry into the liberated city of Thebes.

[90] B. Gavoty, ibid., p. 147-148.

[91] B. Gavoty, ibid., p. 146.

[92] B. Gavoty, ibid., p. 151.

Speaking about this quality of the composer's music, it is worthwhile pointing out that he knew how to combine it with the greatest care in the choice of details. This is very well exemplified by his use of the musical saw which he introduces into the orchestra at the moment of Sphinx's death.

[93] It is possible that the roots of this theme should be sought even earlier. Its prototype might have already been contained in the descending figure from the waltz theme with which the last movement of the *Octet* begins (viz. ex. n 12).

[94] As a point of interest let us mention that these notes, if taken in inversion, form a descending semi-tone so typical of the opening of the leitmotiv of Fate. This small detail illustrates the constructive trend in Enesco's thinking which is

always made to serve an artistic purpose.

⁹⁵B. Gavoty, ibid., p. 144.
⁹⁶B. Gavoty, ibid., p. 146.
⁹⁷B. Gavoty, ibid., p. 145.
⁹⁸B. Gavoty, ibid., p. 146.
⁹⁹B. Gavoty, idem.
¹⁰⁰A. Tudor, ibid., p. 54.
¹⁰¹*Vox maris* was first performed in September 1965 at the third "Georges Enesco Festival" in Bucharest.
¹⁰²B. Gavoty, ibid., p. 163-164.
¹⁰³B. Gavoty, ibid., p. 162.

Chapter 7

¹⁰⁴H. Corredor, ibid., p. 285.
¹⁰⁵"Revista muzicala", 1928, n 1, p. 9.
¹⁰⁶"Scinteia", April 6, 1946, n 495.
¹⁰⁷The word "sympathy" had a special meaning for Enesco. It can best be grasped by bearing in mind his following words: "I know by experience that the best and the single way to understand someone is to grow fond of him." ("Georges Enesco", Editutura mizicala a uniunii compozitorilor din RPR, Bucuresti, 1964, *p. 20).*
¹⁰⁸"Democratia", March 25, 1945, n 21.
¹⁰⁹"The Washington Star", January 14, 1934.
¹¹⁰B. Gavoty, ibid., p. 162.
¹¹¹Enesco was greatly helped in playing Bach by his experience in composition and orchestral conducting. In his "Souvenirs" he offers very valuable advice as to how one should work on Bach. For example, he thought it necessary "to declare war on speed in order to insure a correct accentuation." Without proper accentuation, a prelude by Bach, in his opinion "was like water running from a tap." While playing a Bach melody it was essential to make its design look as clear and logical as possible. To achieve this he recommends taking the more complex scores in which the melodic line is interwoven with a contrapuntal tissue. To save a violinist from the risk of going astray in the *Chaconne*, for instance, Enesco suggests scoring the musical text in four parts. "Observe the timbre of each voice"—he says. "Try to imagine the first and the second soprano, the first and the second contralto; everything will then get clear." (B. Gavoty, ibid., p. 115).
¹¹²The Continental Record Company Inc. issued an excellent recording (Ta-33-016-021) of Bach's *Solo Sonatas and Partitas* played by Enesco. These three records provide priceless documentary material which every student of violin art will analyze with the utmost attention.
¹¹³See Enesco's letter to the Director of the Russian Musical Society of September 15, (28) 1909 (M. Glinka State Central Muzeum of Musical Culture, f. 80 N 2592).
¹¹⁴From E. Uminska's letter of June 27, 1978 (The Central State Archives of the MSSR, f. R-2960).
¹¹⁵How firm was his self-discipline as an interpreter in general, and in particular with regard to the concerto by Brahms shows in the following episode which the author of these lines had personally witnessed in the mid-thirties. The programme of one of his concerts in Liège (Belgium) included this work. During the interval the famous violinist first played the D-major scale in thirds several times, carefully verifying the intonation, and then took up the main theme of the Finale playing it over again very slowly seeking the most accurate bow-attack. When one of the

violinists assembled around him behind the stage inquired whether the maestro still needed to work on this concerto, he answered: "In such a work lies the great secret of how to master the intonation and bowing, and I need it no less than anybody else."

[116] Enesco, who had a phenomenal musical memory, learned this concerto by heart in only a couple of days.

[117] The Central State Archives of the MSSR, f. R-2960.

[118] A. Ginsburg, "A.A. Brandukov," Muzgiz. M. 1951, p. 24.

[119] Enesco also liked to play the viola, an instrument of which he was very fond.

[120] Among many occasions when Enesco played together with Casals, mention should be made of their concert given in 1937 to raise money for the International Brigade formed in Spain to fight against the fascist rebellion led by General Franco.

[121] This sonata is available on record ("Electrecord" 95) the study of which will provide the student of the performing art with the most valuable data.

[122] On this occasion his partners were some of the best Rumanian musicians: C. Bobesco (second violin), A. Radulesco (viola) and F. Lupu (cello).

[123] "Muzica", 1955 N 5, p. 15.

[124] D. Oistrakh and Y. Menuhin performed Bach's Double Concerto in Bucharest with George Georgesco as conductor to commemorate the achievements of the great Rumanian musician at the Festival "Georges Enesco" in 1958.

[125] In this connection it is interesting to note that at a concert given in Iasi in 1919, Enesco was the soloist in the *Violin Concerto* by Beethoven and the *E-flat major Concerto* of Liszt. Enesco took part as a pianist in the performance of Stravinsky's "La Noce" under L. Stokowski in New York; the other three piano parts were played by A. Casella, C.Salzedo and the French woman composer G. Tailleferre ("Scateia", 6 aprilie 1946, N 495).

[126] F. Litvin, "My Life and My Art", Leningrad, 1967, p. 71.

[127] The numbers are given according to the Augener's edition of 42 Studies by R. Kreutzer, N 5671.

[128] "Gazeta", 25 decembrie 1935, N 538.

[129] "Viitorul", 13 (26) Ianuarie 1908, N 65.

[130] "Neamul rominesc", 24 decembrie 1936, N 281.

[131] "Georges Enesco", edit, muz. a Uniunii compozitorilor din RPR, Bucuresti, 1964, p. 69.

[132] "Soviet Music", 1966, N. 7, p. 111.

[133] "Cuvintul", 1942.

[134] "Rampa noua ilustrata", 19 iunie, N 279.

[135] "Dimineata", 19 octombrie 1936, N10713.

[136] "Russian Music Newspaper," 1909, N 42, p. 3.

[137] "The New Time," 10/19/09, N 12064, p. 3.

[138] A. U. Siloti, "Reminiscences and Letters," L. 1963, p. 437.

[139] M. Paléologue, "La Russie des tsars pendant la grande guerre," Paris, librairie Plon, 1922, vol. III, p. 216.

[140] "Letter from a Rumanian Desk," G. Enesco, May 9, 1917.

[141] "Scanteia", 6 aprilie 1946, N 495.

[142] "Femaia si caminul," 6 mai 1945, N 22.

[143] "Viac nou", 29 decembrie 1945, N 4.

[144] At this concert he conducted the *Symphony N 7* by Shostakovitch, Balakirev's symphonic poem *Tamara* and the *4th Symphony* of Tchaikovsky.

[145] "Muzica" 1955, N 5, p. 327.

[146] "Music," 1946, N 5, pgs. 9-11.

[147] L'indépendance roumaine" , le 26 octobre (8 novembre) 1915, N 12229.

[148] "Music", 1946, N 5, pgs. 10-11.

[149] "Muzica", 1955 N 5, p. 30.

Chapter 8

[150]"Muzica", 1955, N 5, p. 14.
[151]"Scanteia", 6 aprilie 1946, N 495.
[152]"Cuvatul liber", 17 martie 1934, N 19.
[153]Idem.
[154]"The American Hebrew", 1937.
[155]"Je sais tout de Bucareste", le 20 novembre 1939, N 7-8.
[156]"America", 19 februarie 1924, N 41.
[157]"Muzica si poezia", 1936.
[158]"Dimineata", 27 septembrie 1942, N 3.
[159]"Femeia si caminul", 6 mai 1945, N 22.
[160]"The American Hebrew", 1937.
[161]"The American Hebrew", 1924.
[162]"Scanteia", 6 aprilie 1946, N 495.
[163]"Cuvantul liber", 17 martie 1934, N 19.
[164]R. Dumesnil, "La musique en France entre les deux guerres 1919-1939", édit. "Milieu du monde", p. 43-44.
[165]"Democratia", 25 martie 1945, N 21.
[166]"Femeia si caminul", 6 mai 1945, N 22.
[167]Idem.
[168]The concert programme of the Chicago Symphony Orchestra for the 1931-1932 season.
[169]"Jurnalul de dimineata", 6 mai 1945, N 143.
[170]Idem.
[171]"Lumina carasului", 1930.
[172]"Femeia si caminul', 1945, N 195.
[173]"Rampa", 26 septembrie 1931, N 4096.
[174]"Rampa noua ilustrata", 19 iunie 1916, N 279.
[175]"La revue musicale", juillet-aout 1931, p. 158.
[176]"Timpul", 6 iulie 1939, N 781.
[177]"Propasirea", 17 decembrie 1938, N 75.
[178]I. Nestjev, "Ideology and Aesthetic to study of Bartok's Heritage", "Soviet Music", 1965, N. 4, pgs. 99-102.
[179]"Femeia si caminul", 6 mai 1945, N 22.
[180]"Dimineata", 19 octombrie 1936, N N 10713.
[181]"La tribune de Geneve", le 7 mai 1924, N 108.
[182]"Dimineata", 19 octombrei 1936, N 10713.

It goes without saying that, as we already know, there was no simplification in Enesco's approach to the subject. The importance he attached to melodic expression can be illustrated by the following episode kindly related to the author of this book by the director of the "Georges Enesco" museum in Bucharest, R. Draghici. The latter recalls his encounter with Enesco in the Iasi home of their common friend, the composer E. Caudella, soon after the end of the First World War. They talked about certain tendencies in music of the time and particularly about the lack of melodic expression in a number of contemporary works. Discussing the matter, Enesco remarked that he did not envisage music outside melodic expression (from R. Draghici's letter, The Central State Archives of the MSSR, f. R-2960).

[183]An interesting essay on the zonal nature of auditive perception is written by Prof. N. Garbuzov ("Nature of Music Hearing," Muzgiz. M. 1956).
[184]This affinity of style, besides personal relations, might have prompted Ysaÿe to dedicate his third solo violin sonata to the Rumanian musician (L. Ginsburg, "Eugene Ysaÿe," Muzgiz, M., 1959, p. 124).
[185]C. Taranu, "Confluenta Enesco-Messiaen si reflectarea ei in muzica contemporana romaneasca", Lucrari de muzicologie, vol. 3, Cluj, 1967, p. 17.

[186] This interesting feature of Honegger's style is mentioned by L. Rapoport in his book "Arthur Honegger", L. 1967, p. 288.

[187] For instance, in the *C-major Symphony* string players reach the number of 76 while in *vox maris* there are 6 horns and 4 trumpets. The first symphony is scored for two cornets à piston in addition to two trumpets. Among additional instruments introduced in several works the most frequently used are: flute alto, clarinet in Es, trumpet in D, trumpet and tuba tenor, saxophone, xylophone, celesta, harmonium, organ and piano.

[188] O.L. Cosma, "Oedipul enescian", Editura muzicala a Uniunii compozitorilor din RSR, Bucuresti, 1967, p. 240.

[189] "Muzica", 1955, N5, p. 16.

[190] Ibidem.

Index

Page numbers in *italics* refer to illustrations.

A

Alessandresco, Alfred, 184, *185*
Altchevsky, I., 168
Auer, Leopold, 151, 177

B

Bach, Johann Sebastian, 8, 10, 11, 25, 122, 155, *157*, 157, 159, 165, 168, 171, 177, 178, 182, 224
Bachrich, Sigismund, 21
Balzac, Honoré de, 23
Bartók, Béla, 166, *198*, 199, 205
Basarab, M., 185
Beethoven, Ludwig van, 8, 12, 18, 26, 49, 70, 120, 122, 152, 154, 155, 157, 160, 163, 165, 166, 171, 177, 182, 183, 184, 186, 224
Berlioz, Hector, 23, 39, 40, *40*, 69, 125, 129, 175, 183
Bizet, Georges, 23, 140
Blumenfeld, Felix, 177
Böhm, Joseph, 21
Brahms, Johannes, 12, *19*, 26, 52, 53, 122, 156, 157, 160, 161, 162, 168, 177
Brandukov, A., 165
Briushkov, I., 180

C

Casadesus, Henri, 166, *177*
Casals, Pablo, 27, *30*, 30, 31, 47, 105, 165, 168
Casella, Alfred, 166, *167*
Chaliapin, Fedor, *155*, 156, 166, *177*, 177
Chausson, Ernest, 152, 155, 163, 164, 171, 182
Ciolan, A., 185
Cocteau, Jean, 108
Colonne, Edouard, 27, *27*, 37
Cortot, Alfred, 27, 30, *165*, 165, 166, 168
Corneille, Pierre, 110
Cosma, O.L., 224
Couperin, Louis, 25, 155

Cristesco, M., 185
Cuclin, D., 184

D

Daniélou, J., 108
Debussy, Claude, 39, 45-47, 155, 156, 157, 163, 164, 184
Dinicu, Dimitrie, *162*
Dont, Jakob, 21, 172
Dragoi, S., 184
Dukas, Paul, 184
Dumas, Alexandre, Sr., 8
Dumesnil, René, 184
Dvorak, Antonin, 175

E

Elizabeth, Queen of Rumania, 71
Enesco, Georges (illustrations), *6, 8, 10, 12, 14, 15, 20, 22, 23, 32, 33, 41, 44, 48, 51, 55, 58, 61, 63, 65, 71, 72, 78, 93, 95, 96, 133, 141, 150, 153, 156, 159, 162, 165, 167, 168, 169, 172, 173, 177, 179, 180, 181, 182, 184, 185, 186, 187, 190, 192, 195, 196, 199, 200, 208, 211, 212, 215, 216, 220, 229*

References to musical works:
A Chamber Symphony for Twelve Solo Instruments, 149, 218
Concert Overture on a Rumanian Popular Theme, 86, 103
Concert Piece for Viola and Piano, 210, 217, 218
Concert Symphony for Cello and Orchestra, 42
Concerto for Violin and Orchestra, 55
Concerto for Violin, Cello, and Orchestra, 56
Dixtuor, 20, 73, 74, 199, 201, 218
Impressions of Childhood, 20, 70, 86-103, 164, 201, 204, 206, 217
Octet, 31, 36-42, 66
Oedipe, 12, 46, 68, 102, 105-148, 202, 206, 210, 213, 214, 220, 221, 224, 225, 228, 229
Quartet No. 2 for Strings, 149

Rumanian Poem, 27, 28, 29, 41, 42, 73, 87, 176, 184, 199, 213
Rumanian Rhapsody No. 1, 9, 41, 42, 95, 176, 184, 199, 201, 213
Rumanian Rhapsody No. 2, 41, 42, 73, 176, 184, 199, 213, 222
Rustic Suite, 70, 86, 87, 103
Sonata No. 1 for Piano, F-sharp minor, 128, 203, 206, 209, 213, 214
Sonata No. 2 for Violin and Piano, 31, 33-36, 41, 45, 97, 164, 201, 206, 209
Sonata No. 3 for Violin and Piano, 62, 70, 73-87, 95, 102, 103, 122, 126, 127, 146, 164, 166, 202, 203, 204, 206, 209, 210, 211, 214, 215, 217
Suite for Orchestra, 42, 97
Suite for Piano, op. 10, 213·
Suite for Piano, "In Old Style," 29, 213, 217
Symphony No. 1, E-flat major, 49
Symphony No. 3, C major, 50-71, 78, 102, 128, 194, 203, 204, 209, 211, 213, 214, 215, 216, 221, 222, 224, 225
Three Melodies, 29
Vox Maris, 148, 220, 221, 224, 225

Enescu, Costache (father), *14, 15*
Enescu, Maria (mother), *14, 15*
Ernst, Heinrich Wilhelm, 21

F

Fauré, Gabriel, 26, *27*, 27, 107, 151, 156, 168
Fleg, Edmond, 109, 110, 111, 112
Fournier, Louis, 166, *167*
Francescatti, Zino, 179
Franck, César, *11*, 11, 12, 23, 36, 152, 156, 157, 163, 182
Fuchs, Robert, 21

G

Gedalge, André, 26, *26*, 211
Georgescu, George, 159, 185

Ghertsen (Herzen), Alexander, 109
Gilels, Emil, 182, *182*
Glière, Reinhold, 177
Gluck, Christoph, 184, 224
Golestan, S., 184
Gorky, Maxim, 45, 85, 139
Grieg, Edvard, *36*, 36, 152, 182

H

Hahn, R., 168
Handel, George Frideric, 155, 224
Hellmesberger, Joseph, Sr., 18
Hellmesberger, Joseph, Jr., *18*, 19, 21, 25, 151, 165
Hellmesberger, Wilhelmina, *18*
Hindemith, Paul, 194, 218
Hofmannsthal, Hugo von, 108
Honegger, Arthur, 12, 107, 148, 205, 206

I

Ippolitov-Ivanov, M., 178

J

Joachim, Joseph, 21
Jora, Mihail, 182, *184*, 184, 186

K

Kastorsky, B., 177
Khatchaturian, Aram, 154, 164, *164*, 182
Koch, Henri, 170, 172
Kodály, Zoltán, 220
Koechlin, Charles, 30
Koussevitzky, Sergei, *177*
Kozolupova, M., 180
Kreisler, Fritz, 26, 30, 165, 168, *168*, *179*, 179
Kreutzer, Konradin, 171, 172
Kruglikov, S., 177

L

Lalo, Edouard, 23, 152, 155, 163
Landowska, Wanda, *47*, 177
Lemaître, J., 29
Lipatti, Dinu, *32*, 35, 166
Litvin, Felia, 170, *177*, 177
Liszt, Franz, 8, 125, *128*, 129

M

Maeterlinck, Maurice, 194
Mahler, Gustav, 49, 175, 224
Marsick, Marcel, 26, 151, 165
Massenet, Jules, 23, *24*, 25, 26, 211
Mendelsohn, A., 184
Menuhin, Yehudi, 156, *156*, 158, 166, *167*, 168, 175
Messiaen, Olivier, 205
Miaskovsky, Nikolai, *176*, 177
Milhaud, Darius, 107, 209, 218
Mounet-Sully, J., 105
Mozart, Wolfgang Amadeus, 155, 157, 160, 162, 168, 177, 178, 179, 182, 184
Mussorgsky, Modest, 140, 184, 224, *224*

N

Nardini, Pietro, 155
Nestev, I., 199
Nikisch, Arthur, 176

O

Oborin, Lev, *180*, 180, 182
Oistrakh, David, 162, 166, 168, *169*, *180*, 180, 182, *183*
Orff, Carl, 107
Otesco, I.N., 18
Ovid, 107

P

Paganini, Niccolò, 171
Paléologue, M., 179
Perlea, I., 185
Prokofiev, Sergei, 177, *178*, 180
Prudhomme, Sully, 29
Pugnani, Gaetano, 171
Pushkin, Alexander, 97

R

Rabinoff, Benno, *86*, 86
Rachmaninov, Sergei, *177*, 177
Ravel, Maurice, 30, 39, *45*, 45-47, 154, 155, 157, 163, 164, 166, 217
Rembrandt, 161
Richter, Hans, 20
Rimsky-Korsakov, Nikolai, 10, 175, *177*, 177
Risler, Edouard, 166
Rode, Pierre, 172
Rogalski, T., 184
Roger-Ducasse, Jean-Jules, 30
Rolland, Romain, 25, 28
Rubinstein, Anton, 7

S

Saint-Saëns, Camille, 23, 26, 29, 30, 152, *152*, 163, 175, *177*, 177
Sarasate, Pablo, 26, 155
Satie, Erik, 107
Schmitt, Florent, 30, 31
Schneider, Fritz, 166
Schönberg, Arnold, 218
Schubert, Franz, 18, 50, 90, 206
Schumann, Robert, 50, 87
Shafran, Daniel, 166, 168, 180
Shakespeare, William, 108
Shelley, Percy Bysshe, 194
Shneerson, G., 182, 185
Shostakovich, Dmitri, 168, 180, *181*, 183
Sibor, K., 177
Silvestri, S., 185
Sophocles, 105, 108, 110, 111
Strauss, Richard, 49, 107, 108, *109*, 156, 166, 184
Stravinsky, Igor, 107, 108, *109*, 144, 179, 205, 218
Szymanowski, Henryk, 91, 199, 205

T

Taneev, Sergei, 107
Taranu, C., 205
Tartini, Giuseppe, 172, 173
Tchaikovsky, Peter, 140, 155, 182
Thibaud, Jacques, 30, *30*, 151, *159*, 168, *168*
Toscanini, Arturo, 176
Totenberg, Roman, *170*

U

Uminska, Eugenia, 161

V

Vieuxtemps, Henri, 152
Vivaldi, Antonio, 217
Voltaire, François Marie, 110
Vuillermoz, E., 121, 124, 221

W

Wagner, Richard, 20, 21, 25, 60, 64, 120, 122, 125, *126*, 129, 183, 184, 224

Weber, Carl Maria von, 129, 184
Wieniawski, Henryk, 26, 151, 152, 155, 171
Wilde, Oscar, 108

Y

Ysaÿe, Eugène, 30, 155, 165, 168, 169, 171, 179

Z

Ziloti, Alexander, 177, 178, 179